JOURNEY INTO DARKNESS

For Leonard

With hope

Stephen Arrington

STEPHEN LEE ARRINGTON

Huntington House Publishers

Fifth Printing

Huntington House Publishers
P.O. Box 53788
Lafayette, Louisiana 70505

Library of Congress Card Catalog Number
91-72961
ISBN 1-56384-003-0

Dedicated

to all those who think themselves lost.
There is hope in knowing that shadows are defined by light
—and the light is there for all of us.

Special appreciation to Jean-Michel Cousteau
whose commitment to recycling extended to
an ex-felon who needed a second chance.

The Cousteau Society is a membership sponsored,
non-profit organization dedicated to improving the
quality of life for present and future generations.
For membership information please write: The Cousteau
Society, 930 West 21st St., Norfolk, VA 23517

Epigraph

This story is written in the first person because I lived it. Everything here is true. Only the names of the innocent have been changed. What follows is a *journey into darkness* as I step from the proud world of being a navy frogman and Vietnam veteran into the corrupt world of organized crime. The ticket to ride on this journey is purchased with a single marijuana cigarette. If you will join me, our path is a downward spiral that takes us to a secret jungle hideout for the Medellin drug cartel. The way home again begins by being arrested and leads to being a co-defendant in the John DeLorean drug trial of 1982.

On this journey we will travel into the federal prison system to discover what life is really like inside a cement-walled jungle where primate law rules. I must warn that *Journey Into Darkness* is written in the intensity of the moment and contains situations that may be disconcerting to some, but are absolutely necessary if I am to convey the magnitude of the horror that awaits those who would dance the criminal waltz.

Journey Into Darkness is also about hope—the hope that, by refocusing my life towards the good, I might once again rediscover happiness. When I began to write this book in my prison cell, I never would have believed that I would finish it on a Cousteau Expedition vessel.

We exult in our tribulations, knowing that:
Tribulation brings about perseverance;
and perseverance, proven character; and proven
character, hope;
and hope does not disappoint.
(Rom. 5:3-5)

"Drugs are a pollution of the mind"—Jean-Michel Cousteau

Dangerous Reef, South Australia

I need a volunteer to jump inside an experimental, completely transparent LEXAN shark cage. We are amongst the Great White shark. Steve Arrington is an instant volunteer, just like he was with ammunitions in Vietnam when deactivation was required.

As you read Steve's book, you will discover Steve's sense of courage even as it gets confused with a blind acceptance of orders—perhaps submission due to an "overdose" of confidence. It is easy to abuse such people and Steve Arrington was taken advantage of and misguided. Imagine if I had asked Steve to jump into a shark cage that did not work.

I feel good to have contributed to the recovery and success of this kind human being. People should receive a second chance when they have been abused.

—Jean-Michel Cousteau

Foreword

by James Walsh

My job is the prosecution of serious federal crimes—for the most part, narcotics crimes—and it brings me into contact with a broad cross-section of humanity. Most of those contacts are in court, and very few of them are pleasant. So why am I writing introductory remarks for a book written by Steve Arrington?

I first met Steve Arrington in my professional capacity, as a narcotics prosecutor. He was there in court, in handcuffs, wearing a prison jumpsuit, looking somewhat dazed. Well he might, since he had been arrested by federal drug agents as part of one of the most celebrated narcotics undercover investigations of the past decade—the DeLorean Case, as it came to be known to most of the civilized world. Steve Arrington's role in the events of that case was minor; he was the side-kick of Morgan Hetrick, the man who supplied the cocaine that John DeLorean bounced on his knee in that famous videotape.

Steve was processed in the usual way in the case. His lawyer made efforts on his behalf and eventually negotiated a plea agreement for him. He was convicted on his guilty plea and received a four year term of imprisonment. He went off to prison, and I continued with the prosecution of the case, never expecting to hear from him again.

It is one of the strange aspects of my job that I almost never see or hear again from people upon whom I have an impact. This is not surprising, for although the interaction that I have with them is a very memorable event in their lives, it is also usually the worst thing that has happened to them, and they don't want to relive it, and I don't, either. When I do hear from one of "my people," it is usually because they have gotten out of jail and back into trouble—they are going around for another cycle of arrest, trial, and prison.

You can easily imagine, then, how surprised and pleased I was to receive a telephone call from Steve one day several years ago. He told me that he had done his time in prison and been released, and he was calling to invite me to attend an award ceremony being given by the Red Cross to recognize his successful effort to save a person from drowning in Long Beach. You see, Steve had been a diver in the Navy and had done several tours of duty in Vietnam. He told me that he had landed a job with the Cousteau Society as a diver and, among other things, wanted to have the government's permission to travel with the Cousteau Society. Since he was still on parole, the government's agreement was necessary. It was one of the easier things that I have been asked to do in my job.

I went to the ceremony and was impressed with the friends of Steve's who were there to help him celebrate the occasion. It is an unusual pleasure to be able to see tangible proof that someone who has descended into the underworld of drugs and danger can resurface, with his character intact, and make his way to a successful and fulfilling career. It is even more of a pleasure to see such a person be willing to share his experience with others in an effort to ensure that they won't have to make that full journey themselves.

A few years after Steve invited me to share in his award from the Red Cross he called again, this time to offer his services as a lecturer to civic groups and schools on the perils of the drug culture, gangs, and prison. He knew that I was involved in a Boy Scout troop in the Long Beach area and asked if he could come and speak to the troop about his experiences. Now, anyone who has ever been involved in Boy Scouts can tell you how difficult it is to hold their attention for even a few minutes. Steve came to the meeting and held them spellbound for the better part of an hour as he described his own experiences, in prison and out. The message—that drugs and gangs lead to jail and perhaps even worse—is a message that can bear frequent retelling, but it comes most convincingly from someone who has "been there." It will never be told more convincingly to that audience of Boy Scouts.

So, while I can claim no credit for the resurrection of Stephen Arrington, I am pleased and flattered to have been a part of the publication of that project. The raw material was sound, and so the job was perhaps deceptively easy. Nevertheless, his story is an important example to make the point that you *can* go home again, if you really want to. He did, and we are richer for it.

–*James P. Walsh, Jr.*
March 24, 1992
Los Angeles

*NOTE: The views expressed are solely those of Mr. Walsh, who continues to be employed by the Department of Justice.

CHAPTER 1

At first light the runway looks like any other air strip, but this time the white interrupted line painted down the middle of the black tarmac points toward the corrupt world of criminal enterprise. We pause at the end of the runway in the specially modified twin-engine Aztec. With the plane's eight custom wing tanks and a hundred gallon fuel bladder resting behind our seats, we can stay airborne for almost fourteen hours. I listen to the throaty roar of the engines as the pilot increases the throttle rapidly toward maximum rpm. With a glance and a nod toward me, he releases the brakes. The Aztec lurches forward then rapidly begins to accelerate down the runway. At eighty miles an hour, the nose lifts off, followed almost immediately by the main gear. With a gut-wrenching feeling, I watch the ground falling away, knowing that my life has been forever altered in a terrible and unforgiving way. The powerful twin climbs quickly. Looking out the window at the desert terrain below us, I suddenly feel cold inside. Is it because of the chilly high-altitude air as we level off at eleven thousand feet, or is this icy feeling in my gut brought on by the fear of doing something criminal and terribly wrong? My fingers tremble slightly as I reach for the switch that activates the heater. Then, sitting back in the seat, I close my eyes, and while waiting for the heater's warmth, think about the events over the last twenty-four hours that have so completely changed my life.

It all began just yesterday afternoon. Morgan and I were driving down Century Boulevard in his silver Cadillac Fleetwood. I was behind the wheel; Morgan sat in the passenger seat counting money—a lot of money.

"I'll bet you don't know where all this money really comes from?" he stated cheerfully, holding up two thick bundles of hundred dollar bills.

"From your overseas investors?" I answered casually, knowing that Morgan's main source of income came out of the Bahamas from investors who sponsored Morgan Aviation, Inc., and its many private assets.

Morgan turned in his seat to regard me more directly; his fixed gaze seemed to look right into my soul. I could see miniature twin reflections of myself mirrored in his thick glasses as he chuckled, "Yeah, but do you know why they send me so much money?"

I shook my head, "No." The sun glinting off his thick prescription glasses prevented me from seeing his eyes. I looked carefully at the man I trusted, the man who had become the father image I so desperately wanted. His hair was a uniform silver. It made me wonder if he dyed it. His waist had thickened over the years. Morgan, a multi-millionaire, lived well.

Morgan smiled inwardly, then as if noting my fascination with his glasses, he removed them and set to polishing the lenses with a handkerchief. He peered myopically at the result before putting them back on. "Because I fly their cocaine," he said suddenly.

"You what!" I blurted.

"I'm a smuggler, Steve," Morgan's grin showed teeth as he leaned toward me, "I bring it up from Colombia through the Gulf of Mexico a quarter ton at a time."

I gaped at him. The twin images of myself reflected in his glasses were oddly distorted. They magnified the dark hole of my open mouth into a ghostly siren of a scream.

"No!" The word leaped out of the hole.

"Oh, I'm quite serious," replied Morgan. "Smuggling has made me a very wealthy man." Then, focusing the full force of his awesome personality upon me, he dramatically held up the twin bundles of money. "This is fifty thousand bucks. It's yours if you will co-pilot one of my planes to Colombia."

I felt my heart thumping wildly as I realized that Morgan was trying to lure me inside a criminal web.

"No, Morgan," I growled in sudden anger, "I will not be a part of this." Morgan looked slightly flustered. "But, Steve, you already are . . ."

"What do you mean?" I asked in sudden panic.

"Don't be stupid," raged Morgan, "you're spending my money—drug money—and that makes you a part of my operation whether you like the idea or not."

Morgan glared at me, then took a deep breath like someone who is about to tackle a difficult obstacle. "Look, I'm not asking anything of you that I haven't already asked of my own sons. It's just not fair that they should take their share of the risks while you benefit from the money and do nothing in return."

"Morgan, I'm not flying to South America," I argued, though there was now a trace of doubt in my mind. I wondered for a moment if Morgan would try to force me to make that flight.

Though mad, Morgan managed a forced smile. "Look, just think about it, O.K.?"

In the airplane, a sudden loud crackling noise, like popcorn frying in hot bubbling oil, startles me from my thoughts of the previous day. Sitting up quickly in the co-pilot's seat, I glance nervously toward the pilot just as the sharp reek of high octane gasoline abruptly fills the cockpit in an all but visible volatile cloud.

"The heater," yells the pilot, "shut down the heater! Hurry before this thing blows up!"

I flip the switch to *off*; then, thinking that the fuel bladder behind our seats must have ruptured, I turn to check it. Surprisingly, the hundred gallon bladder is full; the black rubberized skin is reassuringly taut to my touch.

The pilot, unsure what is wrong, alters course for Blithe, an isolated desert strip, then begins a rapid descent.

Five miles out from Blithe the starboard engine, without any advance warning, sputters and dies. The heavy plane loses speed rapidly. The pilot frantically cranks the idle engine. The propeller turns in short jerks, but the engine refuses to catch. The plane begins vibrating as the airspeed decreases toward a full stall. A violent shudder runs the length of the fuselage. The stall warning horn blares loudly in the small cockpit; then the nose drops sickeningly as the plane falls into a steep dive. Thrown forward against the instrument panel, I awkwardly reach between the seats switching the fuel selector to the main tanks.

The desert floor is rushing up at us, and I know I am about to die when the starboard engine coughs once loudly belching a thick cloud of black smoke. The propeller turns once; then the engine fires rapidly to life. The pilot slams the starboard throttle against the stops to full power. The super-charged engine races to maximum rpm, yet we are continuing to rapidly lose altitude. The pilot fights for control, pulling vainly back on the wheel. Slowly, the nose of the Aztec begins to respond. At two hundred feet, with the desert floor flashing beneath us in a blur, the plane finally levels out. The pilot immediately points the nose back toward the Blithe runway.

The pilot's hands shake on final; then, the wheels hit the tarmac with a heavy, but reassuring, jolt.

We taxi to a vacant side of the small airport before shutting down the engines. The air reeks of gasoline inside the cramped cockpit. I jump out onto the runway. Looking beneath the plane, I first hear, then am stunned to see a solid stream of aviation gas spilling from the fuselage onto the hot tarmac. The entire bottom of the forward fuselage is awash in high octane gasoline. Above the heater, a fuel line nut is completely loose. The volatile gasoline is spilling in a steady stream directly onto the heater. The fuel is washing over the heater casing and dripping down its sides. A pool of gasoline smothers the spark ignition inducer, which fires the heater.

For a pregnant moment I wonder if this is indeed an accident. Did the nut loosen from vibration or is someone else looking for a way out of Morgan's cocaine business, too? I have an all too vivid vision of the aircraft going down trailing black smoke with the cockpit awash in flames while the two of us scream our lives out.

We thoroughly check the rest of the plane for other possible "innocent mistakes" then taxi to the fueling station to refill the outer wing tanks. The failure of the starboard engine was a direct result of the right wing-tip tank emptying its twenty gallons of gasoline straight into the heater compartment.

Barely an hour after our emergency landing, the plane is once again charging full speed down a runway before it lifts off into the clear desert sky. Stunned, I sit in the copilot's seat wondering why I'm so foolishly risking my life. It certainly isn't for the money. It's fear that drives me. I am in this scary situation only because I'm afraid not to be. It doesn't make sense. I wonder how many other criminals began their felonious careers because they feared the people who manipulated them? I think about Max and know that I'm right to be scared. Max is Morgan's link to the drug underworld. I had the misfortune of meeting him last night at the LAX Marriott Hotel.

Listening to the steady drone of the twin engines, I return to my thoughts of Morgan and the events of last night that lead to my being here.

After dropping the bombshell about his being a smuggler, Morgan was now content to make the rest of the drive in silence. I mistakenly thought he might have accepted my initial refusal. Actually, Morgan was just changing ploys as he ordered me to pull into the parking lot of the LAX Marriott Hotel.

Morgan paid for a suite; then we went upstairs to the fifth floor. Once inside the room, Morgan walked over to a dresser and carefully set down a black briefcase. With his back to me, he opened the lid; then, abruptly turning around, he slapped a .45 caliber automatic pistol into my hand.

I was totally taken by surprise. The gun felt inordinately heavy. Almost by reflex I began to check the weapon: my military training demanded that I know it was loaded. I pushed the release button dropping the ammunition clip into my other hand. Two shiny brass and lead cartridges were plainly visible at the top of the clip. Sliding back the cocking mechanism, I ejected a brass round in a shiny trajectory that landed it upon the bed. Like an ugly statement, it lay there waiting to be picked up and used.

I was in a complete state of shock. "What in the world is going on?" I demanded angrily.

Morgan shrugged his shoulders, "We are here to pick up a lot of money, I just want to make sure no one takes it away from us."

I threw the now empty pistol onto the bed along with the loaded clip, "Forget it."

"O.K., O.K.," he yelled, "leave the gun, but you don't have a problem with helping me carry the money, do you?"

Walking down the hotel corridor, I kept thinking about how

stupid I was being while Morgan practiced his manipulations on me.
I was his puppet; he pulled the strings while I danced for him.

Morgan stopped at a door and knocked once sharply, then twice
more softly. The door swung silently open.

The corridor was poorly lit, yet it was even darker in that room.
A large Latin man stood just inside. His face bore heavy scarring,
like someone had once run upon it with track shoes. He was wearing tan pants and a black T-shirt that stretched tightly across a barrel
chest and bulging biceps. Dangling nonchalantly from his right hand
was an Ingram MAC-10 machine pistol. He casually used the gun to
wave us inside.

The room was larger than Morgan's suite. Against two of the
walls stood two more men, but my attention riveted on a fourth
man standing in the room's center, his hand extended in greeting,
yet even with empty hands he somehow seemed the most threatening of all.

Morgan smiled warmly as he quickly crossed the floor and took
the proffered hand in his. "Hello Max," he said, then turning
toward me added, "This is Steve, the new right-hand man that I told
you about. I trust him with my life."

The salutation was not lost on Max whose cold, reptilian eyes
shifted to me like a snake sensing prey. Max, a professional smuggler, understands the need for reliable people. He offered his hand
like it was a loaded weapon. I watched my hand disappear into his.
Holding it tightly, he said, "Morgan has told me a lot about you. I
understand that you used to be a frogman in the navy and that you're
an expert with weapons and explosives."

Scar Face, apparently not impressed, snorted contemptuously
then chuckled lightly. Max ignored Scar Face's interruption, "You
do any time in Vietnam?"

"Four tours," I answered, "mostly rescuing downed pilots."

"Ever kill anyone?"

"No, thankfully," I wanted to free my hand from Max's grasp,
but he had tightened his grip.

Max nodded toward one of the Colombians, "He has and so has
Juan, who's leaning against the door." I glanced at Scar Face whose
face bore an amused sinister smile as he held up four fingers. "So
you know how this works," Max's voice was deadly serious. "All my
boys are shooters, and they enjoy their work." Max squeezed my
hand, forcing me to look back at him. "You understand what I'm
saying, don't you?" he asked sternly, letting go of my hand.

It was difficult to break eye contact with Max's steely gaze. I
glanced down at my hand. It looked unchanged, but I knew I had
just been pulled into a living nightmare. Morgan now wore a smug
look as if all of his problems had just been solved.

Max snapped his fingers impatiently at one of his men who obediently picked up a heavy suitcase and dropped it onto the bed. Max motioned with his chin for Morgan to open it. Morgan rubbed his hands together greedily as he approached the suitcase. He flipped the latches and slowly opened the lid. It was full of money.

"It will take too long to count," offered Max, "but it's all there, seven hundred thousand in used bills, just like before."

Morgan took a deep breath and sighed as if mentally reliving a sensual memory, then he closed the lid and headed for the door. "Bring the suitcase, Steve," he said over one shoulder (master to puppet) without bothering to look at me. I was surprised at the weight of the suitcase; it matched the heaviness of my heart as I followed Morgan out.

We went back to our room only long enough for Morgan to fetch his briefcase and the pistol; then, we went down to the Cadillac and began our return trip to Mojave.

The sun was low on the horizon, silhouetting the cactus and other desert shrubbery on the west side of the highway when Morgan turned toward me and said, "Want to know who Max really is?" I shook my head not really wanting to hear Morgan's explanation.

"His full name is Max Mermelstein." Morgan chuckled, "With that dark skin of his you wouldn't think that he's Jewish. Well, old Max is the number one man in the United States for the Medellin drug cartel. His boss is Rafael Cardona Salazar who is one very bad hombre." Afraid to ask any questions, I sat in dazed silence.

Morgan didn't seem to mind the one-sided conversation, the words tumbling freely from him as he pulled me deeper into a dark abyss. "Rafa, as he is known by his friends, answers directly to the Ochoa family." Morgan sat back in his seat looking very smug, "You know you're going to have to make that airplane trip, don't you?"

With a fluttering heart, I replied, "Morgan, I don't want to do it." Both of us were aware of my choice of words, "will not" had become "don't want."

Morgan smiled, at that moment he was closest to the father image he played so well as he said the words that hurled me into the criminal underworld, "You don't have a choice anymore, Steve, you have to do it to prove yourself to Max ... and to the Medellin cartel."

With no street lights the corner of the car where Morgan sat was cast in near darkness. The headlights of passing cars flickered off his glasses. Though I couldn't see Morgan very well, I could certainly smell him. Morgan always had severe body odor. It rose from his side of the car in a musky funk that, like an ill-begotten beacon, enveloped me—sapping the will from my body. I felt like the devil himself was reaching out to take possession of my soul.

I knew that I was hooked. If I tried to run now, Morgan would tell Max. There was no doubt that Max would send Scar Face for me. I also knew that his search would carry him to my mother's house. The thought of Scar Face knocking on her front door was an arrangement I chose not to face. I was powerless to resist, and Morgan knew it.

In a tone of voice that expected no argument, Morgan ordered, "Pack a bag when we get home; you'll be leaving in the morning."

A tapping on my shoulder stirs me from my thoughts and pulls me back into the airplane. "Are you ready to take the controls for a while?" the pilot asks. I nod and grab hold of the wheel while he lies down in back and goes to sleep using the fuel bladder as a pillow. We continue to fly all that day and through most of the night. It's three in the morning when we land at New Orleans to top off the fuel tanks before heading south into the Gulf of Mexico.

The long dark runway glistens from a light but steady rain as we taxi to leave America. Through the cockpit windscreen, I watch jagged bolts of lightning strike across a broad weather front masked in thick, black clouds that is marching against the coastline from the Gulf. The rolling thunder of the electrically charged night all but drowns out the roar of our engines as we race down the slick runway and fly out into the dark sky . . . right into a major thunderstorm.

At first, the pilot likes the storm, which shrouds the small plane from coastal radar, but the storm keeps getting worse. The plane is enveloped in total darkness broken only by the flash of lightning bolts that paint towering thunderheads advancing before gale force winds. The Aztec tosses and bucks in the heavy turbulence like a bronco. I know that if we stray too close to the massive thunderheads the violent shear winds could dismember our plane in an instant.

Weaving and threading our way between the dark, massive, nebulous walls is like flying through the Grand Canyon of the heavens. Thunder crashes and reverberates against the plane's thin skin while lightning shatters the night sky with its blinding strobelight effect. Violent air pockets rocket us upwards or drop us like a stone hundreds of feet at a time. In the darkened cockpit, lit only by the dim glow of the instrument lights, the pilot fights the controls. A sheen of sweat glistens on his face as the rank odor of fear, laced with the lingering smell of gasoline fumes, fills the restricted cockpit.

The storm buffets us throughout the rest of the night; then, with the dawn, we finally pass from its embrace into a blue sky filled with puffy white clouds.

The pilot, tired and weary, slumps at the controls. He jerks upright then looks at me with red-rimmed eyes, "You better take the controls, I'm going to sleep in the back."

I glance at the stained air chart, "Where are we?"

The pilot shrugs, "Somewhere southeast of Cuba. Just stay on a compass heading of 187 degrees, and you better keep an eye out for Cuban fighters. That storm drove us too close to their air defense perimeter."

Sitting alone at the controls, I can't believe that I am actually on the lookout for Cuban fighters. I briefly wonder what a Cuban prison would be like. Why I am doing this just doesn't make sense. My fear of Max and Morgan is driving me right into their criminal world—a world where terror and murder are but tools of the trade.

Eleven long hours later, the green coastline of Colombia finally appears low on the horizon. We determine our location by tuning in the main airport's radio signal at Bogata, then turn southeast toward the deeper jungle. The pilot keeps tapping the fuel gauges, but the needles adamantly stay in the red. Fighting our way through the storm has cost us our small fuel reserve.

From three thousand feet the dense jungle canopy seems to stretch forever, its vastness broken only by wide, winding rivers and long mountainous ridges. The pilot looks anxiously at the landmarks comparing them to his air chart; sweat drips from his chin to splatter onto the stained map. I notice that the engines are running hot, that the needles of the fuel gauges are bouncing on empty, and that we are totally lost.

Suddenly, a static-filled whistle blares from the radio—relief floods the pilot's face. Anxiously, he whistles back into the microphone then converses in rapid Spanish. They have seen our plane from the ground. Following instructions, we bank to the right and dip toward the jungle. Ahead of us four trucks camouflaged in foliage move to reveal the hidden dirt airstrip. We slip in low over a tall tree not far from the foot of the short runway and quickly set down. The hot engines roar and cough as we taxi off the bumpy dirt and gravel strip to park the plane under the canopy of a large tree, which shields it from government observation aircraft. The pilot cuts the engines. Their loud, rumbling roar stops. The sudden silence is broken only by the sharp metallic creak of the engines as they dissipate their heat and the low murmur of Spanish-speaking voices as a dozen armed men surround the airplane.

Cautiously opening the door, I feel the sweltering heat of Colombia invade the plane while staring anxiously at the fierce-looking cartel soldiers. Raising an empty hand in a mute, but hopefully friendly way, I stare at the Colombian men, noting the calloused hands that carry an assortment of rifles and shotguns. A man taller than the rest, wearing a bandoleer of red and brass shotgun cartridges and carrying a small radio, says, "You're late, gringos."

Dusk descends on the jungle as we finish refueling the airplane with five-gallon jerry cans passed along a human chain from hand to hand. A cloud of blood-thirsty mosquitoes descend noisily upon us while we work.

Standing with the last full jerry can in my hands, I could not help but think that if we're attacked, I'd be nothing but a running target, not knowing friend from foe. This wasn't like Vietnam where I at least knew what I was risking my life for. Looking at the coarse cartel soldiers standing about me, I realize that my stupidity could easily cost me my life, and no one back home would even know. I'd just be a pile of meat rotting in the jungle, another unknown victim of the cocaine wars.

It occurs to me that with the fuel leak and the storm I have twice brushed against death in the last twenty-four hours. Stunned by the thought, I momentarily pause and stare without seeing into the dense jungle, until the man on my left nudges me and says irritably, "Hey gringo, finish."

Glancing at the coarse, bearded outlaw, it's a shocking realization to know that I'm actually on the side of the bad guys.

Topping off the last wing tank, I feel the icy bite of the gasoline as it spills down my bare arm in cold rivulets, chasing mosquitoes from the sweat-covered skin.

Darkness envelopes us as we stagger wearily along a jungle path toward a crude cement-walled house with a thatched roof. Through gaps in the weathered wood-plank door, I see the yellow flicker of an open flame. Spanish music weeps gently upon the air to us, along with the smell of roasting meat, eliciting hungry growls from the men about me.

The door squeaks loudly on unoiled hinges as one of the men jerks it open and shouts a greeting at the cook inside. The cook glancing over his shoulder laughs as he continues to turn a charred animal carcass over an open fire pit. He is a big man with a huge belly that bulges against a greasy apron. A large butcher knife, half hidden by a roll of fat, protrudes from his leather belt. He says something in Spanish, which sends the men scurrying toward a rough-hewn table.

For a paralyzing moment, I stare at the animal carcass, watching thick globs of fat dripping wetly into the fire where they sizzle in a loud searing hiss. The cook motions with a jerk of his head for me to join the rest of the men who are noisily taking seats around the table. The outlaws lean their rifles and shotguns against the wall, but their pistols lie within easy reach next to the plates. I take a seat between the pilot and a man with a beard and yellow, broken teeth.

The cook brings out blackened pots of beans, brown rice, *chorizos* (sausage), and fried onions along with a pan of cornbread. With a flourish, he carries in the animal carcass on a platter and dumps it in the middle of the table. The men boisterously attack the charred carcass with gusto, ripping chunks of meat away with their knives and bare hands. Blood and grease leak from the wooden platter onto the table then run across the rough surface to fall in a wet splatter on the dirt floor below.

Though desperately hungry, I stare with reluctance at the half-stripped carcass. I know it's not a pig. From its small size I figure it to be lamb. I look hopelessly at the pilot next to me. The pilot, who is loading his plate, pauses. "Are you going to eat?" he asks.

"I'm a vegetarian," I whisper.

"I wouldn't tell them that," laughs the pilot.

The cook, mistaking the reason for my hesitation, leans across the table and knuckles me good naturedly in the chest; he plunges his butcher knife shoulder deep into the half-dismembered animal cutting away an entire limb in a single brutal slash. He proudly drops a kilo of blood-red meat, bone, and gristle onto my plate. Leaning close, his handle bar mustache fluttering in the gruffness of his voice, he rumbles, "Eat, gringo," then he piles on scoops of rice, beans, and fried onions in heavy-handed flourishes. Almost as an afterthought, he grabs a hunk of cornbread and drops it on the plate then lumbers back into the kitchen.

I attack the plate mimicking the coarse behavior of the feeding men. The cook is delighted when he sees me gnawing meat directly from the bone. Slapping my back vigorously he proclaims, "Mos mocho hombre, eh?"

Looking at his open, friendly face, I can't help but wonder if this is how he gets his kid to eat at home. I am almost in a good mood as I look back at the plate then notice a stub nose .38 revolver casually laid where my napkin should have been. The lead bullets are plainly visible inside the six-round cylinder. Across the head of each bullet a deep "X" has been gouged. The bullets have been made into Dum Dums to ensure maximum damage on impact. When a Dum Dum hits a person, the bullet splits into four pieces, each independently wreaking havoc with human flesh and bone. The outlaw to my right notices my stare then possessively slides the revolver a little closer to himself. The gun is an instant reminder that this is the depths of the criminal world. The realization shatters the momentary easiness I had felt with the cook.

The outlaw, maybe seeing the sudden sadness in my eyes, snags a bottle of Ron Caldos rum from the table and urges me to drink. Taking a deep pull, I feel the Colombian rum burning as it courses down to my stomach where its heat immediately flares upwards, numbing my brain. He grunts his approval then raises the bottle to his own lips and drinks thirstily in big gulps.

After the dishes have been cleared, or just shoved to one side, the cook opens a brown paper grocery sack onto the middle of the table. Clods of marijuana spill across the grease-smeared wood planks. The men roll thick cigar-sized joints with yellowed corn paper, which they light with burning twigs from the fire. The room quickly fills with the pungent marijuana smoke. It rises thickly into the still humid air, curling around the smut-stained rafters before drifting out into the night through the thatched roof.

I don't hesitate to take a long pull when a fat joint is passed to me. The corn paper cigarette burns fiercely, its harsh smoke irritating my throat, and despite the burning in my chest, I hold the smoke in, anxious to get stoned. I hope for the stoned drowsiness that might help me to sleep.

Later that night, paranoid and alert instead of drowsy and stoned, I toss and turn upon my grass mat. I lie awake most of the night listening to the guards converse in soft Spanish outside the window. Finally, I fall into a troubled sleep only to be prey to bizarre dreams.

We are out early to load the cocaine, which is packed in plastic-wrapped kilo bricks. The cocaine is taken from a dirty, cement-walled room where the bricks are stacked in rows almost to the ceiling. There must have been over two thousand of them. The head man counts out three hundred bricks, which are then stuffed into sea bags and loaded onto the grossly over-burdened airplane.

While the pilot supervises the loading of the last bag, I look at the plane's bulging tires and note how heavily it squats on the crude runway. Though it is early morning, it is already hot and humid. This will reduce lift and make an already dangerous takeoff even more tricky. Climbing into the plane, I can only hope that the gravel runway is long enough.

The pilot starts the engines. The cartel soldiers help to push the heavy plane into position. The pilot crosses himself, then with his feet applied firmly to the brakes, he runs the engines up to full rpm. The Aztec begins to shudder and vibrate as it strains against the brakes. With a lurch, the plane begins to roll ponderously, slowly building up ground speed as it plows through the soft gravel. The airspeed indicator laboriously climbs to sixty mph as the end of the short runway looms closer. At eighty mph the waiting tree begins to fill the windshield as the wheels finally leave the ground. They touch again briefly. Without waiting for the command, I jerk up the lever that retracts them into the fuselage even as the tree sweeps just beneath us. The engines strain to gain altitude in the thin air.

At five hundred feet we begin a slow, banking turn, heading the nose of the Aztec toward North America. The chemical reek of cocaine fills the close space of the cockpit. Lingering beneath its acid sharpness is the residual smell of the spilled gasoline. I know that the airplane is a potential flying torch just waiting for a spark.

Ten hours later I am light headed and half sick from the toxic fumes. The coastline of Louisiana lies just beyond the horizon, which is shrouded in the dim light of dusk. We're coming in low following Morgan City's radio beacon. The pilot, knowing that airborne and ground-based radar will be actively searching for us, takes us down closer to the waves. With a sinking feeling I realize that if we lose an engine now, we'll have the flight characteristics of a heavy rock. Ahead, offshore oil platforms begin appearing low on the horizon. Pulling back on the wheel, the pilot begins a slow climb, gaining a few hundred feet of altitude.

Surprised by the maneuver, I ask, "Why are we climbing?"

"If we fly below the level of the oil platforms, they will report us for sure," answers the pilot.

As the pilot levels off the plane at four hundred feet, he looks over and grins, "This is just high enough that the workers will think we're oil executives inspecting the rigs."

"But what if radar picks us up?" I ask.

The pilot angles the plane to fly parallel to the distant coastline, then reduces speed. His grin broadens as he looks at me. "I'm betting that on a radar screen we're going to look like a company chopper flying from rig to rig."

His ploy works. No one is waiting for us when ten minutes later we fly across the coastline and into the United States.

Two hours after sunset we land at a small mom-n-pop run airfield where we fill only the regular wing tanks so as not to look too suspicious. Yet even with the reduced fuel, we can't risk landing again for at least six hours without the very real threat of collapsing the landing gear from the excessive weight. While replacing one of the fuel caps, I happen to look toward one of the wheels and see a small shredded green twig caught in the brake pad. A chill passes the length of my spine as I realize that our brush with that tree in Colombia had been closer than I thought.

It is night when we land in west Texas, our last fuel stop. An hour later we are both glad to get out of there because Texas hands out man-sized sentences to criminals, particularly drug smugglers.

Twenty-four hours after leaving Colombia, we arrive in the air space over Los Angeles. It's three o'clock in the morning, and ours is the only plane in the air. We have no doubt that every air controller in Los Angeles is watching the sole blip of our airplane as it transits their fluorescent screens.

We fly almost directly over my mother's house. I look for but can't locate her porch light in the sleeping residential neighborhood. I think of the warm security of her house and wish with all my might that I could be there now, sleeping harmlessly in my old bed without a thought for the real-life crime drama that has caught me in its web.

Flying over the San Gabriel Mountains, we slowly descend approaching Mojave Airport from the southwest. The broad desert floor is blanketed in darkness except for the glowing lights of the small town of Mojave. Reaching for the radio, I dial in the frequency of the tower then key the microphone three times, which automatically activates the runway lights; twin running ribbons of liquid light leap out of the desert floor darkness.

We bring the Aztec straight in and set down quickly. While shedding airspeed, we taxi off the brightly lit runway and head toward Morgan's hanger. Through the windshield, I see the hanger doors sliding open, revealing the cavernous interior and remember the hot, dusty day—was it only two days ago?—when Morgan sprung his little surprise on me. I have changed since then; my past innocence hangs about me in tattered shreds. I wonder if I could ever be my happy, buoyant self again. It seems doubtful.

Opening the door and stepping wearily from the plane, I'm glad that our job is finished. A couple of Morgan's sons quickly move to unload the airplane. One of them is quite young, still a teen-ager, and easily impressed. I had known him when I worked for Morgan seven years earlier. Then he had been just a happy-go-lucky kid with nothing but thoughts of baseball rummaging around in his head. Now he is a criminal, and he isn't even a man yet. I think how he couldn't have stood much of a chance against his father's manipulations. He looks up and smiles a greeting as I walk swiftly by.

I waste no time exiting the hanger and climb quickly into Morgan's Cadillac. Spraying gravel from the rear tires, I race straight home. Inside Morgan's desert house, I go directly to the refrigerator and take out two bottles of dark Mexican beer, and I chug one after the other. Only then do I telephone Morgan who is awaiting my call in the Bahamas aboard his yacht the *Highland Fling*. He chuckles over the phone when he hears that our flight has been a success then tells me to take the next plane out to join him on the boat; it seems he is anxious to celebrate.

Later that evening, while riding in the first class section of Pan Am Flight 501 to Miami, I think about all that has happened to me over the past three days. I'm awed that I have so pointlessly risked my life, but most of all I think about something else—I'm a criminal now, and somehow I know that I will wind up in prison. With that thought looming over my shoulder like a dark shadow, I drink my beer and stare idly out the window with hopeless thoughts as my sole companion.

CHAPTER 2

The lights are dim in the first class section of the 747. With my eyes closed, I pretend to sleep, but actually my mind is actively pursuing the past. I'm tracing the path that brought me to the criminal twist that my life has now taken. I know that Morgan's wanting to manipulate me is not completely to blame. No, most of the fault is my own. My fall from the right side of the law began simply enough; it started with an event that happened two years ago on the day I was diving from the *USS Arizona* Memorial in Pearl Harbor, Hawaii.

The *USS Arizona* was one of four battleships that had been sunk in Pearl Harbor during the Japanese surprise attack, the prelude to World War II. The ship had gone down fast—taking almost the whole crew with her. With the need to raise the least-damaged ships first in order to return them to combat, the *USS Arizona* was left on the bottom. They didn't even make an effort to get the bodies out. Divers sealed her hatches closed with welding rods and underwater blow torches. Over a thousand sailors and marines were unceremoniously entombed beneath the old ship's decks.

My team of bomb disposal frogmen had been tasked with making an underwater sweep of the sunken battleship and its memorial to ensure that they were free of terrorist bombs because the King of Tonga was slated to visit the site later that day. He wanted to drop a flower wreath into the water at the memorial to honor the fighting men of the United States Navy and Marine Corps who had fought so valiantly to free his tiny island nation during WWII.

With great anticipation, my dive partner Bill and I stepped to the edge of the memorial and peered down into the dirty brown water; neither of us had ever dived on a battleship before. The other two members of our team would monitor the dive from the surface. Bill's eyes twinkled with excitement through the clear glass of his face plate; then in unison, we both leaped into the muddied water.

Beneath the surface the visibility was very poor. We could see only about fifteen feet into the gloom of the dirty water. The topside divers would keep track of us by watching the trail of our bubbles bursting on the surface. It took but a few minutes to check the sides and bottom of the floating memorial; then, we descended deeper to explore the dreadnought. The battleship was sitting perfectly upright on the soft mud bottom. The big guns had long since been salvaged off her, yet the incredible bulk of this once formidable fighting ship slumbering on the bottom was staggering in its immensity. There was a great deal of damage still apparent from the attack. The massive hull had been savaged and bent from the Japanese bombs and torpedoes. It felt weird to be swimming along her ghostly decks. Each stroke of our fins lifted a thin veil of black silt that rose slowly in a dark, mushrooming cloud and blotted out the already minimal surface light.

Swimming past a steel hatch that had been crudely welded shut, I wondered what it must have been like for the hundreds of men trapped within these now rusting decks. Perhaps the sailors were sleeping off a rowdy Saturday night ashore in Waikiki when the Sunday morning calm was shattered by violent explosions that racked the length of the ship, throwing the sleeping men from their bunks onto the convulsing metal decks. Trapped within the restricted space of the dark hull with repeated explosions, spreading smoke and fire, and sudden rapid flooding, had to have been horrifying for the peacetime sailors. In a span of mere minutes more than a thousand men died, most of them drowning in complete darkness inside the fast sinking ship, without even knowing that Japan had just thrown down the gauntlet of war.

It was very unnerving swimming in the dirty water along the foreboding decks of the long-dead ship. Nothing grew upon the silted wreck. There were no fish or even empty mussel shells to hint that anything had ever lived here. A ghostly fear crept into my bones with the cold water that seeped into my wetsuit. I would have felt the same fear visiting a graveyard alone on a mooncast night. Both of us were intimidated by this eerie ghost ship shrouded in its veil of silt and muddied water. Our dive lights barely penetrated the deep gloom that surrounded us. I played my light's dull yellow beam upon Bill's face plate and saw by his wide eyes (they looked like fried eggs) that he shared the same fear as I. We both looked toward the surface and nodded in unison.

Swimming slowly upward, I stared down at the gray lady who had lost her fleet. The silted water slowly enveloped her like the closing of an open grave. I took a final look downward at the foreboding, muddied darkness and realized that we had indeed just abandoned what can only be described as a graveyard, an underwater graveyard where the warm light of the surface sun only dimly reached as a cold lunar glow.

Back on the surface I couldn't shed my wetsuit fast enough. I urgently needed the reassurance of the sun's warmth on my bare skin. Later, while storing the dive gear, Bill asked, "Are you as shook up as I am?" A visible shiver ran through his body.

"Yeah," I responded, "that place is going to be worth a month of bad dreams."

"Well what do you say to stopping off at my house for a little attitude adjustment?" Barely an hour later we were in his front room getting stoned. "So what do you think of these buds?" asked Bill, exhaling a cloud of putrid smoke.

The coarse smoke hurt my throat and lungs, but I suppressed the pain and continued to greedily pull on the thick joint.

Passing the marijuana cigarette back, I croaked between clenched teeth while holding the burning smoke deep inside my lungs, "Stuff's pretty bad, man."

Bill rolled the joint between his finger tips and sniffed contentedly at the putrid joint, "Dude, this is the best . . ." he coughed twice, then added, "it's elephant buds from Maui." Sitting across from him, I was having a hard time focusing my eyes. "I know where we can get four ounces of this stuff cheap," he leered.

"So, get it; I'll buy some for sure."

"I ain't got the dough," complained Bill who, having recently married a sixteen-year-old girl, was now always short on cash. Bill passed the joint back after taking a long hit. I was already stoned out of my mind and didn't need any more pot. I took another hit.

"Tell you what." Bill leaned towards me in a conspiratorial way. "You put up the money and we'll sell three ounces to cover your cash; then we'll split the fourth ounce between us." Bill took the joint from my hand. "It'll be like smoking for free, man."

With my mind going numb I didn't have to think about it very long. I had learned that smoking pot, particularly at Bill's intensity, was a very expensive habit. The idea of saving some money sounded very appealing. Bill's argument made a lot of sense to my drug-dulled brain. *Why pay for the pot when I could get it free?*

"O.K., I'm in," I rasped before going into a fit of coughing. I got up and went into the kitchen to get something to drink. Once inside the kitchen, I couldn't remember why I was there.

From the front room I heard Bill yell, "Bring me something to drink, too." Shaking my head, I was surprised at how thoroughly the dope had fogged my brain. Back in the front room, Bill reached for the glass of juice and said, "Thanks, partner." I didn't realize it then but I had just taken my first step toward becoming a criminal.

Bill was the resident dope supplier for our command. We were attached to the Explosive Ordnance Disposal Mobile Unit One headquarters in Hawaii. I was the chief petty officer in charge of Team 11. We were frogmen (or, more specifically, underwater bomb disposal experts). I had spent thirteen very exciting years in the navy, which included four tours to Vietnam helping to rescue downed pilots, and had every intention of staying in the navy until I earned my retirement. Selling dope with Bill was about to change all of that.

We unloaded those first three ounces in a single night, which of course led to our buying a little more marijuana when our supply began to run out. Secretly, I got a thrill out of selling the dope. I thought that walking lightly on the wild side of the law was kind of cool. However, I didn't much care for some of the weird and crazy people from whom we had to buy our marijuana. They seemed like such low-lifes. There was a big hint there waiting to be noticed, but I guess I wasn't paying close enough attention to realize that my life had taken a spiritual and social downward trend.

One of Bill's customers wasn't a friend of mine. In fact, I hardly knew the guy and certainly didn't like him. He was a shifty-looking character who always looked and smelled like he needed a bath. He was a seaman, about twenty-three-years-old, who had lately been pressuring us to get him a quarter pound of marijuana. The order was out of our league. We had never sold more than an ounce of pot to anyone before. Bill and I were strictly small-time dealers, which is maybe why I didn't see much harm in our illegal activities. I would have been surprised if someone referred to us as criminals. After all, it was just pot. My casual attitude about marijuana was heading me directly for trouble.

The navy had its own thoughts about marijuana, it wasn't as casual as Bill's or mine—a fact that I was about to find out in a big way.

Unknown to us, Bill's shifty friend had been busted smoking marijuana on base. In order to reduce his problems he had agreed to set Bill and me up for a controlled buy. The navy has its own police force called the Naval Investigation Service, and they were taking a very serious interest in our little operation.

It took a while to get that quarter pound together for the dirt bag, which is how I regarded the sleazy dude. I didn't like being seen with him in public, so I asked him to meet me during lunch break over at Bill's house in navy housing.

After handing over the dope, I was quite happy to be rid of the guy. But, instead of getting into his car and driving away, he holds the plastic bag of marijuana in the air and points dramatically back toward the house. Then, I saw men in suits leaping out of cars and rapidly converging on the house. I fled for the back of the house with the remainder of the marijuana in a grocery bag. In the bathroom, I jammed the dope into the toilet and tried to flush it, but the floating marijuana just swirled around inside the bowl. Desperately, I grabbed at the floating leaves and tried to force them down the soiled drain with my bare hands. That was how I was arrested by two agents as they busted open the bathroom door—on my knees with one arm jammed elbow deep into the toilet bowl.

The agents handcuffed my wet hands behind my back then dragged me back into the front room where Bill's young wife was sitting forlornly on the floor. Like me, Judy's hands were cuffed behind her back while an agent stood over her. She looked really scared. "Steve . . . " she started to plea.

"Shut up!" ordered the agent gruffly. She hung her head and stared without seeing at the carpet. The agent glared at me. "Don't say a word, junky, just get down on your knees—now!" he ordered.

Junky? It was shocking to realize that this was how he saw me. The handcuffs made going to my knees an awkward task. Then I looked at Bill's young bride. She and Bill had been married barely two months. She looked far too young and innocent to be wearing the handcuffs that glistened on her wrists. I saw her lips begin to tremble. A shudder ran through Judy's body; then the tears began to flow unhindered. Her head hanging in shame and fear, she started to sway from side to side. "This isn't happening," she whined, "Oh God, no . . . "

"I said shut up!" ordered the NIS agent.

Meanwhile the rest of the men were ransacking the house looking for more drugs. Except for a moment of high excitement when they found my vitamin horde, the agents were very disappointed to discover that Bill and I only sold marijuana on a small scale.

Toward the end of the search Bill drove up in the driveway just in time to be arrested, too. A moment later he joined us on the front room floor where he was made to kneel next to his young bride. She looked at him and sniffled, but the agent gruffly cleared his throat as a warning for her not to talk.

I stared at the young couple kneeling side by side, and suddenly in the theater of my mind, I remembered them on their wedding day. They were kneeling before a minister, their hands clasped together in love, their eyes shining in happiness. The future was full of promise and yet-to-be answered dreams. With the ugly reality of that day, their dreams were shattered and the future became anything but promising. They both stared at the floor; behind them the agent smiled cruelly—he was enjoying himself.

I felt so sorry for my young friends; then I felt the handcuffs biting into my own wrists. I suddenly realized that I too had been very foolish. I remembered seeing the marijuana swirling around in the toilet bowl and knew then that it might just as well have been my career I was watching. I had just flushed thirteen years of hard endeavor down the drain. Yet, in the intensity of the moment, I had no idea just how much I was yet to suffer for this stupid mistake. The mental pain would come later that night when I tried unsuccessfully to sleep, and in the morning when I would have to face my command clothed in the shame of being exposed as a drug dealer, or in the words of the agent, "a junky."

My command couldn't believe that one of their chief petty officers had been busted selling dope. We were an elite unit. All of us had top secret clearances because we worked with nuclear weapons and were involved in some very secret projects. I had abruptly become an acute embarrassment for them. Military justice moves quickly, and soon I was standing before a court-martial board.

I was reduced in rank from chief petty officer to seaman recruit, sentenced to thirty days in the brig, and awarded a Bad Conduct Discharge. As I stood before the board, the words "Bad Conduct Discharge" sped through my mind like a hurling diesel locomotive. My shame couldn't have been greater. I instantly knew that the less-than-honorable discharge would follow me through the rest of my life.

The Command Master Chief escorted me directly to the military brig at Pearl Harbor.

The brig was an imposing two-story building of a simple block design. The exterior walls were a depressing battleship-gray. Crossed-sledge hammers hung over the heavy metal gate. Inside, a stern-faced marine sergeant was waiting. He marched me into the guard room where I was ordered to remove all of the insignia from my uniform. From my collar, I took the silver and brass fouled anchors that symbolized my rank as a chief petty officer and placed them onto a wooden table. Next to the tiny brass anchors, I laid three bars of Vietnam ribbons that had been pinned to my chest, followed by my gold jumpwings and the silver insignia that identified me as a bomb disposal frogman. Then, removing my khaki uniform, and clad only in my underwear, I sat stooped over on a small wooden stool while the marine guard roughly shaved my head.

Completely humiliated, my head hanging in shame, I was led down a long dark corridor and locked into a cold and dimly lit isolation cell. The days passed slowly while I sat alone in that cell rummaging though my thoughts of personal failure.

A close presence pulls me from my memories. A stewardess is leaning over me to take away the empty beer bottle. Keeping my eyes closed, still lost in the solitude of my mind, I see that muted cell block and know that it is waiting for me again.

CHAPTER 3

In Miami, I switch planes for the next leg, which will take me out of the country to the Bahamas. It is only a short flight, and almost before I'm ready, I am stepping off the plane. I'm immediately assaulted by the sultry heat of the Bahamas. I join the press of people heading for the international arrivals gate, and that's when I see Morgan. He is standing off to one side with broad bands of sweat marring his white shirt at the arm pits. He is beaming at me, apparently pleased to be a million dollars richer.

In the taxi on the way to his yacht, Morgan is full of ideas about how best to celebrate the evening. "We're having dinner at the island casino, and wait until you see your dinner date," he brags.

Walking into the plush casino just after sunset, Morgan is still riding high, the flush of money in the bank upon him. Walking at his side, I'm less than enthusiastic.

Morgan, aware of my sober mood, tries to cheer me up, "Your date's name is Kelly; she's tall, blonde, and very athletic."

We have barely stepped through the casino doors, when Morgan and I hear his name shrieked from halfway across the main gambling floor. Moving rapidly toward us through a sea of people are two women; heads turn in the wake of their passage. It doesn't take any real skill on my part to recognize Kelly, who is indeed blond—bleached blond, that is, with pink and blue highlights. Her hairstyle looks to have been heavily influenced by static electricity. She is wearing a chain mail jerkin over surprisingly large shoulders and a body-molding red, leather skirt. As she approaches, I hear a distinctive clicking sound coming from metal studs on the bottoms of her knee-high black boots. Fastened around her waist is a chromed, Harley-Davidson motorcycle chain, and slung playfully at her hips is a wide black leather belt with a silver skull-and-crossbones buckle. As she marches up the steps, I see that she likes black eye make-up, which she apparently buys by the pound. Her midnight eyes lock onto me. For a moment I am distracted by the sparkle of her handcuff earrings. A skunk is tattooed on her left arm. The noisy casino has gone almost completely silent as everyone stares. She stops in front of me and extends her hand. On the knuckle of her middle finger is a ring bearing a Nazi swastika.

I smile weakly at Kelly who anxiously shakes my hand. It's an opportunity for her to try out her grip. Her girlfriend, who looks surprisingly normal, leans toward me and proudly states in complete candor, "Hey, you're going to like being with Kelly. If we get into a fight, she swings a mean belt and doesn't mind going to the pavement for close-in kicking and scratching."

Kelly beams at the compliment then possessively takes my arm in a vice-like grip. Walking across the plush gambling floor toward the restaurant, we are truly an odd-looking couple with me looking like the victim and she like the vampire's bride. We're greeted by the hostess at the restaurant door. She does a double-take at Kelly and displays a grimace, which turns out to be a big mistake.

"How'd you like to have your lips wrapped around your head?" offers a perturbed Kelly.

At the dinner table I soon discover, along with most of the people sitting around us, that Kelly's favorite words, expressed loud and often, are all four-lettered-ear-burners.

A shy businessman sitting at the next table is prompted by his wife to say something. "Excuse me, miss," he says weakly, "but is all that vulgar language actually necessary?"

Kelly glares at the shy man who immediately leans backward toward the dubious protection of his wife. "Mind your own business," rages Kelly, "or I'll use you and that fancy cream suit you're wearing to mop the floor."

Holding my hands over my eyes does not make Kelly disappear. Unable to flee the situation, I instead spend most of the dinner sopping up the champagne. Later that evening we return to Morgan's yacht where the party continues. The last thing I remember is Kelly daring me to drink a tequila shooter, which unfortunately is followed by a chain of others.

The next morning I wake with a terrible hangover to the sound of Kelly snoring. Climbing out of bed, I note with relief that I am still clothed. Looking back at Kelly, whose snores continue uninterrupted, I see that she is still wearing her clothes as well as her boots. *Maybe nothing happened last night*, I think hopefully to myself.

A few minutes later in the shower I discover a rather large double bruise on my upper left arm. The mystery grows. Kelly, wearing a simulated tiger-skin bikini, wanders out on deck around eleven o'clock. She looks at me belligerently then goes to sit in the sun.

"Ahh, Kelly, you're not mad at me are you?" I'm hoping for a clue about last night.

"Leave it alone," she grumbles. A few minutes pass while we both stare at different points in the same ocean.

Finally, I can't contain myself any longer, "Ahh, Kelly, we didn't do anything last night . . . did we?"

"Have you noticed your arm?" snarls Kelly.

I look down at the bruise; the twin blue/black circles look like Mickey Mouse's ears. "Yeah, I was wondering about that."

"It's where I punched you—twice," glares Kelly.

"I did something wrong," I offer.

"Yeah, you wouldn't take your clothes off, and you didn't want to do it."

"I didn't?" My grin is hard to suppress; it slops across my face.

"You want another bruise you just keep grinning like that," threatens Kelly.

Later that afternoon Kelly is still wearing her tiger skin swimsuit as she lays stretched out in the sun. Morgan is sitting behind her. The book he has been reading lays forgotten in his lap. A sly leer plays across his face, then he leans down and whispers something in Kelly's ear. For a moment she looks startled, like Morgan has offered her a bug, then she leaps to her feet and clobbers him in the arm. The blow sends Morgan and his chair skidding across the slick deck. Kelly glares at Morgan, pulls down on the hem of her swimsuit, and storms off.

For a moment Morgan just sits there stunned. He rubs his injured arm then inspects it for damage. A large bruise is already forming. It had been quite an impact. Kelly, an experienced street fighter, had swung from the hip and gotten her broad shoulder muscles into the punch. "Looks like your bruise is going to be bigger than mine," I say with a smile.

Morgan continues to finger the blackening flesh, "I can't believe she punched me so hard."

"She packs quite a wallop," I present my bruised arm for him to see.

Morgan glances at the distinctive mouse ear bruise, "What did she punch you for?"

"I didn't want to do it," I answer with a shrug.

Morgan shakes his head in disgust, "You're not still pining over that Hawaiian girl, are you?"

"Her name is Susan, and she's not Hawaiian," I answer.

"Yeah, well you're still pining over her."

I have no choice but to nod in agreement. Not wanting to remain under Morgan's self-satisfied gaze I climb up onto the flying bridge and watch the bright tropical sunlight dancing on the calm water. Naturally, thoughts of Susan are rampant in my mind. I'm recalling a very special weekend on the Northshore of Hawaii that occurred right after I got out of the brig. It was early January, and the first big winter swell was pounding Oahu's reefs. Later it would become known as Big Sunday; I, however, would remember it as the day I met Susan.

I was standing on the beach taking pictures of some stupendous wipeouts with a long, 650mm telephoto lens. The monstrous waves had closed out most of the Northshore. Only the big breaks like

Waimea, Sunset, and Pipeline were still barely rideable. The tradewinds were holding the three- to four-story waves super critical before they broke with the crashing sound of rolling thunder. Just a few brave, or slightly crazy, surfers were out and riding the out-of-control waves. The others, huddled in a small pack, were just trying to survive long enough to make a hopeful dash for the safety of the beach between sets. A half-dozen broken surfboards had already washed up on the beach, and the morning was only half over.

I had just shot an excellent sequence of an overly brave, or incredibly stupid, marine who tried to conquer a vicious set wave with his little boogie board. When the massive lip had pitched with him in it, the marine swiftly found himself in hydraulic-assisted free fall, heading for an astonishing impact with the bottom. His mangled boogie board was just washing up on the beach when I was distracted by two good-looking blondes walking in my direction.

I, like most of the guys on the beach, watched them striding across the sand. I just didn't expect them to stop right in front of me; then, I recognized Caroline, whom I had met once at a party.

"What happened to your hair?" Caroline was amused by my near baldness. "Kind of short isn't it?" I avoided the topic of the brig.

Caroline stepped closer and ran her fingers through the short stubs. "It feels weird," she quipped. Caroline, who was nineteen-years-old, was on the University of Hawaii's varsity swim team. Her figure was sleek as a seal's. She looked ravishing in her tight, white, nylon, dolphin shorts and red bikini top; however, my attention riveted on Susan, who was absolutely stunning even while standing next to a fox like Caroline.

Susan was wearing jeans, a simple white cotton blouse, and sandals. She had long, blonde hair that fell in a silken cascade, which reached half way down her back. She was only a few inches shorter than my six feet. She wasn't wearing any make-up and seemed totally unaware that my heart was flopping in the hot sand at her feet. Like Caroline, she was nineteen-years-old.

Our eyes locked as Caroline introduced us. Susan's grin was open and friendly as she said, "I hope you're not trying to start a fad; your hair looks horrible."

"It keeps me from looking like every other surfer on the beach," I joked lamely.

Susan glanced about pretending not to notice that all the guys were staring in our direction. "You mind if we join you?" she asked.

"Be my guest," I grinned, subconsciously wiping drool from my lips.

Hidden behind my sunglasses, I ogled Susan as she slid out of her jeans. I couldn't help noticing that she had the kind of figure that surfers dream about while waxing up their surfboards. She checked that her burgundy swimsuit was in place—as did most of the guys on the beach—then lay down on a beach towel just a few feet away. She and Caroline shared a bottle of coconut oil. They took turns helping each other with the hard-to-reach spots. I took off my sunglasses to wipe away the sweat that was beginning to hinder my vision. Meanwhile, I missed shooting some really good, double-over-head, tube rides. My surfer friends were going to be bummed to the max.

The girls were just settling down to bask in the sun when a black Great Dane arrived at a dead run, spraying sand everywhere. Caroline glared at the big dog as she brushed at the sand that was sticking to her oil-covered skin, but Susan didn't seem to mind. She pushed playfully at the big Dane, "Who are you . . . you big mutt?"

"His name is not mutt, it's Puu," I answered while ruffling the Dane's ears, which were naturally floppy. (I don't approve of cropping a dog's ears.)

"Is he your dog?" Susan asked.

Puu was leaning against my legs, sopping up the attention. "Sometimes I think I belong to him. He tends to be rather possessive of me and his dog dish." Almost as if recognizing the words *dog dish*, Puu barked and began to pull on my baggy swimsuit with his teeth.

"What does he want?" Susan asked.

The Dane was bracing his big paws in the sand and was beginning to tug harder on my shorts. "He wants to be fed," I answered. "Would you like to watch? It's amazing what he can do to a twenty-five pound bag of dog food.

"Sure," Susan's smile was radiant in the morning light.

Puu led the way out to the parking lot where he stopped at the back of a very unique, wooden motorhome; it looked like a mountain cabin on wheels. I unlocked the backdoor and stepped to one side so Susan could see. She peered anxiously inside. "Is this where you live?" she asked.

I snapped my fingers at Puu who jumped inside. "It's where *we* live." I nodded at Puu, "He considers it his own mobile dog house, I call it *Revelstoke*."

"You made this?"

"Yeah, it used to be a Chevy truck until I altered it a bit with a hammer and a power saw."

Susan looked about the interior, which was designed along a nautical theme. Two stained glass sky lights admitted a cascade of sunlight for the many house plants that were growing in the nooks and corners. "It looks like the captain's cabin on an old sailing ship," she said in awe.

"I salvaged a lot of the wood from machine packing crates I sent back to the United States from Vietnam."

Opening a cabinet under the sink, I pulled out a heavy bag of dry dog food. I filled monster dog's dish, which was made from the lower third of a large metal trash can. Susan was watching Puu inhale his mountain of food. "Do you need feeding too?" I asked.

"Yeah," quipped Susan, "but I wasn't going to pull on your shorts with my teeth to ask." Later, after both of us had eaten and Puu went back outside to play, I realized that it was a perfect time to ask Susan out. The thought made me tongue-tied. Susan crossed her legs, brushed a wisp of hair from her face, looked right then left, took several deep breaths, and probably wondered why I was not asking her out. "Are you going to ask me out or not?" she finally asked.

"Ahh . . . err . . . I'd love to," I croaked awkwardly.

"You'd love to what?" asked Susan. She was affecting an innocent look.

"I'd love to ask you out," I blurted.

"Well, that's an original idea; why don't you try it?"

"Would you like to go out tonight?" I couldn't believe that there was a distinct quiver in my voice.

"Hmmmm," she placed a finger to her lips as if she were pondering my offer.

"Well?" I asked impatiently.

"I'm thinking about it." There was a mischievous glint to her eyes. Then before I got completely exasperated, she nodded, "O.K., but you'll have to pick me up at the restaurant where I work. I get off at nine, but if you arrive early, I'll make you dinner." I grinned at her. It was a big fat grin that threatened to swallow my whole face. I had absolutely no control over it.

"I'm glad we finally got that over with," teased Susan. "Dare I ask what we are going to do?"

"Dancing would be nice." I could feel the grin pulling at the flesh around my eyes, probably giving me a Quasimoto look. The grin became contagious as it infected Susan who developed a broad grin of her own.

Our faces were only inches apart. I looked into the depths of her liquid brown eyes and unconsciously moved to kiss her. It really wasn't my fault, my lips had apparently decided to take the action on their own. Susan saw it coming, her eyes widened in surprise. Then, she quickly stood up.

"Well, time to go," chimed Susan. A little later, I was leaning against Caroline's car (she drove a pink Volkswagon convertible), trying to look casual while my heart is hammering against my chest. Susan gave me another one of her wonderful, innocent smiles then casually asked, "Would you like to know the address or even the name of the restaurant?" She wrote it down and stuck the paper into my T-shirt pocket. "Don't lose the address."

My heart and I stood there. When they'd driven out of sight, I did a happy little jig about the tarmac. In the middle of a one-legged spin, I noticed two of my surfer friends watching me, their surfboards tucked under their arms. Water was dripping from their wet shorts. They were standing in a puddle of their own making, which meant they'd been there for a while . . . they didn't look happy.

"I hope you're not going to tell us that you haven't been shooting pictures," pleaded Jay.

"Ahh . . . "

"Steve, this is the best surf we've had all year. I almost killed myself out there thinking you were getting it on film."

"Ahh . . . "

"Do you see his dog anywhere?" inquired Jay. "I swear I'm going to kill him, but we better not try it in front of that crazy dog of his."

My shrill whistle brought Puu bounding up a couple of seconds later. He stopped at the puddle at the surfers' feet to get a drink before jumping nonchalantly into the truck. "Well, gotta go, guys," I smiled and made a fast exit.

"Steve!" Morgan's shout pulls me instantly back to reality, "Get down here right now." I see Morgan hanging up the telephone—he's in a complete panic. "We've got problems," he says urgently, "I've just heard that one of my girlfriends in California has been interrogated by the DEA. They know I'm moving drugs, but so far they don't have any hard evidence."

"What are you going to do?" I ask.

"I'm flying to California on tonight's plane. I want you to take the girls to the airport; then move the boat to Fort Lauderdale. Call me when you get there." Morgan rushes below to pack his bags. For a moment I pause to think about the implication of what Morgan just said about his being under investigation. I find it very interesting that the thought pleases me.

An hour before sunset I cast off the lines and carefully maneuver the big boat out of the Paradise Hole Marina and set a course due west. As the yacht plunges lightly into the calm Caribbean Sea, I stare at the fiery orb of the sun, which is slowly sinking into a flat sea. A multitude of stars appears in the heavens. I dim the sweeping green light of the radar then stare into the dark of the night. Standing alone at the helm, my thoughts drift back in time to my date with Susan on Big Sunday.

After parking outside the restaurant where Susan worked, I quickly pulled on a pair of jeans and took out my favorite aloha shirt. Fortunately, it passed my sniff test, which could be a rare event. I put it on and brushed out the larger wrinkles. I took a moment to practice my best Tom Selleck smile in front of the mirror. Puu guarded the truck as I stepped out into the tropical night with my hopeful thoughts.

A small bell attached to the door tinkled as I walked into the restaurant. I immediately saw Susan who strode quickly over to greet me. We stood there for a moment grinning at each other while the little bell jingled merrily above us.

Laulima was one of those Hawaiian hippie-type restaurants where customers sat directly on the floor on top of pillows while eating off low Japanese tables. Soft, environmental music drifted from the walls and sandalwood incense wafted lightly on the air. The place was packed, mostly with strange-looking characters—I knew I fit right in.

On Susan's recommendation, I ordered a bean tostada, then she scurried off to serve the other tables while I tried to appear as though I was not watching her. She turned to smile in my direction then disappeared into the kitchen.

Unbeknownst to me, and despite the protests of the Hawaiian/ Chinese cook, she was building a monster bean tostada. She piled on the frijoles until they began to slop over the side of the plate. Since I was watching the kitchen door as alertly as Puu observes an untended picnic basket, I saw Susan as soon as she exited the kitchen. She was carrying a large plate on which squatted a respectable bean mountain. I was wondering if it was for the family of four sitting at the next table when she abruptly plopped it down in front of me. An ounce of beans slopped onto the table. I stared in awe at the size of this bean volcano. "This is a tostada?" I asked.

"Is there anything wrong with it?" Susan was again affecting her innocent smile.

"No, it looks fine," I offered lamely. "Any chance of trading this spoon in for a shovel?" If my Hawaiian shirt had long sleeves I would have rolled them up.

Ten minutes later, Susan returned as I was sopping up the last of the beans with a corn tortilla. "You ate the whole thing!" Susan was gaping at my empty plate. She ran back into the kitchen and returned, dragging the cook. "Look," she pointed proudly. "He did it all by himself." I felt like the little kid who just completed his first successful attempt at potty-training for his proud parents.

Instead of dancing, we decided to take a long walk on the beach at Waikiki under a full moon. We talked about harmless subjects, discovering each other with words, while sensual energies lurked subtly beneath our social dialogue.

It was Susan's idea to go back to visit Puu, who was on guard duty in the truck. After romping with him in the parking lot we went inside *Revelstoke* together. I put some Hawaiian slack key music on the stereo and lit a few candles. Above us, the stained-glass skylight admitted a soft lunar glow from the full moon. Falling silent, we stared into each other's eyes; then Susan raised a hand to her pony tail, a moment later her golden hair fell in a fan across her upper back and shoulders where it gathered the soft candlelight and seemed to have a sparkle all its own. I took a silken lock into my hand and lightly placed it against my lips. Susan's eyes were very wide and very trusting as I kissed her.

A shrill beep calls my attention to the radar scope on Morgan's yacht. Increasing the brightness on the fluorescent screen, I see that a boat has entered the radar's alarm shield. I alter our course, though the other boat is still miles away. Then, in an unsuccessful attempt to shake off the sadness that suddenly grips at my soul, I step out of the wheelhouse and walk to the lightly plunging bow. I wonder at the unhappiness that so fills my life. I miss Susan and Puu, yet even more I hate the downward-spiralling direction my life is taking. I still can't quite believe that I'm living in a criminal world now. Happiness seems so far in the past that it is but a memory—just like Susan and Puu.

CHAPTER 4

After tying up the boat in Fort Lauderdale, I call Morgan from a public telephone at the beach. "It isn't good news," Morgan says anxiously, his panic approaching a frantic level. I smile inwardly. Although I am involved, I would like to see justice reach out and touch Morgan and company. Practically breathless, Morgan continues, "Just in case things get worse, I want you to ready the *Fling* (Morgan's boat) for an extended trip out of the country."

"I'm going to need some money for repairs," I answer.

"I can't risk sending any from here, you'll have to get the money from Max."

The thought of seeing Max sends a shiver down my spine. "How do I get a hold of him?"

"You don't; he'll get in touch with you." The phone goes dead in my hand.

The next morning I'm returning to the boat with a bag of groceries when I see two Latin men lounging on the stern deck. One of them is Scar Face, the Colombian who was guarding Max's door at the Marriott Hotel. As I board the boat, Scar Face steps between me and the saloon door. He peers into the grocery bag, then, his hand moving quickly, he flicks open a butterfly knife and stabs a green apple from the bag. I carefully keep both of my hands wrapped around the paper sack in plain sight—non-threatening. Scar Face slices off a piece of the apple and bites into it. A second later, he spits it onto the deck. "These apples are sour!" he scowls.

"I was going to make a pie," I answer without thinking.

Scar Face looks at the other Colombian, who is standing to one side of me. "He was going to make a pie," mocks Scar Face. He turns back to me. "I suppose you're an expert with a spatula, too."

I say nothing, knowing that the man is in a dangerous mood. Not getting the response he hoped for, Scar Face closes the knife. "Forget the pie," he snarls, "you're coming with us. Max wants to see you." The ride to Miami in the back of their car is long, hot, and sweltering. Being scared didn't help matters any.

Max lives in a wealthy neighborhood called Miami Lakes at the end of a plush street. His house is white stucco with a red tile roof. It's a lavish affair with a small man-made lake lapping at the back door. According to Scar Face, Max owns the houses on either side of his, thus surrounding himself with the trusted security of family for protection. Scar Face opens the door and pushes me into the shadowed coolness inside.

Max strides purposefully across the front room floor to meet me. He's about five-foot, ten-inches tall with a stocky build. He is wearing a loose, white shirt and black chino trousers that gather at the ankles. His eyes still have that piercing, reptilian look that commands my attention. They are of the darkest brown with large black pupils that hint he may be a little crazy. He exudes a bestial power that lurks within the realm of the sadistic. Max scares me so much that I have to consciously focus on not trembling in his presence.

He places his arm over my shoulder and leads me into his private domain. The ever-present armed soldiers (there are two more of them) stand right and left just outside the kitchen door. Max introduces me to his two cousins who are related to him via his marriage to a Colombian woman.

"I only employ family," he states proudly, "who else can I trust?" Then squeezing my shoulder firmly, he adds, "I want you to get acquainted with my men, Steve, so you will truly know they are from me should I ever have to get a hold of you unexpectedly." The reptile eyes blink. My soul shudders under that cold stare. His meaning is incredibly clear; I am again being subtly warned.

The money isn't there yet, so Max asks me to join him for lunch. There are a couple of things that he wants to talk about. Since I'm supposedly Morgan's right-hand man, Max feels he can speak frankly. First of all, he isn't a bit happy about Morgan's new banking arrangements. Morgan is currently laundering his money through a San Francisco bank that apparently doesn't mind accepting drug money. Max, who doesn't know about Morgan's current problems, says he thinks it stinks of a DEA sting operation. Later, he is proved correct.

Max is also having a little trouble with the attitude of one of Morgan's pilots, the man I had flown to Columbia with. Apparently the pilot has tried to work out his own deal with Max, who is presently shaking his head in disgust. "The guy's a drunk, too. You just can't trust someone like that; he might talk too much. I think we ought to dump on him, you know what I mean?" Max looks at me quite frankly. There is no doubt of his meaning.

My heart races as I realize that Max is actually talking about killing a person. He says it so casually, with all the emotional feeling of a man swatting a fly.

Memories of the pilot leap to mind. This is someone that I know, someone that I drank beer with, someone who has told me about his hopes and aspirations—and Max wants to know whether I think killing him is a good idea? I wonder how Morgan would react to this news. I can't see him sanctioning the death of a friend. Yet, I don't doubt that Max will do whatever suits him, with or without Morgan's permission.

This whole conversation is getting to be a bit much for me. I'm not sure how to answer, I certainly don't want to react wrongly. The reptilian eyes are watching, waiting for the proper response. Fortunately, I'm saved from answering by the arrival of the money in the form of a twelve-year-old kid wearing shorts and a Space Invaders T-shirt. His name is Pedro, and he is carrying a large black leather satchel.

Pedro is accompanied by his father, who is Max's number two man. He is a sharp dresser with sophisticated Cuban tastes. He is wearing a white shark-skin suit and lots of gold jewelry. He moves with the smooth, effortless, flowing quality of a cat. I've seen his type before in Nam. He is the quiet, competent killer.

The boy is obviously devoted to his father; it shows in the way he looks up to him and in how he tries to emulate his habits and mannerisms. Pedro knows exactly what he wants to be when he grows up—a killer just like dad. Meanwhile, he is apparently at an acceptable age for learning the family trade. So much for a happy childhood, I think to myself.

Pedro sets the satchel down on the table opposite me then reaches greedily inside. He takes out two black leather cases and carefully opens one. I'm amazed to see that it contains an Ingram MAC-10 machine pistol. He hands it to Max, who immediately begins checking the action by cocking the slide mechanism. Pedro opens the second case and takes out a second machine pistol, which he handles with a loving caress. I can almost see the bloodthirsty thoughts running around in his little mind. Unexpectedly, he looks directly at me. Hate and hostility leap from those young eyes with such sudden ferocity that the hair on the back of my neck stands on end. I can't imagine this kid playing with other children; on a playground, he would more closely resemble a barracuda among a school of minnows.

Max, who hasn't missed Pedro's look says, "Go ahead, Pedro, give it to him." Tensing, I look back at the kid whose finger is white on the trigger. *CLICK!* The sound of the pistol's hammer falling on an empty chamber is abnormally loud. Max laughs boisterously then leans over and ruffles Pedro's hair, "This kid is going to be one tough hombre." Pedro, suddenly a child again, beams at the praise.

Max sits back in his chair and more seriously says, "Pedro, give Steve what you brought." The small outlaw reaches into the satchel and takes out a four-inch thick bundle of money. He can barely grip it with his small hands. He tosses the money onto the middle of the table like it is nothing. He returns his attention to the machine pistol that is far more interesting. Apparently he has already learned that money is just a tool in the family trade.

Pedro, lost in a fantasy world of ricochetting bullets, spins in his chair and puts an imagined burst into an unknown enemy, "Burrrp, burrrp." Pedro's upper torso shakes as he imitates the shudder of the gun on full auto. I, too, had played with toy guns and imagined enemies as a child, but the MAC-10 in Pedro's hands was no toy, and I don't believe his imagined enemies are the normal villains viewed by the average twelve-year-old kid.

Watching the young, dark eyes seeking out fantasy targets, I think about the childhood happiness that Pedro would probably never know. The family would require that Pedro grow up far too soon. I don't doubt that he will live a violent life, motivated by twisted values and corrupt pleasures.

Our business finished, Max escorts me to the front door. I realize that we haven't actually eaten any lunch. Placing his hand on my back in a friendly way that is very intimidating, he says, "Remember to talk with Morgan and just call if you want me to take care of that little problem with the pilot. My boys are always so anxious to please." The reptilian eyes smile.

After Scar Face returns me to the boat, I rush below and open a secret drawer. With shaking hands, I quickly roll a joint. I am again smoking marijuana as I desperately seek to cope with my out-of-control life. I'm running scared, lost in a criminal world with no one to turn to and nowhere to go. Fear is my constant companion and paranoia my bedmate.

CHAPTER 5

I wake the next morning hating myself. My life has taken a downward spiral that promises only to get worse. Morgan's plan to leave the country doesn't sit well with me. I don't relish leaving my home for an unknown life among outlaws. For a moment I consider what it would be like living with Scar Face and Max as my constant companions. The thought convinces me that the only solution is to flee Morgan and company. A plan has been growing in the back of my mind, and in a single instant, it puts down roots. I will return to Hawaii and disappear into Oahu's Northshore surfing community.

My plan is simple. I'll tell Morgan that I need some time away, maybe a little surf jaunt to Hawaii with my old friend Sam. Actually, Sam is only twenty-two-years-old, but we've been friends for over a decade. We learned to surf together in Hawaii and have since maintained a close friendship. Currently, he lives in San Diego, but I know that he is anxious to return to Hawaii.

A few minutes later I have him on the telephone and drop my idea in a very appealing way: "Sam, how would you like to go to Hawaii and surf your brains out—my treat?"

Sam's wild enthusiasm is instantaneous, "I'll quit my job, drop my girl friend, and be ready to go tomorrow morning."

"Well, don't do anything just yet," I caution, "I still have to run the idea past Morgan."

"So, what's the problem?" asks Sam, who has met Morgan on several occasions.

"Well, he has me fixing up his boat, and it's going to take some time to finish."

"Look, if you need any help," he offers. No one loves to surf more than Sam.

"No," I reply, "you just hang loose. I'll let you know when we are leaving."

I'm about to break the connection when Sam casually asks, "Hey, are you planning on seeing Susan while we are in Hawaii?"

My heart squeezes into itself at the mention of her name, "No, Sam," I answer, hanging up the telephone.

I quickly dial Morgan's number before I lose my nerve.

"What do you mean you need a vacation?" Morgan is not happy. "How could you possibly need a vacation? All we do is play."

"Morgan, I just need a little time away with Sam," I plead, "I haven't surfed in a long time."

"So what, the world doesn't revolve around surfing."

I try to make light of the situation, "You're only saying that because you don't surf, Morgan." Before he can say no, I bring forward my best argument, "Look, with you under investigation wouldn't it be a good idea if I was somewhere else at least for a couple of weeks?"

"How much money do you want to take?" Morgan asks cautiously.

I know this is my chance to sink the hook. Morgan still owes me the fifty thousand that he promised for my trip to Colombia. If I ask for too much money he would suspect that I'm not coming back. "Fifteen grand," I answer weakly.

"What?" Morgan's cry of outrage leaps from the phone.

"You don't understand," I answer quickly, "Morgan, I'm a criminal now. If anything goes wrong with the investigation, I'm going to need enough money to rejoin you wherever you are."

After a moment's pause Morgan concedes, "Yeah, that's true. Maybe you better take twenty grand; it wouldn't hurt for you to have the extra cash."

"Good idea," I answer quickly.

"However you're not going anywhere until you finish with that boat. I want to get it out of the country as soon as possible."

Throughout most of the morning I'm wearing a happy grin, which fades abruptly while scraping paint on a part of the bow section. I have found a large patch of the hull that is showing signs of wood rot. After spending the day cutting away the rotted wood, I call Sam later that evening to tell him I'd be delayed by at least a week.

"No problem," chirps Sam, "because I'm coming out to help."

"What?" I couldn't have been more shocked.

"Yeah, I called Morgan and offered my services. He's stoked, seems he wants to get his boat fixed fast."

"You're not coming out here . . . " I begin to argue.

"It's too late. I've already quit my job, and my girlfriend isn't talking to me anymore—she said I loved surfing more than her. What could I say, she was right."

I try to talk Sam out of coming, but he won't listen. The last thing I want is to have Sam hanging around Morgan, "The Great Corrupter." In any case, Sam arrives the following day. Even with Sam's help the work is still going too slow. I figure we have about two more weeks to go, when Morgan arrives unexpectedly on the pier with a little surprise.

"How would you guys like to leave right away for Hawaii?" he shouts up to us with a broad grin.

I am suspicious of Morgan bearing gifts, so I yell back, "What's the catch, Morgan?"

"What catch?" he exclaims. "Actually, I've got a relatively simple job which I think you will both thoroughly enjoy. I need a new car driven to California." His offer doesn't seem strange because Morgan has been pricing Rolls Royces in Florida to avoid any California record of the sale. Morgan is quite cheerful as he tells us to pack our bags. We'll be leaving first thing in the morning. I should have known that something was up. Morgan only gets that cheerful when he is about to make a lot of money.

Sam and I spent the night foolishly celebrating. The next morning I'm a little late joining Morgan for breakfast. Over the rim of his coffee cup, he says, "Look, you want to be real careful how you drive this car."

I shrug my shoulders, "Of course we'll be careful. It's not exactly like we're going to go racing about in your Rolls Royce."

Looking genuinely surprised, Morgan asks, "What do you mean Rolls Royce?"

"You said you were buying a new car; I just figured it was one of those Rolls Royces you've been pricing."

Setting his coffee cup down, he answers irritably, "I'm not buying a car; we're just doing a favor for a friend. It's his car, not mine."

I know I've been had again. "Morgan," I ask, dreading the answer, "is there anything in particular I should know about this car?"

"Don't ask," Morgan quips, "this way what you and Sam don't know can't hurt you."

"You have got to be out of your mind! I thought you were out of the drug business, and what about the investigation?" Morgan anxiously looks at the other tables while motioning with his hands for me to keep my voice down.

Leaning across the table, he whispers, "Everything is cool. Look, how would you like to take an extra twenty thousand with you on your trip? Do this and I'll give it to you." I know right then and there that Morgan isn't going to let me go to Hawaii unless I drive that car. He still doesn't know that I intend to bail out on him, and I certainly could use that extra twenty thousand. Starting a life from scratch isn't going to be cheap.

The waitress, a cute innocent-looking teen-ager, steps up to the table to refill Morgan's coffee cup. He smiles wantonly at her then pauses in our conversation to watch her walk away. Dropping four lumps of sugar into his coffee, Morgan continues, "Look, the car is going to be a little late; I want you to take my girlfriend to the airport."

I return to Sam's and my room and tell him to grab his bags and meet me in the parking lot. Morgan's latest girlfriend is already waiting in the car when Sam shows up. The three of us cram into the front seat together. The girl is pleased to be riding close to Sam, and she spends most of her time flirting with him.

After dropping her off at the departure terminal, I turn to Sam. "You're getting out here, too. I want you to take a flight home and get everything ready for the trip. I'll join you in four or five days."

Sam is shocked. "No way," he replies, "I'm going with you."

"Sam," I put my hand on his shoulder, "trust me on this one O.K.? It will be much better if you go now, then we'll be ready to leave that much sooner."

That's when Sam drops a little bomb shell of his own, "It's O.K., Steve, I know that there's going to be something in the car. Morgan called up to the room from the restaurant and offered me five thousand bucks to ride shotgun with you. Cool, huh?"

I'm shocked. "He what?!" I scream.

"Five thousand bucks," echoes Sam, "now I'll be able to pay my own way to Hawaii."

"Sam, you don't want to do this; there isn't anything cool about it. Go get on that airplane."

We argue for about fifteen minutes, but Sam is adamant about going with me. Reluctantly I agree, which is, of course, a bad idea. My only excuse is that at the time I'm not thinking too straight. The stress that is my constant companion and the marijuana I've been smoking don't lend themselves to rational thought.

I tell Sam that he can ride with me on one condition only: if we are busted, he must act like he doesn't know a thing about what is in the car. "It's coke, isn't it?" Sam asks with a knowing smile. I look at my young friend and wonder where his innocence has gone. For an instant I remember him as a happy teen-ager whose only thoughts were about surfing and girls. I realize that simple innocence doesn't stand much of a chance around Morgan and his sophisticated manipulations. He has a way of beating the word "No" into submission with a fist full of hundred dollar bills.

Back at the Pier 66 Hotel we wait anxiously for the car to arrive. Max's people finally show up early in the evening. I go outside to meet with them alone. There are at least eight Colombians covering the parking lot. I know there has to be a lot of coke hidden in the car. Max only plays in the big leagues.

I see Scar Face waiting for me. He is leaning alongside a Chevy Caprice. "How was your pie?" he asks sarcastically. Opening the car door, he points to a button hidden under the dash then pats the backseat. I understand. The button is the trigger that will release the backseat, which covers where the cocaine is hidden. Next, he walks around to the back of the car and opens the trunk. It is empty except for a case of fancy pineapples. He picks up two and bashes them together. "The pineapples, they mask the smell of the cocaine."

Scar Face grabs another pineapple and, flicking open his butterfly knife, cuts out a piece of the fruit. He points the tip of the fruit-laden knife at me, "Want some?"

"No thanks." I'm not in a social mood. "Is that all?"

"Yeah," he bites into the slice of fruit. Wiping juice from his chin, he says, "Maybe when you get to California you can use the pineapples to make a pie." Walking toward the lobby of the hotel to get Sam, I hear Scar Face laughing behind me.

As Sam and I are crossing the parking lot, he becomes suspicious of all the Latin men hanging around in the shadows. He sides up to me and whispers that we should be on our guard with all these Mexicans hanging around.

"They're Colombians, not Mexicans, Sam," I'm trying to be patient.

"Well, in any case, don't worry," he says, "if anything goes down you can count on me."

I wonder what he is going to do against eight Colombians armed with automatic weapons . . . threaten them with his pocket knife? "Sam, you're being stupid," I say angrily, "the bad guys are on our side." I am not in the best of moods.

"They're on our side?" Sam is awed.

"Yeah, welcome to the criminal world," I look not unkindly at my young friend. "I tried to warn you, Sam. You know, it's not too late for me to drop you off at the airport. I'm telling you, you really don't want to be in this car." Sam is too wrapped up in the intrigue and the promise of five thousand dollars to be dissuaded. I repeat my earlier warning, "Just remember, whatever happens, you didn't know a thing; promise me you will say that." Sam promises.

I have just gotten on the northbound interstate when I hear the voice of Ronald Reagan, the President of the United States, coming over the radio. He is announcing the formation of a new anti-drug task force to fight organized crime. Even more importantly, he calls on all Americans to help in the country's war on drugs, which implies we are actively losing in a big way.

As an ex-American fighting man, I have an extraordinary commitment to my country. I know I'm on the wrong side of the fence, but I have no idea how to climb back over to the right side and not wind up in a body bag in the process. Having stepped into the criminal underworld, I can't now find my way out. Reluctantly, I continue down the highway and into the dark of the night.

Late that evening we pull into a motel. I'm more mentally fatigued than anything else. I have to crash even for a few hours and don't want Sam driving yet. In the hotel room I lie awake far into the night, wrestling with my conscience.

The next morning, I go out alone to the car while Sam is still on the toilet and push the button hidden under the dash. I have to see for myself what we are carrying. The backseat pops forward with an audible snap. My soul shudders as I stare at row after row of brown-paper-wrapped bricks each containing a kilo of cocaine. When Sam comes walking out, I quickly close the seat. If he doesn't see the cocaine, his story will hold up that much better.

I drive all that day and well into the night. We are now just entering east Texas, and I'm so dog-tired that I finally let Sam drive. He seems pretty out of it himself, so rather than risk an accident, I ask him to get off the interstate and to find us a motel.

We pull into a small town where I have seen a flashing motel sign from the highway. We stop for a traffic light in the left turn lane then wait for it to turn green. All Sam has to do is make a simple left turn into the motel parking lot. Somehow Sam misses the driveway and winds up making an illegal U-turn.

"Sam," I yell, "what the heck are you doing? The last thing we need is a hassle with a small town Texas cop."

Sam drives about three quarters of a mile down the road to where it is safe to turn around. We then proceed back to the light. I look angrily at Sam and snarl, short-tempered, "Now, don't screw it up this time."

He does. I couldn't believe it. "Look, idiot, it's not real tricky, just aim the stupid car into the stupid driveway!" I am livid.

A couple of minutes later we return to the signal. It's red, of course. While we wait I notice that Sam's knuckles are white on the steering wheel. I knew I should say something to calm him down, but I am too upset. When the light finally flashes green, Sam who has been staring intently at the signal, begins to pull out immediately. "Look out!" I scream.

Sam stomps on the brakes stopping the car inches from a hurl-ing eighteen-wheeler that is running the red light. I stare wide-eyed at the huge machine rumbling past mere inches from our bumper; its mammoth tires are flinging dirt and gravel against our windshield. As a cloud of dust settles about the car, Sam sits there in a state of shock. Behind us other cars begin honking their horns anxious to make the light. "Go!" I yell.

Sam floors it. The car lurches forward almost giving me whiplash. Unbelievably, he is in the process of missing the driveway again. Frantically, I reach across and grab the wheel, fighting him for control. The car bounces over the curb, across a narrow side-walk, and into the motel parking lot before coming to a jerky stop. Sam has stalled the engine and is looking at me with panic. I growl at him, my words unintelligible. I'm ready to choke him with my bare hands; my fingers flex like claws in eager anticipation. Pulling the keys out of the ignition, I roar, "Wait here!"

I stomp off into the motel foyer. My mood doesn't improve when I discover that the place is booked. Sam doesn't ask any questions when I get back into the car and drive toward the interstate. He just sits quietly in the passenger seat, sulking.

We are up early the next morning and quickly get ourselves out of Texas. We have just crossed the New Mexico state line, with a sigh of relief, when a speeding black Subaru flies past us. A state trooper going the other way makes a rapid U-turn and speeds in pursuit.

The Subaru hasn't missed seeing the trooper either; he pulls over into the right lane ahead of me and slows rapidly. I have been doing the speed limit, fifty-five mph, but the Subaru has slowed to under fifty mph, and now I'm right behind the idiot trying not to crowd his bumper. The speeding police car is coming up fast. If I pass the Subaru, which has slowed to forty-five mph, I might attract the state trooper's attention to me. I just know the cop is going to pull both of us over. His red light begins to flash as he pulls alongside. Then, at the last moment, he maneuvers between us and pulls the Subaru over.

Watching the red light fade in the rearview mirror, I realize that being a criminal means that mere circumstance could land me in jail. Then, even more startled, I think about the many other life threatening dangers that revolve around being a part of the criminal world. Murder and gang hits are a natural part of the drug underworld, and I was right in the middle of it. Sheepishly glancing over at my young friend, I realize that Sam is in the middle of it also . . . compliments of Morgan and me.

The next day, in the late afternoon, I let Sam drive again. He needed some reassuring, and, besides it being a straight and deserted desert highway, I figure even he couldn't get into any trouble . . . or so I thought.

I'm comfortably napping in the right seat after telling Sam to wake me before we get to the California border. There is an agricultural inspection station there. I want to dump the last of the pineapples so we won't attract any undo notice from the border inspector. There are only a few of the pineapples left. Lately, Sam has taken to eating them when I am not looking. I wake abruptly to the sound of voices raised in heated argument. Opening my eyes, I'm momentarily blinded by intense sunlight. The burning orb of the sun is low on the horizon and its bright glare is shining directly into the windshield. I rub my eyes trying to clear them; then, I see the vague outline of a man leaning into the car through Sam's window. Something flashes silver on his chest. As my eyes focus, I see that it is a badge in the shape of a star pinned to a tan uniform. My heart leaps wildly. It's a border inspector!

Sam and the border inspector are arguing over a pineapple that Sam has smuggled into the front seat. He was probably planning on eating it while I slept. Sam doesn't want to give it up. The border inspector is getting upset. All the while I am seriously entertaining thoughts of throttling Sam. I can't believe he's risking both of us going to prison for an unknown number of years—over a fruit!

Finally, they reach a compromise. Sam rips the leafy top off of the pineapple and hands it to the border inspector who, now satisfied, grudgingly waves us through.

Driving away, Sam glances over at me and, with a big grin, brags, "See, we didn't have to throw the pineapples away. I knew I could get this one through, and I've got two more hidden in my bag in the trunk."

At that moment I can't decide which is more appealing, to strangle him or just to bash him about a bit with that stinking pineapple. "You know, Sam," I answer, angrily, "the only reason you have a brain is to keep your ears from caving in."

Just before the sun completely sets, I relieve Sam at the wheel. The desert seems so peaceful and calm as the day fades to darkness. With our trip almost over, I have just begun to relax, when out of the darkness a mule deer runs onto the road. It is a large buck with a magnificent set of antlers. In the super slow motion that occurs just prior to an accident, I see the deer running gracefully on a collision course with the speeding car. I desperately try to miss it by angling the car hard to the right. For a frozen moment, I see the buck captured in the bright glare of the left headlight beam. Then I hear more than feel a slight jar. Instantly, the buck disappears from sight. The incident happens so fast, I'm not sure whether I have really hit the beast. Slowing rapidly, I pull to the right and stop.

Getting out of the car, I look for damage and find none. Maybe for a hopeful moment I think I might have missed the deer. I breathe a premature sigh of relief; then, I see the brown fur.

It is only a little tuft of hair lodged in the side of the bumper. A tiny wisp of blood tells all the story I need to know. I desperately wanted to go back and check on the animal, but there is no way I can risk having a highway patrolman find me at the scene of an accident. My hands shake on the steering wheel as I drive away.

"Aren't we going to go back and check on the deer?" asks Sam, "I think it may be hurt."

"Of course it's hurt," I yell, "only we can't go back—not with the cocaine in the car."

"What are we going to do?" There is a quiver to Sam's voice, and his eyes are wet with tears. For a moment I don't answer. Instead, I stare at the white interrupted line painted down the middle of the dark highway and remember the Mojave airstrip and my fateful trip to Colombia. I hate the life I am living now and suddenly know that if I don't do something this instant, Morgan and Max are going to own me for the rest of my life.

I look over at Sam and with the confidence of a decision made, "We're going to California, but I'm no longer following Morgan's plan."

"What do you mean?"

"I've had it, Sam. I wasn't planning on coming back from Hawaii, but I'm calling it quits now. Once we get to Los Angeles I'm parking the car and we're walking away from it."

"Won't that make Morgan mad?"

I stare at Sam, thinking he can't be serious, but he is.

An hour later, we cross the Los Angeles County line. It seems like *déja vu* that the interstate passes within a few hundred yards of my mother's house. I vividly remember flying over her home with the huge load of cocaine, and now I am again passing in the night with another load. Thinking of her and knowing how she would feel about what I'm doing only adds to my resolve. I know without a doubt that I was never cut out to be a criminal.

I drop Sam off at the Valley Hilton, then drive the car alone to the Van Nuys Airport where I abandon it at the Sky Ways Restaurant parking lot. Then I call Morgan in Florida. "Morgan," I roar over the telephone, "I've had it. You can keep your drug money, but I want out."

"Hold on, Steve," Morgan cautions, "what's the problem?"

"Your car's the problem," I yell.

"Calm down. Now, where's the car?"

"I parked it. You want it? Come get it. I'm at the Valley Hilton, room 327." I'm glad it's finally over. Maybe, I hope, against all odds, Max will leave me alone once he gets his cocaine. The next day, Morgan calls from the LAX Marriott. He wants me to bring the car by. I have Sam take me to the hotel in his Volkswagon baja bug. I tell him to wait outside while I go into the lobby. Using one of the hotel phones, I call Morgan in room #501. He says he will be right down. A few minutes later, I see Morgan walking towards me across the lobby. When he offers his hand I drop the car keys into his palm.

"Where's the car," he asks, "in the parking lot?"

"No, Morgan," I answer, "the car is in front of the Sky Ways Restaurant at Van Nuys Airport."

He totally flips out. "You mean the car is just sitting there, unattended? Are you nuts?"

I reply fiercely, "Remember, I quit!" I'm in an emotional state.

"Forget quitting," he curses in anger. "Steve, this is not a time for games; we're dealing with some very heavy dudes. These guys are mobsters. Right now they're waiting upstairs with the money on the table. These people don't screw around. If we don't hand deliver that cocaine, you and I are going to wind up in a couple of garbage bags!" He pauses to think for a moment, then snarls, "Don't move." He hurries back into the elevator. In less than a minute he returns with two serious looking men walking at his side.

Both of the men are dressed in dark suits. One of the them is fat and stocky, he waddles as he walks. The other man is lean with a mean look about him. His walk is more like a prowl, I am reminded of a junk yard dog looking for trouble. The lean man is wearing a permanent sneer on his face—it is probably influenced by the heavy caliber pistol he is packing; it causes his tailored jacket to bulge on the right side. I don't doubt that he is Mafia. The fat man I recognize as James Timothy Hoffman. Morgan introduced me to Hoffman a couple of months earlier. I remember Morgan telling me not to trust this guy. The three of them stop in front of me.

"This is Louie," Morgan nods toward Sneer Face, "and you already know Hoffman." Hoffman leers at me. I know that whatever is coming next, I'm not going to like it. "You have to take them to the car." Morgan frowns at me in a way that encourages no argument.

"O.K., but I have to go outside to get rid of Sam." I purposely left Sam out in the parking lot, not wanting him involved any more than necessary. Louie follows me outside and watches as I walk over to Sam's Volkswagon. In the parking lot, I see several other men in the shadows; I figure they're with Louie. Sam looks up from the *Surfer* magazine he is reading. It still hasn't gotten through to him that we are messing around in the deadly serious world of big time criminals. I lean on his door, trying to look casual. "Look, Sam, Morgan needs me for a little while. I want you to go back to the hotel and wait for me."

Sam closes the magazine after dog-earing the page. I momentarily wonder how anyone can forget what page they are on in a magazine, after all, he only has to look at the pictures. It's amazing what passes through your mind when you are under serious stress. "Sure," Sam answers absently, "there's a picture on the tube I want to catch anyway."

I wonder what is going on in his head. There are armed men lurking in the shadows watching our every move. They're probably thinking that Sam and I might try a get away and are prepared to rivet us with bullet holes. And Sam is idly thinking about surfing and catching a science fiction movie on the boob tube.

I step well away from the car so the bad guys will know that I'm not fleeing with Sam as he revives the sooped-up Volkswagon engine toward the red line then peels out of the parking lot. I watch

Sam drive safely away; then looking towards the hotel entrance, I see Louie and his shadows waiting for me. Reluctantly, I walk alone up the driveway. Morgan has sent for the silver Cadillac. It pulls smoothly in front of the lobby entrance. The young, uniformed driver steps out and holds the door open with his hand outstretched for a tip.

Reaching into my wallet for a couple of dollar bills, I think how crazy life is. Here I'm possibly on my way to my own funeral, and I am worrying about tipping the parking valet. "Thank you," chirps the valet taking the two crumbled bills, "have a nice evening." I doubt a nice evening is possible as I watch Louie slide into the front seat next to me. Hoffman lowers his bulk into the backseat. I feel his heavy breathing on the back of my neck.

As I pull out onto the dark street, Louie looks over with what he probably thinks is a friendly smile; actually it isn't much of an improvement on the sneer. "So where are we going to pick up the stuff?" he demands in a coarse Italian accent.

I wonder if he is trying to scare me with his behavior, because if he is . . . it's succeeding. He shifts in the seat and visibly moves the gun under his jacket into a more comfortable position . . . or, I suddenly wonder, is he making it more available?

"We're going to Van Nuys Airport," I reply.

In the rear view mirror I see his smile fade; his hand drops to his coat unbuttoning it. He turns toward me in the seat, his jacket flap opening to reveal the polished wooden grip and black metal of a .38 revolver. Placing his left hand on my shoulder, he asks "So tell me, when we get to your car are you going to have any friends waiting?"

I glance at his eyes, which glare coldly in the semi-darkness, then back to the road. Not knowing what to expect from this character, I almost answer, "Yeah." I thought, but only for a second, that a little insurance might be a good idea. For all I know, this could be a rip-off. Instead I reply, "No," which turns out to be a very good idea, because this guy is wired for sound. We're being followed by four car loads of armed-to-the-teeth DEA agents. It wouldn't have been a very good idea on my part to have gotten them overly excited.

The man riding with me, doing a fine job of impersonating Louie, the crazed Italian killer, is actually a DEA undercover agent named Gerald Scotti. James Hoffman is a drug smuggler turned government informant . . . and me, well I'm totally in the dark, I'm thinking they're both Mafia bad guys from Chicago.

Pulling into the Van Nuys Airport parking lot, I notice Louie/Scotti is surprised to see that the car actually is unattended. "You really left all that cocaine just sitting there?" He is looking at me like he thinks I'm a complete idiot.

I don't answer—feeling that it wouldn't be wise—or healthy—to tell a Mafia hit man that you want out of the criminal enterprise that involves him, not if I want to go on living.

I park the Caddy then go over to get the Caprice with the cocaine in it. My hands are shaking as I park the Caprice next to the Cadillac. Scotti jumps out of the Cadillac as soon as I pull up. He opens the driver's door and glares at me from the semi-darkness. The parking lot security lights cast everything in a harsh jaundice yellow.

"Where's the stuff?" he asks anxiously. He is inordinately excited, even for someone who is picking up a major load of drugs. If I had thought about it, I would have realized that his high level of excitement mimicked the intense, alert behavior of a man about to go into combat.

"It's stashed behind the backseat," I answer quickly. While Scotti frantically tears into the backseat, I cautiously move toward the driver's door of the Cadillac and silently open it. I still am not convinced that this isn't a rip-off and want to be where I can at least attempt a fast get away. As I slide in behind the wheel, I see that Scotti has one of the kilo bricks in his hands. He is ripping at the plastic and brown paper wrapper with a knife. I thought it pretty strange that he would be doing this in plain sight. He sticks a finger into the cocaine and tastes it, then I plainly see him flash a signal to other men who are waiting in the dark shadows. Suddenly, an army of men are running crouched over toward the Cadillac. Their drawn guns are in plain sight!

I desperately reach for the ignition, convinced that it is indeed a rip-off, that my only hope is to flee the scene—my fingers close on an empty key hole. The men are almost upon me; I steal a quick glance at the floor hoping to find the keys before I'm taken. Then the driver's door flies open. The dome light seems inordinately bright as I see a man leaping from the shadows. He jabs toward me, and I duck instinctively then feel cold metal pressing against my temple. I pull slightly down and to the right then freeze when I see the gleaming barrel of a .38 special. The gun sight nicks the skin on my face. Blood runs down my cheek and drips onto my arm. My attention is riveted on the revolver. From this close-up perspective the gun's thick bore looks huge and foreboding—a giant black emptiness about to blow me away. I have an instant visualization of being blasted at close range with my shattered body hurling across the seat in a bloody, pulpy mess. The man holding the long-barreled revolver is half-shrouded in darkness and harsh yellow artificial light as he yells, "Move, scum bag, and I'll blow your head off!"

In an instant, the Cadillac's other doors are thrown open, and guns are stuck in from every direction. I numbly stare at the gaping bore of a riot shotgun aimed at my face from the passenger side. In apparent slow motion, I see coarse hands, matted on the backs with thick, black hair, work the pump action, sliding a shell into the chamber. The *click-clack* of the mechanism is uncommonly loud in the restricted space of the car. The massive barrel lowers and pushes forcefully against the side of my chest. Still convinced that it's a rip-off, I wonder if I will hear the shot that will end my life. I also wonder if it will be painful to die. Then the man with the .38 special yells the greatest words I've ever heard: **"Federal agents, you're under arrest, dirt bag."**

Suddenly, I know that I'm not going to die, that is unless someone screws up. I keep my hands on the steering wheel in plain sight and try not to move though I am trembling uncontrollably.

Unseen hands jerk me from the car and slam me against a black van. A dozen men stand in a half circle with their guns at the ready. To my right I recognize the unmistakable silhouette of an M-16 automatic rifle. A man grabs my hair in a vice-like grip and jerks my head backwards; I feel the cold bore of a pistol pressing against my temple. Someone kicks my feet outwards forcing me to assume a spread-eagle position against the black van. I stare at the distorted image of my face reflected in the dark paint while hands expertly search for weapons, then a man with red hair brutally twists my arms behind my back, and I feel the biting edge of handcuffs cutting into my wrists.

Standing there with trembling knees, agents on each side supporting me, I think I might throw-up. Then I realize that at least it's all over now. I no longer have to wonder how to escape from Morgan and company. It has been taken completely out of my hands. I know without a doubt that I'm headed for prison, probably for a long time, but at last I am finally free of the criminal intrigues. I have a sudden feeling that a tremendous burden has been lifted from my shoulders.

A few minutes later, sitting in the back of a government car, Scotti, who is riding in the front seat, turns around and says gleefully, "Well, I guess this isn't the best day in your life, is it, creep?"

My answering smile isn't forced. "Actually," I reply soberly, "I think it is." Looking mildly confused, Scotti turns away to ponder that one awhile.

That night they take me to Parker Center, also known as the Glass House, because all the cells have thick plate glass instead of steel bars. After midnight they bring in a very bewildered Morgan Hetrick. He is rubbing the angry red welts on his wrists. We talk for a while in whispers. I figure the cell has to be bugged or they wouldn't have put us together. Hours later, I somehow manage to fall asleep to deeply troubled dreams.

CHAPTER 6

In those first few moments before actually waking up, I hope beyond reason that it all might be just a bad dream . . . I slowly open my eyes . . . it isn't.

At 7 A.M., the guard comes for us. We are taken in shackles and chains to the federal courthouse to stand before a magistrate for our bail hearings. Morgan's bail is set at a staggering twenty million dollars. The magistrate doesn't have time to fully consider the case against me, so he temporarily sets my bail at five million dollars just to make sure I am not going anywhere soon. My mind boggles at the value he places on my head. I know that the huge bail amount is a bench mark to gauge the magnitude of my crime. He asks the marshals to bring me back the following morning for a second hearing.

We are returned to Parker Center, where Morgan is finally allowed to make his one promised telephone call, but I reject the opportunity to use the phone. I do not look forward to telling my mother that her youngest son is again locked behind bars. Sitting on the hard cot, staring at the steel door, I have never felt so lost or so alone in my life; tears slide down my cheeks to splatter unheeded on the dirty cement floor of the jail cell.

The next day we are returned to the courthouse where Morgan and I are separated. He is taken to Terminal Island Prison for instant processing from free man to inmate. At 10 A.M., two marshals come for me. They cuff my hands behind my back then lead me upstairs. Stepping from the elevator, I'm surprised to see a mob of people crowding the corridor outside the courtroom. They fill the narrow space with their presence, then the noise level drops off noticeably as the marshals force their way through the dense mass of people. "Who are all of these people?" I nervously ask my marshal escort.

"Reporters," grunts the fatter of the two marshals as he straight arms a thin man in a rumpled suit out of the way. The man staggers against two people who prevent him from falling down. "Dumb gorilla," he silently mouths at the broad back of the marshal. Inside the courtroom, I see why the corridor is so crowded, the room is packed, every seat is occupied and many more people stand lining the walls.

"What's with all the press?" I ask. "Is something special happening?"

"I guess," laughs the marshal, "they're here to see you, dummy."

Surprised, I look anxiously about the crowded room, it has become almost silent except for the excited whispers of the reporters who are mostly staring back at me. Simple drug busts don't command this much media attention—do they?

Then, in the midst of the crowd, I see my mother looking at me. She sits with my brother, Jim, leaning into the security of his arm, which is clutched tightly around her shoulder. Her eyes are red and puffy from crying. The tears have made long sorrowful streaks in her make-up. When she sees me looking her eyes widened hopefully, silently pleading that all of this must be a huge mistake. Some of the reporters notice the eye contact and write anxiously in their notebooks. I look away and stare dumbly down at the table. I feel horrible knowing that there is absolutely nothing I can ever say that will excuse my actions in the slightest. I want to crawl into a hole and die.

A few minutes later, the court clerk announces that the bail hearing is to be postponed. There isn't enough room in the courtroom to accommodate all the reporters, who are continuing to arrive in droves swelling the mob in the corridor. The marshals hustle me back downstairs. The press of the crowd keeps me from seeing my mother again.

An hour passes before my presence is again requested upstairs. The marshals in the holding tank are excited about all of the media attention. They're arguing over who is going to get to escort me. A female marshal with masculine, close-cropped hair and wearing Ray Ban sunglasses comes up with the simple solution, "Why don't we all go?"

A general nodding of heads lends approval to the idea. "Hey, let's really dress him up in chains," offers the fat marshal who originally took me upstairs. A stainless steel chain is wrapped twice around my waist, then my hands are cuffed and padlocked to the chain. In front of the steel exit door eight marshals pack tightly about me whispering excitedly to each other. The fat marshal grabs the door handle then looks at the others, "Everyone ready?" he asks with a grin. There is a lot of head nodding and giggles of anticipation.

"O.K.," he smiles showing teeth, "Then let's rock-and-roll." We hit the lobby going at full speed. My flying wedge of marshals drives straight into the surprised crowd. As people are shoved aside they quickly turn to stare eagerly at the chained criminal.

I hear a woman's excited voice, "It's him; it's the Night Stalker."

An anxious ripple of voices flows through the crowd, "They got the Night Stalker," echoes a masculine voice.

"Who?"

"He's a rapist and a serial murderer," shouts the masculine voice with authority.

We shoulder pass a pleasant-looking, middle-aged woman, I'm surprised to see that she is glaring at me with hate-filled eyes. I want to shout out that I am not the evil person they suspect, but the chains and heavy marshal escort nullify my unspoken words.

The marshals force their way to the elevator bank seizing the first arriving car. All the people who are already inside are rooted out. A man in an expensive gray suit, obviously a lawyer, begins to protest. The woman marshal jerks him out by the lapels and sends him spinning into the crowd.

After the doors close, the marshals laugh happily amongst themselves and compare the individual damage they have done in the crowded lobby; obviously they are having a good time enjoying their role as a posse of bullies.

The elevator doors open at the eighth floor. At the other end of the corridor, a crowd of reporters obstruct the double doors to the courtroom. "O.K.," grins the leader, rubbing his meaty palms together. "Sleaze-bag attorneys and noisy reporters, we take them out."

The crowd in the corridor seeing the determined approach of the flying wedge has enough sense to get out of the way; much to the disappointment of my thug escort.

After they seat me at a front row table, I survey the crowd. Although this courtroom is easily twice the size of the last one, it too is packed. The press has even taken over the jury box, which later proves to be more than appropriate. At a long table opposite mine, I notice a tall, gray-haired man sitting between several attorneys. He looks too distinguished in his expensive dark suit to be wearing the handcuffs that glisten on his wrists. I ask one of the marshals who he is.

"Are you kidding me?" he replies. "That's your co-defendant, John Z. DeLorean, the famous auto maker."

I am confused. What did John DeLorean have to do with Morgan and me? As the prosecutor begins to read off the incriminating facts to the magistrate, I begin to understand. The prosecutor is asking for a bail of twenty million. The magistrate agrees, "John DeLorean, your bail is assessed at twenty million dollars." The announcement stuns the press.

The prosecutor asks the magistrate that my bail remain at five million dollars. The magistrate turns to observe me. Maybe in my surfer T-shirt, 501 jeans, and basketball shoes I don't look the wealthy criminal type. "Mr. Stephen Arrington," his voice booms across the crowded room, "your bail is five hundred thousand dollars." He dismisses the court with a loud bang of his gavel.

The flying wedge of marshals forms and takes me forcefully away. Just before we step through the double doors, I glance back at my mother. She tries to smile encouragingly, but instead tears flood her eyes.

Downstairs the fat marshal cheerfully says my next stop is going to be Terminal Island Federal Prison. "You are not going to like it there," he adds brightly.

I ride down in a marshal's van with eleven other inmates. We are chained together in groups of three. Through the dusty steel mesh on the van's windows, I watch everyday people in their cars hurrying home after a day at the office. Freedom already seems worlds away, a much different reality than the one I'm about to face.

Terminal Island Prison (T.I.) squats at the end of a long peninsula in Los Angeles Harbor. Built at the turn of the century it originally served as a navy prison. It's where Al Capone died of syphilis after it became a federal prison in the 1930s. T.I. is not a pleasant-looking place. The drab, thirty-foot cement walls are surrounded by two tall concentina laced (razor wire) fences.

Entering with the rest of the chain gang through the cement portal of the salle port, I am assailed by a musky, mildew smell that permeates the entire building. Long strips of green paint hang from the thick, cement walls. We mount rust-covered steps that lead upstairs to a holding cell that stinks of urine and stale cigarette smoke. One by one we're taken out, strip-searched, fingerprinted, and issued prison coveralls. It is dark outside when we are led to the cell blocks.

Jail Unit One (J-1) has three tiers of cells stacked in a narrow two-and-a-half-story building. Each cell is twelve feet long, six feet wide, and less than eight feet tall. The stale air in the cell smells rank; I'm reminded of a musky tomb. A toilet, its bowl heavily soiled and missing its seat, squats against the far wall. I place a hand against the wall to steady myself. My hand is slimed by a caking of cigarette smoke that has turned the cement greasy brown. A dim yellow light in the ceiling barely reaches the lower bunk, which is half-shrouded in darkness. A huge black man lies there. He is naked except for a pair of torn and stained underwear. The man emits a heavy musk that fills the tiny cell. I look at his thick muscular arms, barrel chest, and hateful stare—I am instantly terrified. Saying nothing, he glares red-eyed.

"Hello, my name is Steve."

He grunts and shows a meaty fist, "I don't give a damn what your name is, whitey, just stay out of my face or I'll bust you up good."

At a loss for what to do next, and anxious to get out from under his glare, I climb onto the upper bunk. The sounds of the cell block about us are angry and intense. In an attempt to shut it out I jam a dirty pillow against my ears. I look from the jail bars to the dim yellow bulb in the ceiling. By letting my eyes go out of focus I imagine the glow of the bulb to be the light of a setting sun. Slowly the cell block noise fades and becomes rhythmic, like the soft rippling sound of gentle surf breaking on a distant shore. Willing myself away, memories of Hawaii touch then slowly embrace my troubled mind.

In the theater of my imagination, I see a giant yellow/red sun descending into a restive sea beyond the beach at Waikiki. Small waves lapped on the white sand beach where Susan, Puu, and I sat on a blanket. Susan unpacked a picnic basket full of vegetarian treats. Puu smelled hopefully but the basket held little interest for him. Susan playfully offered Puu a leafy celery top, which he consented to smell; then with a disappointed snort he laid his head between his paws and whimpered. While rubbing the Dane's ears, Susan asked, "Didn't you bring anything for Puu?"

From the basket I removed and proudly held up a large can of Mighty Dog. Susan opened the can and dumped the sixteen ounce cylinder of meat onto a paper plate, which Puu inhaled in a couple of seconds; then, he contentedly laid his head in her lap. Susan was thrilled as Puu gazed at her with adoring eyes, until he loudly passed gas.

We settled in the lee of the Royal Hawaiian Hotel's balcony where a Polynesian show was beginning. As the sun slowly disappeared into the calm sea, Hawaiian dancers flooded the stage moving in rapid sync to the beat of drums. I scooped the remains of our dinner, like so much compost, back into the picnic basket. Puu returned to lie at our feet as Susan leaned back into my arms while she listened to the music and watched the exotic dancers through eyes that reflected the flickering light of burning tiki torches. Suddenly fire dancers leaped onto the stage twirling batons tipped with fire. The heavy rhythm of the drums soon matched the beat of my heart . . . I let my hand slip slowly from Susan's shoulder.

"Stop that," complained Susan.

I quickly apologized while moving my hand back to safer ground.

"This is just our second date," Susan continued, "last night doesn't mean you can maul me whenever you want. In fact, I've been thinking about it and maybe we should just be friends." I found her implication of our just being friends a saddening thought.

"Don't give me that hurt puppy dog look of yours," she said angrily.

"O.K.," I held my hands up, "let's just sit here and listen to the music." Susan was incredibly pretty even while glaring at me.

"I'll be good," I lied, adopting my most innocent smile.

She looked at me suspiciously, "You promise?" I shook my head yes, not wanting to lie to her again. Susan smiled and leaned against my shoulder after fluffing it like a pillow.

My revelry is abruptly shattered by a deep, rumbling voice that reaches out from the bunk below, "The name is Mose." The voice pauses, then continues, "Look man, since we're bunkies I guess we gotta talk to each other, but that don't mean we're friends or nothing. If there's a riot, Old Mose is gonna have to waste ya a——, man. It ain't personal, whitey, just the way things be in da joint."

I say nothing, thinking instead about the dark connotations of his words. "Waste ya"? Is he actually telling me that he might try to kill me?

"Hey, whitey," the voice thickens with anger, "you listening to me, man?"

"Yeah . . . you said you may have to waste my a——," I answer.

"Good," grunts Mose, "so longs as ya understands."

I lie on my bunk, memories of Susan and Puu blown completely away by the sudden wondering question of what happened to Mose's last roommate.

"Youze got any cigarettes." I listen for, but hear not the slightest friendliness in that deep baritone.

"I don't smoke."

"They sells cigarettes in duh commissary store."

"I don't smoke."

"I knows you don't smoke, whitey, they still sells cigarettes in duh commissary store, and smoking makes Mose a mellow dude if you catch my drift." I feel the bunk shift as Mose rolls over and farts. *So much for the T.I. Welcome Wagon*, I think forlornly to myself.

We are allowed only four hours of sunshine in the exercise yard a week, not that we always get it. The exercise yard is a tiny enclosure with a cement deck and thirty foot tall cement walls that keep the narrow area in dark shadows most of the day. There is an old rusted universal gym where Mose likes to workout. He has someone stand on the three hundred pound stack of lead plates while Mose does repetitive bench presses. The man is a monster. I can't help wondering about his sexual habits. I don't even want to consider that he might be gay. My skin crawls at the very thought of being attacked by Mose. In a very personal way, I begin to comprehend the rape fear that women deal with on a daily basis.

Prison chow is worse than I thought possible. I gave my first meals to Mose who is stoked to have the extra groceries. Watching him eat would destroy anyone's appetite. He eats with his mouth wide open and likes to talk while gulping his industrious way through the food pile on his plastic tray. When he gets excited, the chewed pieces of meat and vegetables spray from his mouth in moist bits, kind of like an over-stuffed garbage disposal spewing wet chunks. Not wanting to offend him, I have to restrain from flinching at the wet contact of his gross mastications.

We are allowed a shower once every three days, not that we have to take one. Mose needs a shower in a big way, but I certainly am not going to be the one to advise him of it. I just keep my mouth shut and wait. The time passes slowly.

The place is full of continuous noise: people yelling insults at each other, conflicting music blasting from multiple radios, steel gates slamming, inmates fighting, people cussing; the energy level is maddening.

The only natural light comes into the cell block through a single row of grimy yellow windows that are high up on the cement wall. There isn't a chance of seeing anything through them, not even the sky. The muddied light that does dimly penetrate the thick coat of grime casts a hellish glare upon the dirty green walls. I easily understood why the inmates referred to J-1 as the hole. The saddest week of my life slowly ebbs; then, they transfer me to Jail Unit-3.

As I step out the cell door, Mose mutters from his bunk, "Youze gonna pay for not buying me those cigarettes, whitey, duh hacks ain't gonna keep Old Mose in duh hole forever." I turn my back to Mose and walk after the guard. Descending the steps to ground level, the J-1 hack casually asks, "You know what happened to Mose's last cellmate?"

I shake my head *no*. "The guy was black, so we figured Mose wouldn't hurt him. They got in an argument over cigarettes and Mose smashed the guy's head repeatedly against the cement wall five or six times. The dude is still in the prison hospital recovering from a concussion."

I have to consciously keep a stutter out of my voice, "If you know Mose is violent, why did you put me in his cell?"

The guard looks at me in surprise and belly laughs, "Hell, half the cons in this joint are violent. Where do you think you're at anyway, YMCA camp?" The hack is still giggling as he turns me over to the J-3 guard.

J-3 turns out to be a single-level cell block on the lower wing of the prison hospital. Upstairs is the nut ward . . . often we could hear the crazies screaming throughout the night. A passageway runs the ninety-foot length of J-3 with a bank of cells on each side. At one end is a small television room where we eat our chow. I hesitate to call it food. Chow reminds me more of what belongs in a dog's dish. Still, it's an improvement over J-1 where I ate while sitting on the rim of the toilet.

The cells in J-3 are the same size as before, but instead of an open grill, there is a heavy metal door with a little window in it, which at least lends the barest hint of privacy. A forty-watt bulb casts a weak dull-yellow glow from the cement ceiling. It's difficult to read by its dim light. A dented metal locker stands in one corner. I don't have anything to put in it. I'm wearing most of my worldly possessions: a jumpsuit, a pair of old underwear (worn by any number of inmates before me), a torn T-shirt, one pair of socks that bag loosely at my ankles, and the running shoes I was fortunately wearing when arrested. On a rusted shelf in the locker, I put a comb, my tooth-brush, and a half-used tube of toothpaste. Later, someone steals the toothpaste. It looks awfully lonely in that empty metal locker and in my soul as well.

If you're lucky, your cellmate doesn't smoke, snore, pass gas, or have body odor—my new bunky is four for four. Prison food is high in starch, which causes some inmates to pass gas. Air does not circu-late well in a cell block, so bad odor can be a serious problem. The toilets tend to reek, particularly when Morris, my Armenian bunky, is blasting away on it. I find that burning a match helps to clear the air a bit. I learn to keep a book of matches next to my pillow for Morris' regular surprise attacks, which usually occur late at night and just prior to first light in the morning—Morris is a kind of flatu-lence alarm clock.

When not locked in the cell, I spend most of my time walking the corridor. Sometimes there are four or five of us pacing the tile floor. The pacers tend to be lost in their own private thoughts. It isn't considered polite to look another pacer in the eye, so you learn to walk head down, in the classic posture of dejection, eyes on the floor. There are 28 men in J-3 compared to the 250-plus inmates in J-1. All of us are awaiting trial or sentencing, the cell block vibrates with continuous tension and uncontrolled anger. Fights are almost a daily occurrence, and they are always vicious. The goal is to maim or hurt your opponent so bad he won't be a threat in the future.

The J-3 yard has a torn volleyball net stretched between two poles, a bent basketball hoop hanging from a brick wall, and a rusted, only half-functional, exercising machine. A narrow dirt path leads around the tiny perimeter where it is a challenge to run without brushing up against any of the pacers. Inmates take serious offense if you accidently bump into them. In one corner there is a scruffy patch of dried grass covered with years of cigarette butts and other debris. It looks like a miniature garbage dump. The yard is walled in on three sides with the one end looking out on the north yard through a tall chain link fence. Through it, we can watch the men in general popu-lation and vice versa.

My second week in J-3 finds me standing at the yard's chain link fence staring enviously at the manicured green lawns and petite shade trees of the north yard. Turning to look at our patch of scruffy, brown grass, I decide to do something about it. Kneeling on the stiff dead grass, I remove the debris, rocks, and weeds. With my fingers, I rake away hundreds of cigarette butts and gum wrappers. When the ground is relatively clean, I begin carrying buckets of water from the drinking fountain, which I pour over the dry cracked soil.

The other inmates look at me like I'm nuts, but I keep imagining how the grass feels about it. I take a simple inner joy in pouring each bucket of clear clean water knowing that it is washing life into the dry, brittle blades of grass. It is a slow process filling the bucket from the dribble at the drinking fountain, then carrying it to the other side of the small yard, but I just keep looking at the green lawns of general population and continue to carry the water with that much more determination while ignoring the cat calls and shouted insults from the other inmates.

As the days become weeks I slowly begin to adjust to the prison routine. One of the first things I discover about living in a criminal institution is that they are full of rats; and I'm not talking about the long-tailed, four-legged kind. Rats are inmates who are constantly on the lookout for a tidbit of information that they can share with a prison guard or inmate case worker. For their petty snitching, they may receive a little reward like a better job assignment or a favorable statement in their jacket (inmate file). However, if a rat uncovers a tasty morsel of information that aids in the prosecution of a criminal case, the snitch can get a reduction in his sentence. With that kind of incentive there are a lot of seriously dedicated rats sniffing around in J-3.

The only person held in more contempt than a rat is a child molester or rapist. Inmates have families of their own, and there is a code of honor even among felons. Rapists and particularly child molesters don't always live long enough to serve out their sentences.

As an inmate I have to behave according to a long, detailed list of institutional rules and regulations. It's a lot like being back in a military boot camp, except here even simple infractions can lead to a serious increase in the length of one's sentence. Yet, prison rules and regulations can be almost insignificant when compared to the more serious inmate codes of social behavior while incarcerated.

In the courts we're promised that everyone is considered innocent until proven guilty. Inmate justice, however, is not concerned with such trivia. They're not confused by such humane terms as compassion or social responsibility. Convicts are far more interested in the instant gratification of punishment actively administered in person.

For example, if a new, unsuspecting inmate should inadvertently violate certain unwritten inmate codes, he might be brutally raped, just to show how casually his existence is held—prior to being slashed, stabbed, choked, or bludgeoned to death for amusement's sake.

Since inmate codes are not written down, except maybe as graffiti on a wall, a short list might be appreciated, particularly by the young reader who is considering dealing drugs and hasn't a clue as to what is really waiting for them in *chez* clink:

Rule 1—Don't hang out with people of poor reputation. This means rats, rapists, and child molesters. I'd also tend to add dopers and schemers because they're unconsciously heading for extended sentences and often rise to the high aspiration of becoming repeat offenders. Seventy percent of all ex-felons return to prison within three to five years—kind of gives an inmate something to look forward to.

Rule 2—Find a dependable friend. In prison, a good friend is referred to as a road dog or home boy. Prison is stressful and it's important to have someone you can share your problems with and not have them repeated five minutes later to the guard.

Rule 3—"You gotta hang tough." It's a prison expression that means you have to be prepared to react violently in your own self interest. Just because some brute is thrown into prison doesn't mean he or she is about to mellow out. In fact, confinement tends to stoke their fury to a greater intensity, and often they're looking for someone on whom they can take out their frustrations. There is a very simple reason why almost everyone works on their physical conditioning in prison. Either you pump iron and get in shape to defend yourself, or you may wind-up on your belly getting raped by some AIDS-ridden brute. And don't even make the mistake of thinking that the guards will protect you. Usually, the hacks don't care about what they consider an inmate's personal problems. Of course, if you're really scared that someone is looking to kill you or get overly personal, you can always request protective custody. Then they just lock you down in a place like J-1. However, inmates in protective custody can still be stuck through the cell bars with a homemade knife attached to a broom stick. Convicts can be darned imaginative, particularly when it comes to cruelty.

Prison isn't easy on the more gentle types who are usually eaten body and soul. Sooner or later everyone gets tested. At some point you will have to fight for your rights. If you don't fight, you get tagged with the name "Punk." A punk gets used. He does the laundry and cleans up for other inmates during the day. At night he does sexual favors (despite his attitude on the subject) for any number of perverted inmates. Usually, punks are forced to call home for money, which is taken away as soon as it arrives. Life is tough on a punk—suicide is one possible solution for a punk who seeks to escape the terror that stalks his daily—and nightly—life.

Rule 4—If you have a problem with an inmate, you gotta solve it yourself. Never ever go to the guards. It's an easy way to get labelled as a punk. In prison, personal problems with other inmates don't just go away with time.

Rule 5—Stay away from the guards. It's against inmate etiquette to make friends with the hacks. They have a term for guys who buddysup to guards; they say, "Get off the man's leg." Hanging with guards often makes you look like a rat and you just don't need to bring that hassle down on yourself. It can get you stuck.

Rule 6—Never ever walk up on two inmates talking; you might hear something you shouldn't be listening to. Just by accidentally looking in the wrong direction you might see something you shouldn't have—like a drug deal going down. If their stash is ripped off, or worse yet the guys get busted, they may think you are responsible—serious bad luck.

Finally, before I abandon this chapter of the inmate training manual, it helps to remember that all inmates are equal. It does not matter how much money you have on the outside or whether you are eighteen or sixty-five, you can still get punched out, raped, stabbed, or any combination of the above by any number of interested inmates. Everyone is under maximum stress from trials, anticipated long sentences, family problems, and daily prison situations. As such, you learn to walk lightly. A guy might be six foot four and weigh in at 240 pounds of solid muscle. A 90 pound weakling, however, can easily shove a homemade knife into his ribs while he sleeps. Arguments are seldom settled with just fists.

Remember that all inmates want to be treated with respect because they certainly don't get it from the hacks. If you forget this just for a moment, even the most mild tempered inmate can go off on you. Be mellow yourself and don't brag about what you have or how soon you're getting out. Long termers tend to get rather upset when they hear some wimp complaining about their meager six month sentence. It makes them want to give the guy something real to complain about. Once you've gained an inmate's attention, it takes him awhile to forget about you. After all, it's not like they have anything else better to do. Harassing you could be the highlight of their day, or worse yet, their night.

———— CHAPTER 7 ————

I have been down almost a month when the guard comes to tell me that I have a visitor in the attorney counseling room. Calmly waiting in the tiny enclosure is a middle-aged, over-weight man whom I've never seen before. His name is Chapman. He apparently signed in to see one of his clients, another inmate in J-3, but once in the cell block counseling rooms he asks instead to see me. This not only violates the attorney's ethics code, it happens to be against the law.

He wastes no time getting directly to the point, "I know you don't know me, but I have some information you may like to hear." Over the next couple of minutes he rattles off details about Morgan's operation that no one should know about—that is unless someone is talking. He doesn't mind naming the source of his information. It is three of Morgan's sons whom he alleges are now his clients—clients who are apparently eagerly seeking to cooperate to keep from going to prison.

"Steve," he earnestly continues, "there are some very powerful people inside the prosecutor's office who think you are the key to unlocking this case. They know you played only a minor role, and they're prepared to deal. All you have to do is agree to talk, and I can promise that you'll walk."

I'm keenly interested in his offer, but after a moment's consideration shake my head no. Ratting on someone else just doesn't seem like the solution to my problems. Once you begin to cooperate, you have to tell the government everything; and I have no intention of giving up Sam. Luckily, Sam, by following my warning to pretend ignorance, has been able to remain free, though he does tend to overreact whenever someone knocks at his door.

Chapman reaches into his pocket, then dramatically throws a ring of keys onto the table. "Steve," he argues, "think of it this way. I'm holding the key to your cell door. If you agree to cooperate, I can have you out of here—maybe by tonight."

Looking into his eyes, I feel like I am being conned. It's almost as if he is the devil bargaining for my soul. His offer sounds too much like the same kind of deal that James T. Hoffman has cut for himself. I knew I didn't want to be someone's puppet again.

Chapman sees that he's losing me, so he brings forward his heaviest argument, "Don't be an idiot. Morgan's sons are already cooperating, and it's not going to be long before Morgan Hetrick cops a plea too." Chapman irritably slams a fist down on the table making the keys jump, then he points an accusing finger inches from my face, "Mark my words; when Morgan cooperates he is going to dump on you so bad you won't see the streets again for years."

I know that Chapman is speaking the truth, but I just can't see myself as a rat. "I'm afraid that I have to handle this on my own," I answer sadly. Standing to leave, I feel like I've just sentenced myself to a long stay in prison.

The last vestige of Chapman's friendly manner evaporates in an instant. "You're going to regret this," he yells after me as I walk through the security door. "Morgan isn't going to think twice about giving you up and the prosecutor is going to put you away for a long time."

The echo of his words follow me down the lonely corridor. I open my cell door and step inside. Later, sitting on my bunk with my head in my hands, I keep seeing that ring of keys he so casually threw onto the table.

That afternoon I'm sitting in the television room watching the news when an inmate reading a newspaper begins to laugh loudly. "Hey, Arrington," he yells, "you made the funny page."

"I what?"

"You're on the funny page," he repeats. "The *Doonesbury* strip is doing a piece about the DeLorean case becoming a movie."

"You gotta be kidding," I go over to look for myself.

"Listen to this," he giggles, "one of the cartoon characters is telling a bag lady that you kept your boat berthed next to his in Fort Lauderdale, then he boasts that he even loaned you his deck gun for one of your clandestine operations."

The inmate shakes his head. "That's pretty funny stuff; I'm in prison with a real live cartoon character." He turns to stare at me almost as if he is seeing me for the first time. "Hey," he says, suddenly inspired, "How about autographing this for me?"

The next day a toilet clogs in one of the other cells. Two inmate plumbers from general population are admitted into J-3 to fix it. The guard watches them working for a while, then he retires into his office, which is at the other end of the cell block behind a thick security door. From there he cannot monitor the cell block, which is why the two inmate-plumbers chose that moment to walk boldly into my cell.

I'm kicked back on my upper bunk idly reading a paperback book. Completely relaxed and totally engrossed in the story, I don't realize that I'm in danger until I casually look up from the page to see who is coming through my door—the terror is instantaneous.

The two burly inmates crowding into the cell are bikers. The headbands they wear identify them as members of the Aryan

Brotherhood, a white racist gang known for its violence against other inmates. They both have the muscular build of dedicated weight lifters. I immediately realize that a hit is going down—and that I'm it!

The first one through the door has deep set, fanatical eyes that glare from a heavily bearded face. At the corner of his right eye are three blue, tattooed teardrops. "Are you Arrington?" he demands gruffly.

My eyes fall to his right hand, which grasps a long, heavy-duty screwdriver. The shank is covered in rust, but the nicked tip is deadly shiny, like it has been recently sharpened on a grinding wheel. I've never visualized a screwdriver as a weapon before, but now the horrible image of being stabbed by that long, rusted shank explodes in my mind.

I'm literally on the verge of voiding my bowels, I feel them turning watery with fear. I know I'm about to die. It seems so incredibly unfair. I want to flee but there is nowhere to go. I can't even jump down from the bunk to properly defend myself. I'm trapped as death crowds against the side of my bunk.

The brute with the screwdriver leans heavily on the edge of the mattress, "Hey," he growls, "I asked you a question, are you Arrington?" He shifts his weight to his left foot, apparently to give himself driving force. I know he will first thrust for my gut. I want to distance myself from him, but the wall presses coldly against my back. The other inmate glances out the door to make sure the guard isn't coming then whispers urgently, "We gotta hurry man."

I want to scream, instead in a weak whisper I hear myself answer his question, "Yeah, I'm Arrington."

The inmate transfers the heavy screwdriver to his left hand, the tip wavers between my gut and groin. I brace myself to try to prevent the blow that I know I can't block in time.

The brute grins through his dark beard showing yellowed and grossly crooked teeth. I watch his right hand disappear into his shirt pocket and extract a piece of crumpled newspaper. "Mind signing this for me?" he asks hopefully.

It is the Trudeau comic strip. I write quickly to mask my trembling fingers.

CHAPTER 8

A few days later the guard announces that I have another visitor in the attorney counseling room. I half expect to run into Chapman again and am therefore surprised to see William, a musician friend of mine. Apparently he knocked at the wrong door of the prison while looking for the visitor's room, and some guard, mistaking him for a lawyer, accidentally let him into the attorney counseling rooms at the end of the cell block.

His eyes wide with fear, William explains that he has been nervous about visiting me because he doesn't want to see what it's like inside a prison visiting room. William has a serious fear of prisons because of a little side business of selling small quantities of cocaine to friends. Not that he considers himself a dealer, he only sells enough to support his own habit, which sounds oddly familiar. So after building up some false courage by getting high on coke in the parking lot, he is accidentally admitted into a full-blown cell block. Looking wildly about, he is as unsettled as a woman who has just stumbled upon a gang in a dark alley.

I could see the gears turning in his head as he watches the inmates aimlessly pacing the corridor through the thick plate glass of the reinforced security door. This is a cocaine dealer's worse nightmare come true. A long-haired pacer, who happens to look a lot like William, stops at the plate glass and stares idly at my friend. It isn't just any old stare, it's an inmate stare—empty, without emotion.

Visibly shaken, William asks, "What's he in for?"

"Drugs," I casually reply, "he use to be a cocaine dealer. Now he's not too with it anymore. It's hard to get a complete sentence out of him. He still has the habit though," I add almost as an afterthought, "but no money to pay for it. So he trades his favors for whatever he can snort, smoke, or shoot."

The pacer turns and begins to shuffle away with his shoulders slumped like there is no tomorrow. "William," I say softly, waiting for his complete attention; he's looking rather pale, "do you see that brown stain on the backside of his coveralls?"

William nods. "Yeah," he squeaks sensing that I'm about to tell him something that he really doesn't want to hear.

"It's dried blood . . . and his underwear is worse," I add seriously. "I know because as head orderly I have to collect the dirty laundry. Now, do you see that large, thick guy standing in the corner staring at you."

William's eyes flick to Jay Jay, who now glares with added intensity, sensing that we are talking about him.

"Jay Jay is the pacer's main squeeze. The pacer's butt bleeds because Jay Jay likes to be brutal, particularly when he's high on drugs."

William coughs, then gags; for a moment I thought he might throw-up. He tries to say something but is stuttering so badly he can't get a full sentence out. He later writes me that he quit using cocaine forever, let alone selling it, after seeing the pacer and his brutal boyfriend.

William isn't my only visitor, just the first one to come in through the wrong door. On the fifth Sunday of my incarceration, my mother and brother come for their first visit (getting someone on your approved visitor list can take months). For me the hardest part of doing time is dealing with the uncertainty of how my mother is going to take it.

My stomach is alive with the jittery feeling of butterflies as I walk nervously into the visiting room. Mom and Jim are sitting at a small round plastic table surrounded by other inmate families. She stands as I approach and wraps her arms around me. For a moment we stand very still just holding each other quietly, then she asks, "How are they treating you? Are you going to make it O.K.?" She is so nervous that the two sentences run together.

"Yeah mom," I reply, "I can cope, but what about you?"

She laughs, "Don't worry about me; you're the one who's in prison." Mom always did have a practical outlook on life. Anyway the next thing she has to say really shocks me. "Stephen," she says firmly, "I only have one piece of advice to offer you." She pauses to add impact to her words. "Don't cooperate. Just do the time you have coming, then you can come home with a clear conscience."

That is about the last thing I ever expect to hear my mother say. I tell her about the offer from the rogue lawyer.

"Wait a minute," Jim, my brother, is looking wide-eyed back and forth from our mother to me. Hearing what mom had to say has come as quite a shock to him and now he isn't exactly buying my response. "You mean they've already offered to let you walk if you cooperate and you're not going for it?"

We both look at Jim who has a lot to learn about people who rat and their future relationships with upset Colombians. So I tell him about the infamous Colombian Bow Tie, "First they slit your throat, then they pull your tongue out through the opening, and split it lengthwise with a knife." I'm avidly demonstrating with my hands as I talk. "The two pieces of the tongue are then tied together in a rather gruesome knot. Of course they like to make sure that you're awake while all of this is happening. They say it usually takes a while for the snitch to die." Then I add in a soft whisper, "You know, Jim, instead of coming after me directly, they could start with you first as a subtle warning to get my attention." By the look on Jim's face and the way he is fingering his throat, I know that I've made my point. He quickly drops the subject of cooperation.

Mom, seeing how upset Jim is, tries to cheer him up, pats his hand, and says sweetly, "Why don't you tell Stephen about that little piece of news you discovered."

Jim, who is a mortgage broker, brightens visibly. "I ran a credit check on you just to see what the computer would kick-out and guess what?" I shrug my shoulders, thinking nothing could surprise me.

Jim seems a little too pleased with his information. Leaning anxiously across the round plastic table, the words spurting from him, he says with a broad grin, "It seems, little brother, that you have been assessed with a little tax lien for the insignificant sum of . . . " he pauses to reach into his pocket for a scrap of paper, ". . . six million five hundred, twenty-one thousand, three hundred fifty-two dollars, and . . . " he flips the paper onto the table, "fifty-five cents." For a moment, Jim stares wistfully at the scrap of paper, his mind apparently lost in accounting appreciation. "You know, I still can't believe that they have it figured to the nearest nickel." I'm floored; my throat goes dry as I croak, "What?"

"Yeah," expounds Jim, obviously pleased with my reaction,. "Six point five million. Maybe they'll take it out of your prison pay," he adds thoughtfully.

The belly laugh rises from my gut unhindered; I can't stop laughing. "Jim," I giggle, "I only make seven cents an hour as an inmate orderly."

"I wouldn't laugh if I were you," he cautions. Then completely serious, he adds, "Do you know what this is going to do to your credit rating?"

Our visit ends too soon as my family stands to leave, then Jim just has to ask, "So tell me, little brother, what's it really like being in prison?"

"When you get home tonight," I answer sarcastically, "take your dinner into the bathroom . . . then stay there for a few days."

Back in my cell with the darkness closing in around me, I take a cigar box from the locker and climb up onto the bed. I lift the lid and finger the blades of cut grass it contains from my tiny lawn in the exercise yard. I raise the drying blades to my nose and deeply inhale the fragrant smell. The grassy bouquet carries me back to Hawaii and the day I met Susan's parents.

Her father was out watering the lawn as we pulled up in front of the house. A few moments later Puu and I were under close parental scrutiny. It didn't help our introduction when Puu started things off by making a deposit on the man's manicured lawn. Her father and I were standing side by side as Puu dug his back paws into the delicate grass making long scratching scars in the green carpet, which only a few moments ago had been without flaw. Susan's father gaped open-mouth at the small clumps of flying grass.

"Puu," I yelled in frustration, "get over here."

Susan's father took a couple of steps closer to the large offensive pile. He looked somewhat amazed at the size of it, then glanced sternly at me. "That's an awful big dog you've got, son."

"Yes, sir," I answered lamely, not missing his use of the word *awful*, "he's even rather large for a Great Dane."

"So I noticed." Mr. Longway looked again at the large offensive pile as if he couldn't really believe it's there. "I guess you would like to borrow my shovel?"

"Yes, sir, Mr. Longway." I gave Puu a scalding look, which he ignored, while heading for the garage.

I was carrying the shovel back into the garage with its still steaming cargo when I saw Susan and her mother step into the back of *Revelstoke*. I was so anxious to get back outside to make sure nothing else went wrong that I didn't notice that the trash can I was emptying the shovel into happened to be Mrs. Longway's over-sized laundry hamper.

Rushing back outside I see that a neighbor has joined Mr. Longway who is standing at the back of the truck eyeing the interior of *Revelstoke* suspiciously. I arrive just in time to hear the neighbor say, "I don't know about you, Walt, but I sure wouldn't let my daughter in the back of that thing."

Susan's mom stepped out of the truck beaming. "I really like your home, but that bed is a bit tiny isn't it?"

To my stunned amazement, Susan instantly answered, "Oh, no, mom, it folds out into a full-size double; there's loads of room, want me to show you how it opens?"

Walt tried to look past his Susan at the bed under discussion while his neighbor snickered in self-satisfaction. "Well, how do you figure she knows how to do that?" he chimed.

Before anything else could go wrong, I quickly broke in on the dangerous conversation. "Susan, we gotta go, we don't want to keep our friends waiting." We were going hiking in the mountains above Waikiki. Susan stepped out of the truck. I closed the back door and whisked her around to the passenger door and held it open until she was safely inside. Rushing to the driver's side, I quickly jumped in.

"Oh, mom, will you wash my jeans? I need them for work tonight."

"Certainly," answered her mother, "where are they?"

"In the laundry hamper," Susan replied.

"I'll do them right now."

Driving away, I saw Walt and his neighbor talking animatedly. We were just rounding the corner when Susan said, "You forgot something."

"What? What did I forget?" I was exasperated after the stressful encounter with her parents.

Smiling sweetly, Susan said, "Your dog."

CHAPTER 9

The next morning I wake to see sharp-edged shadows of jail bars marching slowly across my cell wall in sync with the rising sun. Upstairs someone flushes a toilet, an event that will be repeated many times throughout the morning. The rushing sound of the gurgling water causes the pipe above me to rattle slightly. The metal bunk bed then momentarily shakes as Morris, who sleeps on the bunk beneath me, rolls over and expels gas. I quickly strike a match to mask the foul odor that seeps into the air. Then while watching a wisp of gray smoke curl upward from the burning match, I faintly hear the distant call of a military bugle.

Two hundred yards from my window, across many walls and fences, stands a Coast Guard base at the harbor mouth. I could easily visualize the brilliant red, white, and blue colors of the American flag ascending the shiny pole while the bugle call brings the formation to attention. Memories of myself in dress uniform come vividly to mind, standing proud at parade rest and saluting the flag as it ripples and snaps in the wind.

Instantly saddened, I burrow deeper under the thin prison blanket. Tears threaten to spill from my eyes as a shudder runs the length of my spine. Closing my eyes against the moisture that clouds my vision, I still see the shadows of those jail bars burning in my mind.

Morris, my middle-aged Armenian cell mate, is concerned. Standing on his toes with his nose just reaching my mattress, he asks, "Steve, why aren't you practicing your karate?" It's his way of politely asking what is wrong. Normally I practice karate in the limited space of our cell in the early morning; the challenge is to be so silent that I do not wake him.

I sadly tell Morris what the bugle call means to me, how it stirs memories of a prouder past that, though now lost, still lives deep within me.

For a moment Morris just stares kindly. "You know, Steve, you don't belong here; you don't have a criminal mentality. Morgan just came into your life when you were the most susceptible. Instead of writing that magazine article (in the cell I'm writing an anti-drug piece for *Surfer* magazine), maybe you should be writing a book about all this. It might help others not to make the same mistakes, and it'll give you something constructive to do . . . I mean let's face it, we're both going to be here for a long time."

Breakfast that morning is eggs over-easy—something we get only once a week. Inmate cooks fry the eggs early in the morning, then the prepared breakfasts are later wheeled over to J-3 in metal carts where they wait for the guard to open the door at his leisure. As usual, the carts have been sitting outside in the sun for the past half hour. Already, the milk in five gallon cartons will have begun to sour. The eggs will need to be reheated in the microwave, which gives them a bland rubbery texture that causes the eggs to stick to the cardboard plates. There will also be dry sausage and stale white bread, both of which I always give away. As a vegetarian, I never get enough to eat; however, there are some advantages to not eating the low-quality prison meats. Half the cell block came down with a raging dose of food poisoning from a batch of tainted chicken last week.

However, being a vegetarian was no protection from one of the other hazards of inmate chow. The inmate cooks sometimes secret little surprises in the food for their own amusement. These hidden treasures often include components not listed in any book—except for maybe the Anarchist cookbook. For example, I used to enjoy the Tuesday morning oatmeal until I discovered a small tidbit lying on the bottom of my half-empty bowl. It bore a remarkable likeness to a rat's claw.

The oatmeal memory keeps me suspicious as I eye my breakfast for unwanted surprises. I stare unhappily at the eggs on my paper plate. The yolks are broken; the egg white is greasy brown. Beside the eggs lay two shrivelled sausages that look very much like something normally buried in a cat box. It's hard to imagine that this is my favorite meal here. In some prisons they use meat loaf as part of their punishment program. After two or three days of eating nothing but meat loaf, an inmate can become anxious to be more cooperative, particularly when you consider that meat loaf is often referred to as "Inmate Surprise." An imaginative cook can shovel a mess of untasty surprises into meat loaf.

At 9 A.M., the guard lets us out into the yard for our one hour of allotted sunshine. I race a crazy old black man with bulbous eyes to my small patch of green grass. For some reason he likes to pee on it. Often our races are quite humorous as he runs his shuffling gate with one hand fumbling for his fly. The other inmates purposefully get in my way to give the old codger a sporting chance. I prefer to do my stretching exercises on the tiny lawn without the benefit of smelling someone's urine.

The other inmates still think I'm nuts to be watering the lawn, but the grass is quite happy about it. Tiny green shoots are beginning to fill in the larger bare dirt patches, and the once lackluster, brown grass has begun to turn a vibrant green.

The small lawn is my refuge from a world of cement and steel bars. I enjoy watching the green grass grow. It makes me feel like

I'm accomplishing something real, something that I can actually see happening. A visible reinforcement of positive action is a rare occurrence in the joint.

Lying upon the soft grass, my head turned toward the cloudless sky, I watch a pelican soar gracefully on the wind. I follow its flight till it disappears over the tall prison wall then stare for an instant at the glittering stainless steel razor wire that lines the top of the wall. The moment galvanizes the intensity of my incarceration. My whole life now revolves around the single wing of a building, this little yard, and the wacko inmates that are my constant companions.

Not wanting to become depressed, I fetch the metal bucket and begin the first of twenty trips to and from the drinking fountain. I patiently watch the water dribbling into the dented bucket then carry it to the grass where I pour the water carefully. My mind rejoices in the crystal clear purity of the flowing liquid as I watch it spill from the bucket onto the grass.

"Arrington! Put that bucket down and get your butt over here." The guard is standing at the gate, from his hand dangle handcuffs and manacles. "The judge is requesting your presence at court." The guard laughs at his own simple joke.

The mesh-covered windows in the marshal's van are dusty as usual. Shackled next to two other inmates, I'm fortunate to have a window seat. I sit with my nose pressed against the dirty window watching the real world passing by. People driving on the freeway do not see me; I am just a shadowed silhouette in a darkened van. I'm outside their boundary of awareness, while they totally fill mine. We are worlds apart. I've driven these same highways as a free man many times, yet never have I noticed these marshal vans with their dark, caged interiors and silhouetted cargo of lost souls.

Up front the two marshals are listening to the FM radio. After a commercial break the disk jockey plays "Working on a Chain Gang," by the Pretenders. One of the marshals increases the volume then turns around to smile brightly at us, "Hey, dirt bags," he yells, "listen, they're playing your song."

The black man riding next to me tells the guard to screw himself then, looking down at the chains hanging from our wrists and ankles, laughs and nudges me good naturedly.

At the courthouse, we are taken to the holding tanks in the basement. In threes we shuffle slowly; you cannot walk shackled in chains. If anyone breaks pace the manacles gouge the skin brutally, which always upsets everyone concerned.

Later, upstairs in the courtroom, it is a rare opportunity to be among real people. While reporters and law students write in their notebooks, caught up in their thoughts, I wonder about them. Free people have an uninhibited quality that prisoners are very sensitive to and envious of. An inmate exists in a world of distrust, where he must always be alert for danger, yet where little actually happens—except for instantaneous sparks of physical terror. It's an artificial environment that lends itself to cruelty and usually twists the human mind in the direction of insanity.

Human incarceration can be compared to what it is like for animals living in a zoo. Imagine the tiger pacing its cage endlessly. The tiger with its finely tuned body is designed for wide open places. Instead, it goes slowly insane as confinement in a small, artificial cell deadens its dynamic personality. Is there any doubt why many wild beasts have trouble mating in a zoo's artificial confinement? The truly sad thing about zoos, however, is that its inmates have done nothing wrong. The tiger has been sentenced to life imprisonment merely for the diversion of man, or even more sadly, because its home was needed by civilization.

At lunch break I watch the real people begin to filter out of the courtroom. They talk animatedly. A man and woman, both in their early twenties, laugh unhindered as they walk hand-in-hand down the corridor. I notice that the woman's long, flowing, blonde hair looks exactly like Susan's. With my solemn marshal escort, we follow the happy couple. While waiting for the elevator, I hear them discussing restaurants and their plans to go out dancing for the evening. When the elevator door opens we go inside together. The grim-faced marshals and I stand on one side, the happy couple on the other. The woman looks at me then whispers to her companion. They both laugh lightly while I stare at the floor.

In the courthouse lobby, I watch them walk through the wide double doors out into a day filled with sunshine and bustling activity; the sunlight halos the woman's hair as it dances in the wind. The marshals walk temptingly close to the light-filled portal then continue leading me down a dark hall and through twin security doors that lead to the building's basement.

In the cold reality of the holding tank I sit idly on a hard metal bench. In my hand I hold a white bread and bologna sandwich. The inmates watch each other looking to see if anyone has something they don't. Almost everyone smokes. A thick gray haze hangs in the air. I sit quietly on the cold metal bench and wait. It is three long hours before the marshals come for me.

John DeLorean is in court today. He sits at the table in front of me. He knows I've refused to cooperate. Turning in his seat during a break he looks at me and offers an encouraging smile. He is pleased that I'm not cooperating. Charisma radiates from the man.

Morgan sits with his lawyers at the other end of my table. He tries to get John's attention with a grin, but DeLorean frowns then turns away. Rumor already has it that Morgan will soon turn government witness. Both men are trying to get their bail reduced.

I've asked my attorney, Richard Barnett, not to bother seeking a reduction in my bail. Already convinced that I am going to be serving some serious prison time, I figure the sooner I get started the sooner I can go home. Besides, I know without a doubt that in the end I will plead guilty. I'm just holding out for some kind of plea bargain that doesn't involve snitching. Knowing that I am going to be inside for a while, I just try to take it one day at a time. Oddly, I find it easier to cope with life in prison than the rich lifestyle I lived while under the bondage of Morgan and company. The hardest part, though, is living with the guilt. My conscience, suffering under a heavy burden of guilt, is a talkative companion who often keeps me up far into the night.

On the ride back to prison, I try to cram as many sights into my mind as possible—visual fodder to carry me through the long, lonely nights yet to come. When the trial is over, I won't be leaving the prison anymore. I think about my father and how he must have felt like this too when he left the hospital for the last time. My stepmother said that he knew he was going home to die. They lived in the mountains among pine forests at Big Bear Lake. She said that he was completely silent on the ride home; he just stared intently out the window of the car looking at the tall trees, the animated people, and the vibrance of life about him. He was storing up memories to lend himself a bit of comfort for the death bed that awaited him at home. My father was a prisoner of his disease, while I sit shackled in chains, a prisoner of society and shamed in my own eyes.

Back at the prison I have missed dinner so am treated to another bologna sandwich, which I trade for a bruised apple from the black man who rode in the van with me. I eat, yet still there is a hollowness in my gut. The emptiness is felt deepest in my soul. I wonder, *Am I an evil person? Have I really been so bad that society must lock me away from itself?* My questions have no answer as I lie awake in the semi-darkness of the prison cell.

At 4 A.M., I'm still awake thinking about the horrible twist my life has taken when a strange memory comes to mind. I remember a day in 1969 when my ship sailed into Long Beach harbor after my third tour to Vietnam. No one was on the pier to meet me when the ship pulls alongside the cement quay. I watched the other sailors being greeted by loved ones. I walked alone down to the highway and began to hitch-hike home. Along the way I was dropped off the freeway at an exit ramp that has no on ramp. I had to walk over a mile in the heat of the day carrying a heavy duffel bag over one shoulder.

I was beginning to feel sorry for myself and was a little bit angry at the world when I saw that I was walking past a school for handi-capped children. There were about seventy kids in a big circle on the playground—all of them were in wheelchairs. A skinny boy of about twelve wheeled his chair over by the fence to get a better look at me. He must have envied the sailor's uniform that promised world travel and my two healthy legs, something this kid would never have. I knew he would have given anything to be able to carry that heavy sea bag. Ashamed of my self-pity, I waved. The kid's face lit up in a buoyant smile; he waved back vigorously with both hands.

I instantly knew that if this kid could face his adversity and still find a smile for me, then how could I in honesty feel sorry for my-self. My self-pity evaporated. I stood straighter and walked on with a swagger to my step despite the crushing weight of the heavy duffel. I was not even as upset as I might have been when I got home and discovered that my mother had unexpectedly moved without telling me.

Opening my eyes in the enclosed half-darkness, I see that the shadows of the jail bars are back on my cell wall, this time painted faintly by the harsh illumination of the bright security lights outside. Lying on my bunk, I decide to take another lesson from that kid. No more self-pity. I have my health. I could have just as easily been shot the night I was arrested and could even now be in a wheelchair my-self. Instead I should count my blessings. I have been saved from a life that was out of my control. Prison won't last forever.

Thomas Milton, a fifteenth century monk/philosopher once wrote, "A monk retires to cloister to become more a part of the world, not to flee from it." I do not know for how long I will be in prison, but I do know I'm going to make the most of it. How many times have I wished for the leisure to really commit myself toward physical, mental, and spiritual development? Certainly I have that time now. Someday I'm going to walk out of that prison gate, and I do not want to think that this part of my life has been wasted. I take out a journal and begin to write with renewed vigor. Then, for the rest of that short night, I sleep better than I have since my arrest.

Later in the morning, I wake refreshed and ready to go. When I hear the bugle call to colors, it just reinforces my determination and commitment. I have always been in good physical shape, so I have a solid foundation to work from as I begin a regular exercise schedule in my cell: sit-ups on the bunk, push-ups on the cement floor, and pull-ups from the overhead toilet pipe. In the yard, I run harder and work out more fiercely on the universal gym. Whenever I start to falter or even slow down, I only have to look at the glittering concentina wire on the walls and my determination is renewed.

At night and in the early morning, I practice yoga and karate. During the noisiest part of the day, I sit quitely, immersing my spirit in simple prayer. I find that the drab cement walls force inward focus. There is little outside stimulus in prison to draw the mind's attention from itself. Since I can't journey outward, I take long trips within. I follow many paths on that winding course that leads to our inner being. I discover secrets that I had unconsciously hidden even from myself. I had sealed them away under the lock of embarrassment. Sometimes I stumble unexpectedly upon one of these uncomfortable memories. They are easily spotted by the habitual mental cringe that I experience whenever they come to mind. Mostly they are about stupid, little things, petty incidents in my life that I am not particularly proud of, mostly childhood blunders and adult embarrassments. I find that by re-thinking them, plunging into their essence, I can forgive myself by understanding what I had done wrong thus wiping away the guilt. I heal many old wounds and can soon freely remember them without the habitual cringe. It's a wonderful discovery, and it actively encourages me to seek out those dark memories as if they are buried treasure. I rejoice in their detection and the revelations they teach me, then I sweep them away like the unneeded baggage that they are.

The book shelf in the J-3 television room holds seven books, four of which are Bibles. I carry one of the Bibles into my cell and open it to page one. Though I have skimmed the Bible many times, I have never actually read it. Now, questions are coming to mind that only the Bible can answer. My biggest question revolves around being a criminal. In the Bible, I read about many people who had fallen and later found their way back. The Bible gives me hope for the future.

Confined within the narrow space of my prison cell, I learn to escape into books. A really good book is like a miniature vacation from prison. Wrapped in my worn blanket to hold off the winter cold, I travel with Mary Stewart's *King Arthur in Medieval England*. C.S. Lewis took me to strange new worlds, and I shared hobbit adventures in the fantasy writings of Tolkien in *Lord of the Rings*. All of these writers shared a common theme; their stories were about good triumphing over evil. I realize that if I am ever to be happy again, I will have to find my way back to the good side of life. It's where I left my once buoyant soul. I become determined to find that happiness again.

I also begin to learn from the inmates around me. I share the lives of people who grew up in the slums. I talk with men born into money and power. Our prisons are full of people from all walks of life and from all over the world. Some teach you nothing except maybe patience because their ways are so darn trying.

Watching television with inmates is in itself a learning experience. They root for the bad guys and boo the heroes. The news, when embellished with inmates' anecdotes, takes on a whole new perspective I have never considered before.

An inmate named Shorty is addicted to the soaps. One morning the guard takes him away to court for sentencing; when he returns in the afternoon everyone wants to know how many years he got. "Oh, I got eight years," he answers, dismissing it with a wave of his hand as unimportant, "but tell me," he asks eagerly, "what did I miss on 'All My Children'?"

Prison is a unique university of life; that is, if one can survive long enough to complete their education. For some, prison is a place where they come to die. It is one of the harsh realities that is just another part of the prison experience.

CHAPTER 10

Wednesday morning is commissary day, the highlight of an otherwise drab week. If an inmate has money on his prison account he can make simple purchases from a shopping list that includes cigarettes, candy, instant coffee, tea, boxes of soup, etc. Many inmates lacking their own funds simply borrow from others or commit assorted acts of extortion on the weaker inmates.

Standing in line waiting for my commissary issue, I glance over my shoulder to see the kindly, old black man, the one who so likes watering my lawn with his urine, disappearing into his cell. A homeless man from the back streets of Los Angeles, I know that he has no family or friends to send him money. He is much too proud to consider borrowing from the other inmates. So, when the commissary cart makes its weekly appearance, he quietly shuffles down the hall and disappears into his cell. As I see his cell door close, I happily think about the surprise I am getting for him.

The old man is a chronic cigar smoker. Yesterday I watched him hand-rolling a cigar from the coarse bulk tobacco issued to the inmates by the government. He began by wadding up a handful of the loose tobacco into a fat cylinder, which he carefully laid into a brown paper towel. After rolling the paper towel back and forth on a wooden bench, he tamped it into a crude cigar. Then he lightly dampened the homemade cigar with water from the drinking fountain, which caught the attention of Shorty, who had to come over to investigate.

"What ya doing?" Shorty asked, leaning over the black man's shoulder.

"I'm dampening my cigar," the old man replied patiently.

"Why don't you just lick it?"

"Because I ain't got that much spit," the old man grumbled.

"Well, how come you gotta wet it anyhow?" Shorty could be real persistent with his endless questions.

The old man turned to regard Shorty; the contemptuous look on his face showed that he didn't think Shorty was very bright as he growled, "Because if I don't wet the paper towel first, the fire will run right up the sides of the cigar and fry my lips."

"Oh," shrugged Shorty.

Finally, I arrive at the front of the commissary line and receive a brown paper sack with my last name printed on it in crude letters. I take the sack to my cell to open it. It is never wise to let other inmates see your purchases. I set the sack on my bunk and peer anxiously inside. For the barest moment a childhood memory comes vividly to mind. I remember being at elementary school and opening my sack lunch in hopeful anticipation of finding peanut butter cookies inside. The memory passes quickly as I reach into the sack and instead of cookies remove two small boxes of cigars.

A moment later I am standing at the door to the old man's cell. I tap twice lightly on the metal frame; in prison it's not healthy to just barge into someone's cell. All kinds of unnatural things occur in prison cells behind closed doors so it's best to knock if you want to avoid unpleasant surprises.

"So come in already," answers the old man, "I ain't got no keys to lock it anyhow." I open the door and step inside. The tiny cell carries the old man's smell like a signature. There is, of course, the lingering odor of cigar smoke, but also there is the sickness smell common to an aged person who is slowly dying. The old man, cast in shadows, is lying on the lower bunk, his bulbous eyes gleam in the half-darkness. "What do you want youngster?" he asks.

I hold up the cigars, "The commissary man made a mistake and put these in my sack. Rather than return them I thought you might want them."

The whites of the old man's eyes flash in the shadows, "I don't want no charity, boy."

"I got them by mistake," I say softly. Taking a step closer I set the cigars on the edge of his bunk. "You might as well have them. It's better than just throwing them out."

I turn swiftly and exit the cell. Outside in the corridor I take several deep breaths washing out of my lungs the death smell that lingers in that cell. Before depression could set in, I quickly return to my own cell and tear open the commissary sack. Inside is the radio I've been anxiously awaiting. To buy a radio is a long, involved process. After submitting the initial request I had to wait six weeks for the prison staff to approve the purchase.

Removing the radio from its protective box, I set it upon the locker. It is just a little mono unit with a single three-inch speaker. Turning it on, I tune the radio to a pop station and hear the opening strains of one of my favorite tunes. Turning the volume up the music builds on itself, the happy beat washing in waves into the silence of the cell. I close my eyes, giving myself up to the music, amazed that the tiny fifty-cent speaker so fills the cell; its sound waves reverberating off the walls and driving away the noise of the jail unit outside my door. I immerse myself in music and am a much more cheerful soul when an hour later I leave the cell to set up the television room for lunch.

Out in the corridor, I see the old black man shuffling along with a big toothless grin wrapped around one of the store-bought cigars. His eyes look even more bulbous than normal as his jaws industriously work that cigar. As he passes he quietly says, "Thanks youngster," then goes tramping off down the corridor followed by a dense cloud of cigar smoke.

For the rest of the week he struts around the yard smoking or just chewing on those cigars. Then on Saturday morning the guard opens the old man's cell door to find he passed away in his sleep. As they take the thin body away on a stretcher, I know that I will always remember him best seeing his lanky frame poised over the small lawn with the stub of a cigar sticking out of his mouth while he happily peed on my grass.

That night in my cell, I dwell upon the vitality of life that I am missing, locked within these drab prison walls. At the cell's window there is little for me to see. A thirty-foot-tall security wall blocks most of the view, and looking up I can't see the stars for the bright glare of the security lights. Yet with the lights off in the cell and listening to the radio playing softly, I am able to ride the winds of the Los Angeles air waves.

When the radio begins to play "Surfer Girl" by the Beach Boys, I open the locker and take out a picture of Susan and Puu to look at it under the glow of the security lights glaring in the window. Susan is on the beach about to throw a stick for Puu to chase. The camera has caught her with one arm over her head, the stick just released from her fingers. Beyond her the surf is running a solid twelve feet, which meant the wave faces were taller than a two story building. In my mind a window into the past slowly opens.

I remember sitting on my surfboard at Laniakea and seeing Susan on the beach making that overhead motion with her hand. I thought she was waving to me and was instantly stoked. Susan never bothered to watch me surf before, and I was in perfect position to catch a set wave that was just forming. I paddled furiously, surging ahead of the other surfers who were after the same wave. At the last instant, I realized that the wave was bigger than anything I'd ever tackled before. From the top of the wave, I had an elevator view of a twenty-foot-tall wall of water. For a heart-sinking moment, I wanted to back away from the vertical edge; then I felt my board falling away as I dropped into the long downward plunge screaming my lungs out. Somehow I maintained enough control to make the bottom turn, the board was flashing across the wave face; I was going faster than ever before—but not fast enough.

With a sinking feeling I saw that the whole wave was pitching as it washed over a shallow inner reef. Then the thick lip came down like a liquid door closing. I was caught inside a spinning liquid barrel that was rapidly collapsing upon itself. About to be mangled, I turned the board hard into the wave face in a desperate attempt to arrow the board, followed hopefully by my body, through the thick wall of water.

I almost made it. I could see that I was within a foot of the surface as I strained to punch out the backside of the wave. Looking through the shimmering distortion of the water, I saw a bird flying in the sky . . . then I was pulled irresistibly backward. It was like being in a high-rise elevator that broke its cable. This rapid backward flushing sensation I was experiencing is referred to by surfers . . . in hushed whispers . . . as "being sucked over the falls," and it ranks number one as the last thing that a surfer ever wants to have happen to him. As I watched the rapidly receding sky, I knew that I was about to get trashed in a very big way.

The thick lip, weighed down with many tons of water slammed its small human cargo toward the bottom. The air I had gulped seconds before was hammered out of my lungs by the massive hydraulic impact. All about me bubbles swirled distortedly in a wild, spinning vortex of tons of crashing water. The surfboard leash on my ankle stretched to double its normal length then broke. Curled into a tiny protective ball, I bounced along the rocky bottom, wondering if I was about to drown before Susan's eyes.

Desperately I made it back to the surface just in time to get hit by a second wave. My surfboard had long since departed for the beach as I began my second underwater excursion, which was a lot like being caught inside a giant Maytag washer stuck on the heavy rinse cycle.

I finally landed on the beach just in time to catch my surfboard washing out with the morning tide. I walked wearily across the beach with my broken surfboard leash dragging in the sand behind me.

That's when I saw Susan throwing a stick, which Puu was fetching back to her. Staggering up to her, trying hard not to wobble at the knees, I asked hopefully, "Hey, Susan, did you see that magnificent wave I caught?"

Susan looked at me like she didn't know what I was talking about. "No," she said, shrugging her shoulders, "I was playing with Puu. Why?" Standing there with wet sand in my ears and filling the crotch of my swimsuit, I realized that the throwing motion Susan was making with the stick looked exactly like the waving motion I saw from out in the line-up.

"Oh, no reason," I replied, dragging my thrashed body toward the truck.

I had only gone a few steps when Susan caught up with me. "Steve," she said, taking my hand in hers, "you don't have to try to impress me with your surfing; I already love you." I could feel the surfboard wax melting in my back pocket.

Stepping close against me, Susan raised her face and smiled in a way that needed kissing. As I begin to lower my face to hers, Susan closes her eyes, and . . . my sinuses abruptly drain their cargo of salt water that the big wave had impacted into them. In shock, Susan's eyes fly open as sinus-slimed water runs across her face.

In the darkened cell I can't help the laughter that explodes from me. A moment later a flashlight beam probes into the cell through the small window in the door. I see the guard's face; he is probably wondering what this inmate is doing standing in the dark and laughing. The beam of light switches from me to my bunk; the meaning is clear. Climbing up onto the bunk, I turn my face to the wall hoping to recapture my memories of Susan and Puu; instead I fall asleep.

The next morning I'm up early to prepare and serve breakfast. Afterward, the guard locks the rest of the inmates out of the television room while I mop the floor. They pace anxiously behind the locked grill waiting for me to finish so they can come in to watch television. When the floor is dry the guard opens the grill and the inmates rush to place chairs in front of the boob tube.

Again the guard locks the grill, only now I am on the other side as I begin to mop the corridor. From the television room, I hear the inmates shouting at each other as they argue over what they are going to watch. Shorty wins the argument, and the guard switches on a soap opera. The two guys who wanted to watch cartoons sit angrily at a back table playing cards.

Pushing the mop side to side, I think about the impact that television has on us inmates. For many inmates our only contact with the outside world is found in the glaring orb of the television set. From its two-dimensional image, we sample the essence of life beyond prison walls. Television programing can act as an alternate reality through which many convicts mix their own bag of memories and experiences as their imagination projects itself onto the screen. Many of the convicts are so hungry for stimulus that they almost seem to be feeding as they stare hungrily at the flickering screen of the television.

Above the yelling of the other inmates I hear the high-pitched squeal of Shorty. I can't help but wonder if Shorty's fascination with the soap operas is because they serve as an alternate reality for him. He's not just watching "All My Children;" he's living it as he sits in front of the tube shouting threats at the actors and cursing the women for their sexual intrigues.

After finishing the floor, I retire to my cell to read a book. As the cell door closes behind me the noise from the television room diminishes. Anticipating that I will have a quiet hour or two to read, I recline upon my bunk, not knowing that in the next few minutes I will be locked in confrontation with another inmate.

As head orderly, I have the collateral duty of changing the channel on the television when the guard isn't there to do it. If left to themselves, inmates will fight over the television. Convicts have been killed in fits of rage because someone objected to the choice of programing. So a vote is taken on channel selection, though usually it's the biggest bicep that makes the final decision.

I haven't read more than two or three pages when Shorty opens the door and asks me to come change the channel. A moment later standing before the television, I'm reaching for the knob when I hear a frightening growl of outrage directly behind me. Spinning about I see a large, muscular black man hurling a chair from his path as he comes at me, shrieking, "I'm going to rip your honky face off!"

The paperback falls unnoticed from my hand. I can't show fear as he stomps right up to me. His face is distorted with fury as he growls, "I'm going to kill you!"

Abruptly, like a furnace door swinging open, my own anger blazes to instant fury. I have contained myself too long. This is the last straw as my sanity flees before the fiery winds of a burning rage. Unconsciously, my body adopts a karate fighting stance. Focusing on my adversary, I've become a primal male animal ready to fight for its survival. The other inmates scatter, clearing a fighting area for us.

I prepare to block his attack and counter with my own. Ten years of intense karate training are focused in this instant of time. My hands cup like a preying mantis as my long frame adopts the stilted movements of this insect, which I had been taught to mimic by my Gung Fu master in Hawaii. His teachings crystallize into a fabric of mind and body coordination that will react without conscious thought on my part. Though I'm besotted with rage, an icy calmness settles upon me as I remember my teachings and will my muscles to relax. A stressed muscle moves slower than one that is relaxed.

There is a rage in the man's eyes. I glare back. Hot blood pounds at my temples. Just as I think he is about to attack—he doesn't. Instead he hesitates even as he threatens, "I'm going to waste ya, man!"

Instantly I know that he is going to back down. Unexpectedly I've already won. In a voice almost calm, I answer his verbal challenge, "A man does what a man has to do." Later I'll think how stupid that statement sounds. Yet it isn't a threat I'm voicing, just a simple commitment. I'm ready to fight, and he knows it. I guess he expected me to cower down because of his size. The thought makes me angry again.

"Hey, man," I finally yell, "do it now or get out of my face!" I brace for fury; my anger almost wills him to attack. Then the fire just blows out of him. He curses and struts about while glaring at me fiercely, then, diminished from the monster he was an instant before, he sits down.

For a moment, I'm not sure what to do. In a daze I go back to my cell and close the door. Alone, I shake uncontrollably. When the guard hears what happened, he offers to transfer the troublemaker into the hole (J-1). "No way," I quickly reply. "This problem is between him and me. If you get involved, that's going to bring all kinds of heat down on me."

The guard shrugs his shoulders and walks away, probably thinking about the futility of helping inmates. I don't have any more problems with the angry black man, though I often catch him watching me through hooded eyes.

A few days later during lunch, two inmates viciously attack each other. The guard breaks it up, but not before one of the inmates bashes the other alongside the head with a heavy metal mop wringer. The guard locks down the entire cell block, then lets me out to clean up the mess. Angry puddles of red blood lay splattered upon the white tile floor and a broad splash of wet crimson scars the bulletin board. I mop the grisly mess up, then while washing out the mop in the deep sink, I watch the blood mixing with the water as it swirls down the stained and cracked drain. I think how prison is like an unfeeling machine designed to suck life force for no useful purpose. The thought is not reassuring.

CHAPTER 11

Being in prison means getting back to basics. There are some thugs that have nothing going for them but brawn and a general lack of restraint. What little intelligence they may have once had has long since been burned away by alcohol and drugs. The basics tend to be big guys with unusual sexual habits. I wound up with one for a cellmate on a cold and humid December night.

It's only an hour before lockdown when the guard opens the cell door, "Hey, Arrington, I got a new bunky for you." Instantly attentive, I sit up on the bunk.

A brute of a man lumbers through the door. He stands six foot four and weighs over three hundred pounds. The huge man has a seriously depraved look about him.

Bruno dwarfs the cell; it is like a grizzly bear has entered its lair. He sniffs at the stuffy air, growls his dissatisfaction then glares at me red-eyed. "I swore I'd never wind up in a d—— prison cell," he curses. Bruno tramps over to the metal locker and throws open the door, bashing it against the wall. He glances over at me as if daring me to say something. I set down the letter I had been writing; all thoughts of home evaporating in the flush of fear that envelopes my heart.

Bruno jams his few possessions into the locker then kicks the door closed. He turns aggressively, an angry bear looking for trouble. "They set me up with that d—— lie detector test," he rages. "It wasn't my fault the old lady died. The jerks acted like I killed her on purpose."

There isn't enough air in the cell to fill my lungs, "You killed an old lady?"

Bruno shrugs his massive shoulders, "Yeah, some old woman who had been purposely flirting with me. I wouldn't have been interested but I was drunk and she had been asking for it." He stomps two steps to my bunk and leans heavily on it, his foul breath washes over me as he grumbles, "We were on a cruise ship where I worked as a mechanic, which is what makes it a bloody federal offense."

"But why did you kill her?" I'm in a state of shock.

Bruno's anger flares as he begins to passionately argue his defense, "D—— it, man, the old lady had been asking for it, wasn't my fault that she couldn't take it. Hell, I was so drunk, I didn't even know that she had stopped breathing."

"She had stopped breathing" The words explode in my mind. Listening to him telling his macabre story and hearing the way he absolves himself of any blame, or even simple compassion, convinces me that Bruno is a full-blown lunatic. I feel the hair on the back of my neck standing on end.

Bruno abruptly spins around and slams a meaty fist into the wall—once, twice, three times! He stops and stares at the torn flesh on his thick knuckles then licks at the blood. He spits red saliva onto the floor, then slams the wall two more times, a right and a left. "I'm going to get them," he rages, "Old Bruno is going to waste them all."

I stare at a spreading red stain where his fists impacted against the wall. I have no idea who "them" was but knew there wasn't a chance of me falling asleep with Bruno the insane murderer in my cell. Sitting upright on my mattress, I am so glad that I have chosen an upper bunk. It's easier to defend yourself from attackers when you have height on your side. From a bottom bunk there's no place to go; a rapist has the advantage of leverage and weight. People in bottom bunks sometimes wake up with their faces pressed downwards into their pillow as they are savagely attacked without warning.

From the somewhat doubtful security of my upper bunk, I lie awake throughout the dark of the night listening to the monster beneath me snoring heavily.

The next morning I go directly to the guard and tell him that he has to transfer Bruno out of the cell because there isn't a chance of my going back behind a locked door with that lunatic in there. The guards sudden laughter catches me off guard.

"No problem," he casually grins, "you're right about him being a lunatic. He was supposed to go to the nut ward upstairs last night, but the watch commander made a mistake and routed him to J-3."

"Made a mistake!" I'm livid. "That mistake could have gotten me killed."

The guard is still laughing, "I think you're lucky that Bruno didn't take a fancy to you."

I can't believe that to the guard it's a joke; for me the implications of what could have happened in that cell might have impacted the rest of my life. I didn't return to my cell until after Bruno had departed for the nut ward. I tried to clean the blood smears from the wall, but they wouldn't completely wash away. The stain of Bruno was persistent on the wall and in my mind, where it left another type of scar that would last much longer than any simple stain.

CHAPTER 12

Mail call is at 4 P.M. It's the highlight of the day. We all desperately hope to hear our name called. "Arrington," shouts the guard, bringing an instant smile to my face. The letter passes from hand to hand to me. Anxiously looking at the return address, I happily see that it is from a girlfriend in San Diego. I return to my cell and recline upon the bunk to enjoy the letter. Then with heavy-hearted sadness, I read that she won't be writing anymore. Her father forbids correspondence with a man who is in prison. Enclosed I find a picture on which she has written, "Please, don't forget me."

With a growing knot in my stomach I stare at the picture. Though I indeed understand, the hurt is still there. It reaches way down inside of me and tears at my inner fiber. I feel so terribly alone, lost in a hostile environment where hate and malicious intent prowls the halls, and now another valued and trusted friendship quietly slips away. I sit in my cell prepared to pay for my mistakes, but the inner hurt of forfeiting friends in the process is a soul-rending wound that pains me deeply.

My incarceration has been a real test of my friends. Some of them just don't care to know me anymore. They instead choose to sit in judgment without knowing why I became involved with Morgan and his smuggling operation. Fortunately, my family and some of my closer friends still believe that I am basically a good person. Yet their support and my incarceration is taking a toll upon them, too. My mother's social standing in her community of friends has suffered. After all, her son is a known outlaw.

This is one of the unexpected things that new felons don't often consider when they begin to dance the criminal waltz. It's not only the felon who is going to suffer; family and close friends must also bear the burden of an incarcerated loved one.

Some of my friends are being tested more than others. They are actually being harassed by the government because of their association with Morgan and me. Under DEA scrutiny, they have had their telephone and bank records examined, sometimes they are followed, and worst of all, their homes are being broken into by federal agents.

Michelle is my best friend. A shared interest in diving brought us together. Over the years our friendship grew, and she became the sister I never had. Now, for the crime of being my friend, her life is being actively invaded.

It began when her neighbor called on the telephone. "Michelle,

I don't want to alarm you," she said, "but I saw a man in a white station wagon watching your house yesterday, then when you drove away this morning he followed you."

Over the next couple of days Michelle indeed became aware of a white station wagon that haunted her about the city. Then returning home late one night from a diving trip, she discovered that someone had broken into her house. Nothing had been taken, which made the incident even more scary. Did that mean someone would be coming for her in the night? A home that had once been a safe haven now lay violated. Unable to sleep in the plundered security of her house she fled to the dubious safety of the beach where she spent the night huddled in her car.

The next day a concerned friend of Michelle's stopped by. When he drove away, a white station wagon fell in behind him. That night his Volkswagon camper was broken into. The only thing missing was a pair of tennis shoes probably taken as an afterthought to mask the real intent, which was the active pursuit of evidence by any means. The owner of the tennis shoes was very upset; they were his favorite pair. A good pair of well-broken-in tennis shoes can be awfully important to a high-school swim coach. This particular coach was nick-named The Whale because of his impressive size.

The Whale was still brooding over his lost shoes when he noticed the white station wagon parked just down the street from his house. The Whale slipped out the back door and snuck up behind the car. The man inside, engrossed in a paperback, was completely unaware that a very upset whale was lurking but a few feet away. That is until a giant fist crashed down on the top of the car directly over his head. The whale stepped to the window of the now-dented car and glared inside. "I know you got my sneakers, creep," rumbled the whale. "I want them back or next time it won't be the top of the car that I'm caving in."

The next morning, The Whale opened his front door to find the missing pair of sneakers sitting squarely in the middle of his porch. Meanwhile, the break-ins continued. Sam had his baja bug broken into twice; apparently no one wanted the expensive stereo system, just the two letters I had written to him. A man in a dark business suit was seen trying to break into my attorney's office. The sound of breaking glass alerted the neighbors who chased him away.

Finally, as reported in the *Los Angeles Times*, July 15, 1983:

Attorney Howard Weizman told U.S. District Judge Robert Takasugi that "corroboration" had been obtained Wednesday from a private detective that Gerald Scotti, a federal drug agent whose conduct has been called into question in another case, was involved in the alleged break-ins.

Three break-ins have been "corroborated," said Barnett (Arrington's attorney). He said they occurred both before and after the arrests of DeLorean, Hetrick and Arrington last October.

In a declaration submitted by Weitzman and later unsealed by Takasugi, the private investigator described an interview with Hetrick's son, Harry (Jinx) Hetrick, who claimed to have found Scotti going through papers in the Hetricks' Tehahcapi home. The younger Hetrick reported that a police officer from the Tehahcapi Police Department was in the back yard at the time.

Jinx stated that Buzz (his brother) jumped Scotti and dragged him out of the house, and that Scotti admitted he did not have a warrant and said, "You got me cold," according to Fecheimer's statement.

The *San Diego Tribune*, July 14, 1983, also reported on the alleged break-ins:

Weitzman told U.S. District Judge Robert Takasugi that he believes a specific federal Drug Enforcement Administration agent, Gerald Scotti, was involved in the break-ins.

Scotti, who has been described as having a minor role in the DeLorean case, was a key figure in another recent drug trial of the so-called "Grandma Mafia," in which Weitzman was defense attorney and government misconduct by Scotti was alleged.

"I think it's obvious that Scotti was involved in the illegal break-ins," Weitzman's co-counsel, Donald Re, told the judge. "If so, why hasn't the government told us about this?

"If the government was not aware of it, why were they not aware that one of their own agents was using burglary as an investigative tool?"

Sitting in my jail cell, I couldn't help thinking that I had justifiably given up many of my constitutional rights for my crimes, but my innocent friends had done nothing wrong. These illegal break-ins were a direct threat to their security and well being. After all, the people whom we trust to enforce our laws are also supposed to be subject to them.

Yet, some inmates are having even more outside problems than I. A new kid has just checked-in to J-3. He is only eighteen-years-old—too young to be an accessory to armed bank robbery. A high-school friend encouraged him to drive the get-away car while they were both high on crack.

The kid is using the corridor pay phone to call home; his parents do not yet know that he has been arrested. I am buffing the tile floor so am present to hear the whole conversation.

"Hello, Dad," the boy's voice trembles on the verge of breaking, "It's Billy." Billy pauses while his father shouts into the phone.

Though several feet away I hear the anger in his voice. "Dad, listen," pleads Billy, "I'm in jail." The voice on the phone is furious with anger.

"I . . . I drove my friend Larry to the bank," sobs Billy, "I swear I didn't know he was going to try to rob it."

"Hello, hello," Billy looks blankly at the handset. "I can't believe it," says Billy, looking at me, "my father hung up on me." For the next couple of hours Billy repeatedly tries calling home but there is no answer. I'm serving dinner when Billy finally gets through on the phone to his brother. "Elliot, it's me Billy, I need. . . . " There is a short pause. "What!" shrieks Billy. "How can he be dead? I was just talking to him this morning!"

Billy's face goes pale as he listens. "Heart attack? Dad had a heart attack?" Billy leans against the wall for support. "What do you mean, it's my fault?" he asks stunned. A moment later Billy hangs up the phone and turns to face us, tears streaming from his eyes. "My dad had a heart attack while I was talking with him on the phone. My brother says it's my fault," Billy shutters as uncontrollable sobbing racks his body. "He doesn't want me to call home anymore." Billy turns and flees into his cell.

Not a week later the kid's public defender comes to see him in the attorney counseling rooms. When Billy returns to the cell block he is crying again. It isn't until later that we learn that his grandmother, grief stricken over the loss of her son (Billy's father), apparently died of a broken heart. Billy's family is blaming him for the double death. Unable to cope with the sad situation, the teenager turns into a walking zombie. Except for meals, he stays mostly in his cell or paces the corridor, refusing to talk with anyone.

In my own way, I understand Billy's grief because I too lost someone very special to me, my grandfather on my mother's side. He and I had always been very close. He was the father I never really had. My real father divorced my mother when I was fourteen. I used to take leave from the navy just to help out on my grandparent's farm. Grandpa use to tell me stories about the old days and taught me how to do practical things like repair engines, frame a house, and drive a tractor. What I enjoyed the most was the practical wisdom he shared. He was a simple, upright man. It hurt a lot not being able to go see him when he was sick. He kept asking, "Where is Stephen?" No one could bear to tell him that I was in prison. I desperately wanted to explain what had happened, but one morning he just didn't wake up. I felt like I had failed an important trust—maybe I had.

I've been down almost three months now, and Christmas is fast approaching. I can hardly bear to watch television and its continuous reference to the holidays. On the outside people are festive and in the spirit of Christmas; on the inside we are depressed and argumentative.

Each cell block is issued a small plastic, made-in-Korea, Christmas tree. On Christmas Eve, while everyone else is locked down, the guard lets me out of my cell to set up the tree. He gives me a crumpled box full of old Christmas decorations, most of which are in sorry condition. I dress the tree, carefully placing each ornament so that the plastic pine needles hide most of the cracks and chips. I wrap our best, unstained sheet around the base of the tree then set the Christmas cards I've received in the folds of the sheet. There are two short strings of small colored lights; one goes on the tree, the other around the stout bars on the window. I mold a reflective shield for each colored light with tin foil that I have been saving off the food cart. From the nut ward upstairs, I get popcorn—I never really understood why only the nut cases got popcorn—which I drape around the little plastic tree.

It is dark outside when the guard releases the rest of the inmates for our Christmas Eve dinner. Everyone is surprised to see the tree. For most, the evening turns festive. Some of us sing a few Christmas carols until the other inmates complain about the pitiful quality of our singing.

"What do you expect," rages one of the singers, a convicted bomber who has a thing against tax offices, "the Mormon Tabernacle Choir?"

A few of the harder inmates are angry about the tree. A Mexican bank robber down for the third time curses, "Christmas is the last thing I want to be reminded of in the joint."

"Ah, he's just sore he didn't get a new bike last Christmas," quips one of the other inmates. The Mexican had been arrested while fleeing his last bank robbery on a bicycle; he is often harassed about it.

Billy is late for chow as usual. When he sees the tree, his face lights up in a broad and enthusiastic smile that warms my heart. At the dinner table a new inmate, who doesn't know Billy's tragic story, inadvertently asks, "Hey kid, I bet your family is really missing you, it being Christmas and all." Billy's spoon pauses in mid-air, then his face crumples into itself, uneaten beans spill from his mouth and tears from his eyes as he flees back to his cell. The Mexican slams down his own spoon. "I'm getting real tired of the sissy."

"Hey, leave it alone," I caution, forgetting to mind my own business.

"What do you mean 'leave it alone?'" rages the Mexican. "I have to share a cell with that cry baby."

"He's going through some tough times," I offer, trying to calm the Mexican down.

"I'm going to show that punk a tough time," yells the Mexican.

I try to defuse the situation, "Look, it's Christmas Eve."

The Mexican shoves his plate away and stands up, "Well, d——Christmas, and d——you, too, man!" He stomps out of the television room.

The television room has gone completely quiet. No one has anything else to say as the men finish their Christmas Eve dinner, then by ones and twos the inmates retire to their cells. At nine o'clock, I unplug the tree and go quietly to bed.

The following morning, the bugle at the Coast Guard base wakes me up. I get up to prepare the television room for breakfast. The tiny Christmas tree looks a lot more humble in the daylight. Plugging in the colored string of lights doesn't help. Breakfast is depressing: stale cornflakes, white bread, soured milk, and weak re-heated coffee.

The highlight of the day occurs at ten o'clock when the guards come to each cell to give the occupants a small box of chocolate and a can of Coca Cola. It's nice to be receiving something in the spirit of giving; it kind of makes you want to look at the hacks a little more softly. The image won't last very long. Too often the guards get their kicks abusing inmates.

I unwrap the little box and count the chocolate squares; there are six of them, each wrapped in colorful foil. Looking in the box makes me wonder how many Christmases I'll be celebrating in the joint. The thought that I might be down for a long time, like twenty years or more, depresses the heck out of me. I'm living in DeLorean's shadow, all of the media attention isn't going to help at my sentencing, particularly since I know I will never cooperate.

The holidays pass slowly. The prison staff knows that inmate stress is up around Christmastime and New Years. There are more suicides, fights, and escape attempts during Christmas than at any other time. The staff makes an extra effort to keep things mellow; the food is better, which isn't much of a challenge, and the guards are friendlier, which can be a mixed blessing.

The best part of the holidays is that each inmate is allowed to receive one small box, a care package from home. It can weigh no more than fifteen pounds and must contain only store-bought items to reduce the amount of drugs that are smuggled in.

One of the black inmates is ecstatic to receive a bean pie from home. I've never seen a bean pie before and stand anxiously at the door to his cell hoping for a small piece. To my great surprise, Leon jams his fingers into the pie and tears it apart. Gobs of creamed beans splatters onto the table. Leon grins as he stops poking about in the mashed beans, then he removes a small plastic bag to the oohs and ahhs of his friends. They go shuffling off with their bag of cocaine leaving me alone with the bean pie. I poke my fingers into the goopy mess and lick them. Surprisingly, the pie is quite tasty, kind of like pumpkin pie. Not all of the inmates receive boxes from home. In fact, most don't; for them it is a sad Christmas indeed.

I've sent a friend some money through my attorney to buy me a few things. The crumpled package heavily handled by the prison post office arrives late because my friend smokes too much pot. Whenever he gets the munchies he can't resist rummaging through my box. Carrying the shredded carton to my bunk, I see that he has blown the carefully written instructions. I asked for a pound of hard candy, which I intended to put under the tree, and for two pounds of herbal tea, hopefully enough to last me until next Christmas. Instead he sent four pounds of Christmas candy, which goes in about two minutes after the word gets out that I've gotten a Christmas package—it is January 14th and the only thing that remains of the other boxes is fond memories. The inmates descend upon me and my tattered box like a flock of vultures. Luckily they don't show any interest in the herbal tea, which I have to strictly ration. My friend sent a mere eight ounces.

On New Year's Eve, the problem between Billy and the Mexican finally comes to a head. At 11 A.M., the guard lets us out into the yard even though it is lightly raining. Most of the inmates stand against the cement wall smoking cigarettes and complaining about the weather. Because of the light rain, I decide not to water the lawn. Instead, I begin to work out on the universal machine. Billy is pacing the yard oblivious to the weather. He takes a candy bar from his pocket and begins to unwrap it. As he walks past the inmates lining the wall, a tall black man suddenly steps out blocking his way.

Instead of backing up or trying to walk around the black man, Billy just stands there speechless; the candy bar is poised halfway to his mouth. The black inmate snags the candy from Billy's hand then very deliberately raises it to his mouth and bites off half of it. Billy, unsure what to do, just stands there.

Another inmate steps away from the wall. It's the Mexican. He slithers over to stand next to the black man. "What's the matter, punk, too afraid to fight for your candy?" Billy still hasn't moved. The black inmate passes the rest of the uneaten candy to the Mexican who pops it in his mouth and begins to chew purposefully. Finally, Billy begins to step backward, but the Mexican's hand shoots out and grabs Billy's shirt. "You know, punk, if you won't fight for your candy bar, I guess you won't fight for your candy a——, will you?" leers the Mexican. I'm tempted to go to Billy's aid, but hesitate because Billy needs to stand up for himself. I also know that nothing is going to happen with the guard watching from the other side of the fence.

Billy is still just standing there. The Mexican looks him up and down then, with a snort of contempt, walks away. Later that day I ask the guard if he shouldn't move Billy out of the Mexican's cell. The guard looks at me and shrugs, "Hey, this isn't a boy scout camp we're running. Billy is just going to have to learn to stand up for himself."

That night the storm hit full force. Thunder reverberates through the cell block and echoes off the prison walls. Rather than go to sleep, I decide to stay up until midnight to hail in the new year. The passing of time is always an event for inmates—it means we're that much closer to going home. I stand at the window, wrapped in a blanket against the cold, watching raindrops, driven by gusting wind, splatter against the glass. The dark of the night is intermittently shattered by bold flashes of lightning.

Staring out into the storm, I recall a memory of Susan and Puu. It took place under an incredibly pretty night sky that had just been washed clean by a passing storm. There was a multitude of stars splashed across the dark tropical heavens. A crescent moon hung low on the horizon closely accompanied by the glowing orb of Venus. The evening was warm with fragrant trade winds blowing lightly through the trees, causing the leaves to rustle and setting a dense stand of tall bamboo to clacking and thumping like a giant wind chime.

Susan, Puu, and I were at an outdoor garden party at the University of Hawaii. Though Susan and I had been together for over a month, she kept it a secret from her friends. As such, I was not allowed to touch her in public even though I promised not to be gross about it.

I noticed a couple of guys giving Susan the eye. I was considering how much fun it would be to slam their heads together when I felt Susan tugging on my sleeve. She'd been eyeing a happy couple that were obviously in love, their arms wrapped around each other and looking quite snug about life in general. I guessed Susan liked what she saw because she turned and looked at me with those incredible liquid brown eyes of hers and shyly said, "If you want you can put your arm around me."

I was surprised and naturally stoked. "Does this mean that you're my girl?" I asked hopefully.

Tucking her head into my shoulder she nodded, "Yeah, I guess."

My heart has entered its flopping-on-the-floor stage again. I couldn't have been more pleased as I pulled her close.

I looked down into the liquid brown eyes that own my heart. "If you're asking if I love you, the answer is *yes*, with all of my heart."

Later we found a broad banyan tree to sit under. I leaned against the thick, mossy trunk while Susan settled her head in my lap, her arms wrapped tightly around my waist. Puu lay down beside us under a gardenia plant with white velvety flowers that emitted a potent flowery bouquet. A quiet chomp announced the demise of a gardenia flower—*chomp, chomp*; Puu was otherwise occupied as Susan sighed contentedly and snuggled closer into my embrace, seeking warmth and comfort. With her face burrowed into the hollow of my neck, her breath caressing my skin, she said in a little girl voice that has been lodged in my mind ever since, "Steve, I love you so much; please don't ever let me go."

Standing before the prison cell window, a sudden chill runs through my body causing me to shudder. I see the rain splashing against the window like an ocean of tears. The thick drops run in long rivulets down the panes to puddle on the sill and suddenly I am crying . . . not crying in self pity, but rather for the wonderful happiness I have known. The images I am recalling are a bandage that caresses my battered soul. Turning away from the window, I see lightning strobe against the cell wall; for a moment it paints abrupt shadows of the jail bars; then the cell fades to darkness.

CHAPTER 13

The next morning the guard lets me out of my cell at 5 A.M. as usual to begin getting the television room ready for breakfast. The cell block is cold enough to be almost frosty this first morning of the New Year. The building's antiquated heater, installed in the early thirties, does little to hold off the winter chill. Rubbing my sides to promote warmth, I go to the cleaning locker for a bucket to wash the tables. Passing the door to cell nine, I hear a muffled sobbing. I pause for a moment wondering if Billy is O.K., then shrug off my curiosity; Billy often cries.

For the next hour, I am busy cleaning the television room.

At 6 A.M., the north yard guard opens the door and pushes in the food cart. Opening the doors, I look at the plastic trays stacked one above the other. The twenty-eight meals are all exactly the same: oatmeal, blackened bacon strips, toast, milk, and coffee. Everything is ice cold to the touch. While stacking the bowls of oatmeal in the microwave, I notice some contain coagulated lumps floating in the browning goo. Though I truly enjoy oatmeal, I know I won't be able to eat it because of the suspicious nature of those lumps.

Looking down the corridor to ensure that the guard is still in his office, I climb up onto a table and—pushing up one of the ceiling tiles—reach into my secret food hoard. There isn't much there, a couple pieces of fruit and several small boxes of cereal. While the oatmeal is cooking, I secretly munch a bruised apple and am wolfing down a box of corn flakes when I hear noise out in the exercise yard.

I see an inmate gardener from general population wrestling a power mower through the yard gate. He lifts the heavy machine over a cement curb then pushes it to my tiny lawn, where the grass is now standing five inches tall. Already angry, the inmate becomes furious when the mower refuses to start. He curses and kicks the machine while jerking repeatedly on the rope start until finally, spewing black smoke, it reluctantly kicks over. Two short, vicious strokes later the lawn is mowed—butchered, more like it.

Standing at the window, I wave in a friendly way to the inmate gardener, pleased that the small lawn has recovered so well. In return, he dramatically shakes his fist at me and shouts, "You're the idiot who's been watering this lawn, aren't you?"

I'm watching the inmate wrestling the machine back out the yard gate when I hear the J-3 guard beginning to unlock the cell doors.

The inmates flood into the television room. None of them are happy to see the oatmeal. Leon uses his spoon to dip out one of the lumps. "I hope the cooks aren't being creative with the dead rodents in the kitchen again," he says hopefully.

Shorty smashes one of the lumps with his spoon and carefully eyes the flattened goopy mess. "It looks like cooked spit," he assures the inmate sitting next to him. The man pales as Shorty picks the flatten glob up and pops it into his mouth. He chews grinning, "Yep, it's spit."

The Mexican swaggers into the television room and, sitting down at one of the tables, begins to spoon the oatmeal into his mouth without comment. The guard surveys the room and notices that one of the chairs is vacant. Turning abruptly, he marches back down the corridor. "D— it, Billy," he shouts, "get out here and eat breakfast."

At cell number nine he pulls the door open, "Hey, get out of bed; you know the rules."

"Leave me alone," Billy's high-pitched voice carries easily into the television room.

"Get your a— out of that bed."

I see the Mexican whispering to his three friends. They look in unison down the corridor and laugh.

Shorty, who had been monitoring the hushed conversation, turns to pass the news on to Leon. I'm taking four more bowls of oatmeal to the adjoining table when I hear Shorty saying excitedly, "The kid gave it up last night." The words stop me in my tracks; "giving it up" is an inmate way of saying that someone got raped.

As the news travels from table to table in an excited wave, I turn to stare at the Mexican. He is grinning, pleased to be the focal point of so much attention. For a moment our eyes lock; he smirks and looks away. The noise in the television room slackens as the inmates strain to listen to the argument going on in cell nine.

"I'm not going to play games with you, kid," rages the guard. "Either get out of that bunk or you're going to J-1."

"I don't care," shouts Billy.

"That's it," yells the guard, slamming and locking the door. "Pack up your stuff; you're going to J-1." He stalks down the corridor to lock the grill to the television room, then raises his radio and calls for the north yard guard.

They take Billy out through the back door. He is crying and walking hunched over. The inmates are standing three deep at the grill watching the drama unfold. A tall, lanky inmate with acne scars on his face turns to Shorty, "Sure be handy having a girlie right in your own cell," he says wistfully.

I'm furiously cleaning the tables. My anger is hard to contain.

Among his small crowd of friends the Mexican is being treated like some kind of perverted hero. They are anxiously asking him for details. I am finishing loading the trays back into the cart when the guard returns to unlock the grill. "Everyone get ready to go outside."

The inmates crowd through the door while the guard counts heads as they pass out into the morning sunshine. The Mexican—Carlos—and I are the last ones to pass through the door. He sees me staring angrily at him. He smirks, "I told ya the kid was a punk."

I resist my desire to grab the Mexican by the throat and choke him. Watching Carlos step out into the yard and walk arrogantly away, I know that he and I are heading for a confrontation. I just don't expect that it will happen so soon, nor that it will be resolved with a volleyball.

The Mexican joins his friends at the volleyball court. He playfully punches one of them then makes a grinding motion with his hips. The inmates laugh at the crude motion.

Leon, my black inmate friend, is standing on the opposite side of the net. "Hey, Arrington," he yells, "come on, the South of the Border gang wants to challenge us gringos to a game." Leon is standing at the net opposite Carlos. I stride over and lightly push Leon over one position. My heart is hammering as I face Carlos, who rises to the challenge.

"In your face, I'm going to put the ball in your face," he threatens. Saying nothing, I settle into a stance and eagerly wait for the ball to be served.

The ball bounces from side to side. Then Carlos, who has been yelling for a set, gets one. The ball is set high and close to the net. He waits for the ball to descend before jumping. His eyes are locked on the ball as he leaps; he hasn't noticed that I'm already airborne. Carlos is still going up as I reach over the net and slam the ball. All the anger and hate pent up inside me is focused in the spike. I actually growl as I spike the ball into Carlos' face. The impact knocks his head backward and drives him down hard onto the cement deck. For an instant he is dazed; blood trickles from his nose. I'm stoked as Leon hoots, "Yeah, great spike,"

Carlos leaps to his feet. "He cheated; he reached over the net."

Leon picks up the ball then looks at Carlos, "We're inmates, you stupid idiot; we don't give a damn about rules—our serve."

Carlos glares at Leon then faces me, "You're going to pay," he threatens.

The ball is served. When the other team hits it back, Leon lobs the ball directly to Carlos. It almost seems intentional. Carlos moves under the ball while yelling directions to the short Colombian smuggler next to him. Obviously Carlos is going to pass the ball so he can get a proper set back. With spread fingers Carlos delicately pops the ball up. He is still under the ascending ball when Leon, who has timed his jump perfectly, reaches over the net and sledge hammers the ball straight down in Carlos' upturned face. Carlos buckles at the knees and falls heavily to the ground.

He comes up cursing, then grabbing the ball, he viciously slams it toward Leon. The poorly directed ball flies straight into the anti-personnel wire lining the top of the wall, which instantly punctures it. The ball deflates with a short hiss while hanging obscenely from the wire, then it falls to the ground with a flat plop.

"Carlos, you stupid idiot, I saw that," yells the guard, "get your butt over here."

Leon snickers as Carlos stalks past us, which proves to be more than Carlos can bear. He takes a wild swing at Leon—and misses. "All right, that's it," the guard grabs Carlos and cuffs his hands behind his back, "you're going to the hole."

Watching the guard leading Carlos away, I wonder what will happen to Billy. The rumor of the rape will spread through the prison like a wild fire. Everyone will know that Billy won't fight for himself. It means he will be a target for other inmate homosexuals.

I force the thoughts of Billy and Carlos from my mind. I just don't want to deal with it anymore. With the volleyball punctured the game quickly breaks up. I walk over to my lawn and pick up a handful of the cut grass and hold it to my nose. I fill my lungs with the rich smell and for a moment lose myself in an explosion of boyhood memories that revolve around yard maintenance. As the sudden memories begin to fade, I breathe deeply, trying to maintain contact with my lost youth.

A few minutes later the guard blows his whistle, "All right, we've had enough excitement for one morning; everyone back inside, lockdown time."

I'm serving the evening meal when the north yard guard brings over a couple of inmates from J-2 to take the two empty places in cell nine. Glancing toward the two inmates, I do a double-take. It's Morgan.

"Oh, no," I think as I look at him standing in the corridor. He is holding a large cardboard box filled to the brim with a wealth of possessions. It figures that he'd "be having things" (a cell block expression for inmates rich enough to buy without restriction from the prison store). I watch him carry his bulging box to his cell, as do the other envious inmates. I go in reluctantly after him.

Morgan and I have talked very little since our arrest. I only see him in court, and even then we have little opportunity to exchange words with the marshals staying in close attendance. I actually considered our separation a blessing. It makes it a lot easier dealing with him. Lately I've had an uneasy feeling about his upcoming cooperation. After all, there are only two defendants in the case for him and his sons to give up.

Morgan is unpacking his box when I walk in. It's full of candy bars, cigarettes, sugar, coffee, and toiletries. "What are the cigarettes for?" I ask.

"Favors," replies Morgan. "So how are you doing?"

"I'm doing time, Morgan," I answer sarcastically, "how do you think I'm doing?"

"Look, Steve, I feel sorry about that," offers Morgan, "but I've got it all figured out, and I think you should cooperate."

I see two of the cell block snitches standing just outside the door. Inside dope on the DeLorean case is considered first-class snitching material. I close the door before saying, "Forget it, Morgan, I'm not a snitch."

"Steve, you can't hurt me or my sons," Morgan says anxiously, "because we've already decided to cooperate. The government wants you out of the case. They're afraid certain embarrassing questions will be asked if you go to trial."

"Oh, really," I reply, "like questions about illegal breaking-and-entering by the DEA."

"Who cares why they want to deal; just do it."

"Morgan," I answer tiredly, "I'd really like to be able to cooperate, but I can't. It just doesn't seem right. Besides, we both know that I don't have anything significant to tell, not with you and your sons cooperating."

Morgan thinks I'm nuts and says so. He also keeps encroaching upon me to snitch. He's good at that. He hadn't been popular in J-2 since the word got out that he is going to cooperate against DeLorean. He also has a knack for stirring up trouble with the other inmates, which is maybe why he needs all those cigarettes. He is probably using them to buy protection. Cigarettes are inmate money. Sometimes punks are sold just for a carton of cigarettes, and two cartons can be enough to get someone killed.

As I watch Morgan, I try to remember the man I once knew and respected. In 1975 when I first met Morgan he was a generous person, who really seemed concerned for his fellow man. But then he lost his aviation company to some con artists. I guess that is what made him bitter. He now rationalizes that he is just too old, fifty-two, to spend the next twenty years in prison.

I think that it's important to note that Morgan did not look upon himself as an evil or even as a bad person; most criminals don't. Sometimes they take pride in their wild streak—"a man living a rebel cause," a point of view regularly romanticized by television and films. Unfortunately, this perception allows some criminals to commit crimes with little remorse. This attitude is one of the reasons why I hope my future lecture program might be effective with teen-agers and young adults.

The true nature of crime is that it leads to unhappiness, paranoia, and sometimes even to deviant behavior. Living outside society is exactly that. A criminal is almost always a lonely person. Morgan has proven it.

I really don't want to sit in judgment of Morgan; in fact, I would like to help him but just don't know how. I'm awfully busy just trying to cope. I'm dealing with some heavy thoughts. I was caught outside society's laws; I am shamed before my family and friends, and I am now facing a long prison sentence. The future is looking pretty bleak, the only positive aspect is totally dependent upon my ability to make my incarceration a constructive experience. My own doubts are my worst enemy.

With Morgan hanging out in the television room and wandering the halls, I wind up spending a lot more time in my cell. I'm not into watching television, which reminds me too much of the free life I'm missing, nor am I into shooting the bull with the guys who are mostly interested in discussing crime. I try to focus on just getting through each day, which I can then mark off the calendar so I can begin on the next one. Sooner or later I am going to be released, and I don't want to think that my sojourn in prison has been a waste of time. I read books, think deep thoughts about life, and write the answers that come to mind in my journal. The journal is my way of carrying what I learn into the future so I will never forget.

Morgan is finally moved to another prison in San Diego and put under protective custody. He is now openly cooperating. Time passes; weeks become months. Outside, the end of winter is still raging. It has been one of the wettest, most storm-ridden winters in California history. My friends at *Surfer* magazine write to me about fantastic waves with stupendous rides. I look at the pictures in *Surfer* magazine and wonder whether Sam is having a good time.

He has gone home to San Diego, and, according to his letters, is surfing his brains out. I yearn to see him, but Richard Barnett, my attorney, doesn't think it would be wise to put him on my visitor's list. The less attention we draw to Sam the better.

My little lawn grows bright and green from all of the rain. We have spent most of the winter locked up behind the thick cement walls. The cell block is always cold. I spend hours wrapped in the thin prison blanket watching the heavy rain beating against my window. I have to fight daily the depression that threatens to bring me down.

The penetrating cold has begun to make my wrist hurt where a large nerve ganglion has filled up with a gelatinous fluid. The bloated sac is beginning to disrupt blood flow to my hand. In my grandfather's day, they would have struck the lump vigorously with a Bible to burst the sac, though there was no guarantee that it wouldn't fill up again.

While fingering the nerve ganglion, I happen to glance over at my new bunkie—they change regularly from month to month. He is researching a thick law book that he has gotten from the prison library. Suddenly I have an inspiration and quickly get down on the floor next to the toilet. I place my wrist across the stained bowl rim with the ganglion facing up. "Want to do me a big favor?" I ask nervously.

I think that Fred is slightly nuts. He has a mean streak and spends most of his time planning revenge on the neighbor who turned him in for manufacturing LSD in his house.

"Would you mind striking my wrist with that book you're reading?" My voice sounds rather high-pitched even to my ears. "You need to do it rather hard to squish this lump, but please do it quickly before I change my mind."

It turns out that Fred doesn't need much encouragement; his eyes fill with glee. "Certainly," he says happily.

I hear a great whoosh of wind just before he slams the thick book down upon my wrist. Intense pain lances up my arm; it feels like it has been broken. There is an imprint on my forearm exactly where the thick book struck. Looking intently at my now throbbing and rapidly bruising forearm, I notice that the ganglion has been flattened—apparently bursting the small sac. My wrist continues to hurt for a week, but the ganglion never comes back—much to the disappointment of Fred, who wants another crack at me with his law book. He has recently requested the thickest reference book in the law library.

Slowly the days wax warm, and, finally, summer comes. I rejoice as the flowers begin to bloom outside my window. I call my attorney weekly. The trial is being continuously delayed while both sides prepare for the coming battle. Then, Richard Barnett calls with bad news. The government has been made aware of my trip to Colombia. Not only have Morgan and sons given me up, but apparently the pilot I had flown with has also managed to cut his own prison-free deal with the government. It seems everyone is rushing to turn me in even though I am the least culpable character in the act. No wonder the press, like the inmates in general population, have taken to calling me "Fall Guy." Everyone thinks that I am going to take the big fall, which I don't find encouraging at all.

The prosecutor's office lay out their terms. If I plead guilty to counts one and two, conspiracy and intent to distribute cocaine, then they will drop count three, possession of cocaine. Not that the cocaine was ever mine in the first place, but they also offer not to press any further charges, like a certain airplane trip to Colombia. They require that I decide immediately; there is no mention of a maximum sentence. Looking at the jail bars in my window, I think about my future life in prison and wonder how much time the judge is going to give me.

I've known since the day of my arrest that I will plead guilty in the end. It is the only way that I can really tell my whole story about the threats and manipulation that so influenced my actions. I have been locked down over eight months when I finally go before Judge Takasugi to cop a plea. However, before he accepts my guilty statement, there are a few things he wants to be sure of.

"Are you aware, Mr. Arrington," the judge asks not unkindly, "that by pleading guilty you can be fined fifty thousand dollars, sentenced to thirty years in prison, and face the possibility of a life time on parole?"

"Yes, your honor," I stammer nervously.

For a still moment, the judge stares solemnly into my eyes while I stand nervously before the bench. "Then I schedule you for final sentencing on September second." Hitting the gavel, he dismisses the court.

Riding in the marshal's van back to the prison, I sit muffled between two other inmates, denied the chance to stare out the windows at the cars and people going by. I try to distract myself with thoughts of Susan and Puu. Instead, my inner vision sticks on the judge's face and the awful sound of that gavel.

CHAPTER 14

Pleading guilty has been an emotionally draining experience. Returning to J-3, I retire to my cell and just want to be left alone. I lie on the bunk with the lights off. In the semi-darkness, I stare at the shadows of the jail bars on the opposite wall, wondering how many years they will be used to fence me away from the rest of the world. I'm too shaken up to even attempt to sleep. All I can think about is that in just over a month the judge is going to decide on a sentence that is going to rule my future for a long, but as yet undetermined length of time. He wouldn't really give me thirty years—would he?

I hear the sound of something scraping along the wall outside my window, followed by an urgent tapping on the glass pane. In the lower right corner of the window, a large black fist is knuckling the glass. The arm and the rest of the man is hidden in the dark shadow of a bush. Jumping down from the upper bunk, I move cautiously toward the window ready to bolt. My heart is hammering against my chest. A black face leaps out of the darkness. The harsh overhead security lights cast the man's features in grotesque shadows. It's as if a skull has materialized outside the window. If the cell door had not been locked behind me, I might have fled the cell. The skull is motioning for me to come nearer. It's an inmate from general population, but I have no idea who he is or, more importantly, what he wants.

Face pressed to a cracked pane in the window, he whispers, "Leon sent me." I take a hesitant step closer. "We heard that you copped a guilty plea today." His teeth flash white as he smiles in the darkness. "Leon thought you might be needing this." He pushes something through the window mesh then slinks away into the shadowed shrubbery.

A tapered joint falls silently to the floor. In the dim light, I stare at the marijuana cigarette. For an instant I hesitate; in my emotional state, I'm desperate and tempted to escape the reality of this day. My hand shakes as I strike a flame with the matches I use to camouflage the stink from Fred's eye-burning flatulence bombs.

Soon, the mind-dulling feeling of being stoned settles over me. I think again about the implication of my guilty plea. I stand an excellent chance of spending the next twenty years in prison. Even with the possibility of a third reduction in the sentence for good time, I can easily be in prison for ten years or more. The thought is awfully depressing.

I decide I don't want to do any more thinking on the subject and seek to lose myself in a *Playboy* magazine that Fred received in the afternoon mail. I stand with my back to the window so I can read by the glow of the security lights. I leaf through the pages and stop when I see a feature article about the DeLorean case. It's an interview with an ex-drug smuggler who is commenting on the more subtle implications of the case as seen by the Los Angeles criminal underworld. According to the article, the drug bosses are not as concerned with DeLorean as they are with his two co-defendants. The article claims that those guys, meaning Morgan and I, are undoubtedly being asked a lot of questions by the DEA, questions that the criminal underworld would strongly prefer weren't answered.

It's as if I'm being issued a direct warning from the drug bosses—via *Playboy* magazine. I seriously begin to wonder just how badly they want me shut-up. Don't they realize that I'm not cooperating?

My drug-induced tranquillity evaporates in an instant as serious paranoia shoulders it aside. What if the black man at the window had held a gun instead of a joint? In my stoned state I easily visualize a gunman lurking at my window . . . the window I'm standing in front of with my back in plain view! Dropping the magazine, I leap onto the upper bunk. The shaking of the metal bed frame wakes Fred, "Hey, what are you doing up there?"

"I think I saw something out the window," I answer shrilly.

"So what?"

"So nothing, just go back to sleep," I snap. From the questionable safety of my bunk, I stare out into the darkness, imagining all kinds of enemies lurking in the shadows.

"Hey," Fred sniffs loudly, "I smell pot."

"It must be coming from outside," I say quickly while dropping lightly to the floor. I flush the remainder of the joint down the toilet. Back on my bunk, I think about the inmate who was stabbed last week in general population. According to inmate rumor control, there were seventeen stab wounds in the body. I remain fully alert with my paranoia far into the night.

The next day, Rick, my attorney, calls to tell me that he has hired a legal consultant named Casey Cohen to write a pre-sentencing report for the judge. The report will allow Judge Takasugi to read at his leisure the personal aspects and mitigating circumstances that led to my involvement with Morgan Hetrick.

I like Casey a lot because he really seems to care. We spend a lot of time talking about what I had done and how I had been ensnared in Morgan's criminal activities. Uncle Casey, as he likes to be called, helps me to understand why I erred and lends reassurance that I'm not the evil person that I secretly think I might be. Working with Casey is a cleansing process; I unburden my soul to him.

The eighty-five page pre-sentencing report that he prepares covers most of my life's history; but more importantly, he puts my crimes in a truthful perspective; he tells the human side of my story.

The government also prepares a pre-sentencing report written by a court-appointed probation officer. The probation officer sent in to see me is a lady by the name of Ginger Hartman. When I first meet Ginger, I have to keep from staring. She is a tall, sophisticated redhead in her mid-thirties. Ginger walks like she's well aware of the effect that she has on men. For her visit to our cell block, she wears a white, silk blouse with the top two buttons undone and a tight, gray, business skirt, the hem of which is cut high enough to complement her long legs.

Sitting down at the table next to me, she crosses one leg over the other. The subtle rustle of her nylons command my complete attention. The smell of Joy perfume wafts lightly past my nose, setting it to quivering. When she speaks, I hardly hear her first words as I focus instead on the rouge lipstick that covers her slightly pouting mouth. I haven't been this close to a woman in so long, I could easily spend hours just looking at her, as could the rest of the cell block. The inmates are crowded four deep at the security door.

Ginger gets right to the point, "Mr. Arrington, I'm here to take a statement in your own words as to why you became involved with Morgan Hetrick."

"How do I rate such a good-looking parole officer?" I ask, trying not to grin all over myself.

Ginger laughs. "It's a government plot," she answers with a smile. "You're supposed to tell me everything you know."

Her reference to my talking about the case instantly makes me nervous. "I'll tell you what I did, but I won't snitch on anyone else," I reply seriously.

Ginger almost seems sympathetic as she says, "Actually, with Morgan and his sons cooperating, I doubt there's anything you can tell that we don't already know."

Suddenly it becomes very important for me that Ginger understands my motivations for not snitching. "Look, you should know the reason I'm not cooperating is because I understand that I deserve to do time. Snitching would make my incarceration a lot more difficult. I'm trying to find myself again, and attempting to put my time off on someone else just doesn't feel right."

Ginger is surprised. "You're not going to argue for probation?"

I manage a weak smile. "I know my answer is going to sound square, but I'm going to say it anyway because it's true. I can't completely blame Morgan for what I did. When he told me he was a smuggler, I should have run, but I didn't. I guess I was too greedy. The bottom line is I'm guilty."

Ginger sweeps a lock of red hair from her green eyes. "So what kind of a sentence are you expecting?"

My answer just springs out; I don't even know what I'm saying until the words are already said, "Five years." Even I'm surprised at my answer, then I add, "A five year sentence would mean I could be out in three years with good time, doesn't it?"

Ginger sits back in her chair and regards me carefully, "I've already interviewed Morgan. He admits that he twisted your arm, but you're right that you still have to be punished. Yet, I think in the end you'll come out of it O.K. . . ."

September second is a cold, blustery day. Riding to court in the marshal's van, I watch the wind strip trees of their leaves while I chew my fingernails to the quick. Two nervous hours later, I'm sitting anxiously in the courtroom watching the prosecutor begin to present his case. He turns and points an accusing finger at me, then says loudly, "The United States of America charges Stephen Arrington . . . " His words hammer at me like a physical blow.

The prosecutor continues arguing that by not cooperating, I'm hindering society's war on drugs. He mentions my prior trouble in the navy and several times refers to the huge amount of cocaine that I helped to smuggle in from Colombia. But then, surprisingly, he seems to run out of steam. It's like he doesn't have anything else bad to say, just that he is asking for a long sentence. He concludes and moves to sit down.

Before he makes it to his seat, Judge Takasugi abruptly asks a few questions of his own. "Mr. Prosecutor, do you have any evidence that Mr. Arrington knew anything about this drug deal before he took possession of the car or that he was involved in the supposed conspiracy with Hetrick and DeLorean?"

"No," answers the prosecutor.

The judge continues, "Do you believe that Mr. Arrington has made any money off of this or any other crime, and is there any possibility that he may have hidden any money away?"

The prosecutor looks unhappy. "No, with Mr. Hetrick fully cooperating, we have complete access to all the appropriate bank records."

"You may sit down," says the judge.

My defense attorney, Richard Barnett, then stands up. He begins by referencing a long list of community service that I've done over the past years. He notes that I've been a CPR and First Aid instructor for over fifteen years. He talks about my fourteen-year military career during which I made four combat tours to Vietnam, and how I had risked my life as a bomb disposal frogman while engaged in dangerous missions for the Navy, Secret Service, and the C.I.A.—yet he can't even give specifics in my defense without violating the Secrecy Act because of the clandestine nature of the operations. He points out that I resisted involvement in Morgan's criminal enterprise and that Morgan had to resort to gross manipulations to force my cooperation.

Then, Rick concludes his arguments: "We admit that Mr. Arrington is indeed guilty, but we are talking about two multi-millionaires allegedly involved in a conspiracy and a young man who only had twenty dollars in his pocket when he arrived on the scene. A severe sentence is not fair when you consider the level of his involvement and his resistance in participating."

Next it's my turn to take the stand. The press poises with their pens; the courtroom is packed with reporters as usual. I want to honestly define my situation, to admit to my crime, yet I also want my words to have an impact—a message to others about how things can go completely wrong in life, particularly when drugs are involved. I have to begin twice because my voice cracks with emotion as I try to speak:

"The greatest words I have ever heard were, 'Federal agent, you're under arrest.' Those words freed me from a nightmare. I had been living a life of deceit. I did things I was afraid not to do. When I was arrested by agent Scotti, he later said to me, 'Well, I guess this isn't the best day in your life.' I replied, 'Actually, I think it is.' I knew that my arrest was really a new beginning. I had been rescued from a life that was totally beyond my control.

"From my jail cell, I asked Rick, my attorney, not to request a bail reduction because in prison I was coming to terms with what I had done. I knew that the sooner I began serving my sentence, the sooner I could again become a productive member of society.

"As a Christian, I know that good must come of all things. I want to share what I have learned from this situation. As soon as I'm able, I'd like to begin a lecture series for high-school students based upon drugs, crime, and the realities of prison. I want to prevent others from falling into the same traps I have.

"I know that my crime calls for punishment, and I'm prepared to pay my debt to society. Your honor, I am sorry for what I've done and am ready for sentencing."

In the next couple of moments, my whole future is going to be determined. I know that the judge's decision will be heavily influenced by my airplane flight to Colombia and by my careless involvement of Sam. Despite the fact that I had actually tried to protect Sam from Morgan's influence, it certainly wouldn't look that way to the court since I can't mention that Sam wasn't the unknowing victim they thought him to be. In their eyes my involvement of this young man was inexcusable, and it totally detracts from my credibility as a victim myself. Yet, I can not tell of Sam's eager

participation without jeopardizing his freedom. Remaining silent on
that point, even to my mother, isn't easy.

The clerk's voice is loud and impersonal. "The defendant will
stand for sentencing." The judge peers solemnly at me over his glasses
then calmly reads the sentence from his notes. I focus on his words,
wanting to freeze the moment, so I'd remember it always.

"Mr. Arrington, for count one, I sentence you to five years."
I'm unconsciously holding my breath. "For count two, I sentence
you to an additional five years."

Ten years? I'm staggered by the sentence. After a pregnant
pause—maybe Judge Takasugi is being dramatic for the press—he
adds, "Both sentences will run concurrently."

There is a heavy thump directly behind me. Spinning around,
I'm astonished to see that Ginger, apparently moved by the sentence,
has fallen from her front row chair to the floor. After a moment's
pause to smooth her skirt, she quickly re-takes her seat as the judge
concludes the sentence by awarding me three years special parole.

I tear my eyes from Ginger just in time to see the judge smack
his gavel down, "Court dismissed."

The marshals stand and begin to lead me from the courtroom. I
try to give the thumbs up sign to my mother so that she will know
that I'm O.K., but she doesn't see as she sits huddled against my
brother Jim. It won't be until I call her from prison that night that
I'm able to explain that I've gotten five, not ten years. A concurrent
sentence is kind of like two crimes for the price of one. I could be
out in less than three years because of the eleven months I've already served.

I arrive late back at the cell block, bologna sandwich on stale
white in hand. All of the other inmates in J-3 are waiting for me.
When I come through the north yard door they cheer. The news of
my sentence has already been broadcast on three separate television
stations. The inmates feel that I've received a fair sentence, as do I.
In fact, I've received exactly the sentence I told Ginger I felt I deserved.

A friend has saved my vegetarian dinner, so at least tonight I
don't go hungry. The prison cell's forty-watt bulb snaps off at
exactly ten o'clock. Lying there in the dark, my eyes wide open because I am too excited to sleep, I feel like my life has taken on a new
meaning. I can finally reconcile myself to serving a sentence that has
a completion date. It's like seeing the light at the end of a long, dark
tunnel; though dim . . . the light is at least visible.

I await the rights and privileges of a sentenced inmate in general population—which may not sound like anything to get excited
about, unless you've been locked down in a cell block for the better
part of a year.

CHAPTER 15

On September 16, 1983, eleven months after my arrest, the guard tells me to box up my things. I'm being moved into general population. I've set a record at Terminal Island for the most time served in Jail Unit 3. Gathering my few meager possessions from the cell, I'm surprised at how little I own—my whole world fits into a tiny cardboard box, which I only half fill.

For over an hour, I stand anxiously before the north yard door, waiting for the hack with the key. Whenever someone leaves the cell block, it's always an event. The rest of the inmates, locked behind the metal grating, shout words of encouragement and wave good-bye. There are last minute requests. Some of the Mexicans want me to smuggle Jalapeno peppers to them on the food cart. It's a petty, in-house crime, but the penalty for getting caught is severe.

When the guard arrives to open the door, it's as if I'm paralyzed. Despite the beckoning sunshine and the alluring smell of ocean-fresh air, I am not sure what to do. Every time I've passed through this portal before, I have worn manacles and chains. Conditioned to orders, I look dubiously at the guard who impatiently says, "So, take off, Arrington, you've been here long enough to know the way."

With my pitifully small box held tightly under one arm, I begin to walk disjointedly across the immensity of the north yard. Actually the north yard encompasses but a few acres of cement and grass, however my perception of space has changed significantly after living in the restricted space of J-3 for the better part of a year. Walking alone, I feel naked and totally exposed under the hard, uncaring glare of the general population inmates.

When new meat—meaning me—hits the yard, the other inmates stop whatever they are doing to watch. It is a cold, impersonal stare that greets me. Most of the inmates know who I am, and activity in the yard comes slowly to a standstill.

Fifty feet from the J-3 door, I pause to look at the expanse of green lawn before me. Then glancing over one shoulder, I look back for a final time at the small J-3 yard and its tiny oasis of green grass surrounded by a field of cement. Sudden inspiration encourages me to remove my shoes, then, tying the laces together, I sling them over one shoulder. Stepping off the cement sidewalk, I pad happily onto the north yard lawn that had so intrigued me from the other side of the J-3 fence. With my toes pressing into the coolness of the cut grass, an irresistible smile begins to play across my face. A feeling of sudden freedom flushes through my mind and body as stress and pressure fall away like a heavy cloak. Is it possible, I wonder, to be feeling joy at making the transition to sentenced inmate?

How do I explain the desire to belong somewhere, to have a place I can call my own, even if it is just a bunk inside *chez* clink? At least I'm not going to be alone anymore with just stressed out transients for company. Somewhere in the yard I hope to find a friend, a sentenced inmate who isn't thinking all the time about plea bargaining or sentencing dates. I have been an island too long, a solitary point in a raging sea of emotions and violence. With high expectations I open the door to A unit and step cautiously into the dim interior.

From the guard at the front desk I get my bunk assignment then go to put my few possessions into the locker. I feel like a stranger walking down the hall passing unfamiliar faces that pause to stare yet offer no comment. The hostile silence that greets me is unnerving. I count bunks in search of mine while hoping that my new bunkies will be at least semi-normal. At number thirty-four I stop. This time it is my turn to stare—in acute disappointment. The lower bunk has the poorest excuse for a mattress that I've ever seen. With most of its stuffing gone and covered with a disgusting array of stains, it more resembles a filthy rag than a mattress.

Unfortunately, the bed is the good news when compared with my new bunkies. Four of them are present in the eight man cubicle. They are a mixed bag of druggies who at midday are already stoned out of their minds. One of them is lying on my bunk, drooling into the pillow. Another is squatting in a corner with his head nodding back and forth as he tries to keep loose contact with reality. The other two are staring at me with hostility. I instantly know the situation. They will be up most of the night shooting up with heroin or cocaine. Since all their money goes for drugs, they won't be able to buy commissary items from the prison store, so they will be borrowers, too. It means that there will be a lot of fighting and arguing. Being new meat, I have no options but to make the best of a bad situation. I desperately try to see the positive side of all this but sadly realize that it just doesn't exist.

I step past the two men staring at me. They are a scruffy looking pair with blue bandanas tied low on their foreheads. They are a regular Mutt-and-Jeff combination. One is tall and lanky; the other is short and dumpy. They both glare at me; then looks of interest flicker across their faces as they watch me store my few items in the rusted metal locker. "Hey, you got any cigarettes?" the dumpy one asks gruffly.

I turn to look at the misfits. The dumpy one has shaved both sides of his head in a crude Mohican. I cannot imagine that I would ever purposefully have a conversation with either of these idiots—and now we're going to be roommates. I am not happy as I answer, "I don't smoke."

Dumpy takes a deep breath and throws out his chest; he looks like a puffed-up toad. "What about candy? You got any candy?" he asks, while glaring fiercely from under his bandana.

"Why don't you just watch what I put in my locker, then you won't have to ask me any questions," I reply, not at all intimidated by Mr. Toad and his stork friend.

The stork leans past Mr. Toad to get a better look into the locker. "What's in those little bags?" he asks suspiciously.

"Herbal tea," I answer.

Mr. Toad develops a disgusted look as he glances at Mr. Stork. "Just what we need, one of those weirdo types."

Mr. Toad and Mr. Stork slither down the corridor leaving me alone with the slob drooling onto my mattress and the stoned black youth, which I now notice has vomited recently on his shirt. Holding my nose against the foul odor, I flee the depression of the dim cubicle and head for the beckoning sunlight of the open front door.

Outside again the bright sunlight instantly washes my depression away. I feel wonderfully alive as I pause to watch an inmate raking leaves under a small tree. A sparrow chirps from one of the lower branches. I step a little closer to see it better, but the inmate gardener glares at me in an unfriendly manner. I side-step him and, with great anticipation, walk through a large metal gate that leads to the south yard. I feel like an explorer as I head for unfamiliar territory.

Terminal Island Prison sits on the tip of a peninsula at the breakwater for Los Angeles harbor. Walking along the connecting breezeway, I am totally unprepared for the view that awaits me in the south yard. The open vista is staggering, particularly for someone who has spent almost a year in the downstairs wing of a cement building beneath a nut ward. On the east side stretches the Pacific Ocean. Its deep blue water, lightly driven by the tide, surges against the seaweed-laced rocks at the base of twin security fences. The west side of the prison faces bustling Los Angeles Harbor with its multitude of big ships traversing the channel. Riding the horizon are the rolling hills of San Pedro with its tapestry of old houses and narrow streets.

There are only two small dormitories in the south yard. They're surrounded by grass, shrubs, and trees. The middle of the yard encompasses a football field with thick, lush grass; I wonder who waters it. Everywhere there are sea gulls: floating on the water, flying in the sky, and standing on the lawn, squawking loudly. Even this little bit of freedom is almost more than I can bare. I spend three glorious hours just walking in the sun and breathing in the brisk ocean breeze.

By four o'clock count, I'm back in A unit. I do not look forward to meeting the rest of my new roommates. Walking down the dim corridor, I can already hear them cussing and talking loudly. To get to my bunk, which is now vacant, I have to squeeze past two husky black men, who are doing an extended soul brother handshake. They pause to scowl at me. "What do you want, honky?" demands the larger of the two.

Must the problems begin already? I think to myself. "You are standing in front of my bunk," I answer.

"This ain't your bunk no more," replies the black man, "you've been moved to the other side. Sanchez was already here and cleared out your stuff." Wondering what's going on and where my few possessions have gone, I wander toward the other end of the dormitory and run into Sanchez.

"Hey, Steve, so they finally let you out of J-3." Sanchez is grinning hugely. I grin back, pleased to see a familiar and friendly face. He had been one of the more normal people in J-3. He was down for cheating on his taxes and falsifying a government contract. "Check out this bunk," winks Sanchez. "Do you think it's a bit of an improvement over old number thirty-four and the sleaze patrol that slums there?"

Stunned, I stare where Sanchez's hand is resting. It's a top bunk with an almost new mattress. The bunk stands against a window with . . . dare I believe it? . . . an ocean view! "For me?" I gasp.

"Right on," Sanchez beams. "You just happen to be standing in the celebrity inmate wing of A unit. Come on, I'll introduce you to the guys."

The other men in the cubical are mostly in their forties and fifties, all of them are in for white-collar crimes. By the wealth of books and expensive clothes, it's apparent that they're men of influence and style. I can suddenly look forward to quiet evenings of intelligent conversation and mellow friendship. Lying on the new bunk while waiting for the guard to count us, I stare happily out the window. There is no steel mesh outside the glass panes to spoil the view, just the ever-present jail bars. Ten yards away the Pacific Ocean quietly laps at the moss-covered rocks. The joy I felt earlier in the day surges through me again. I know I will be happy here, at least as happy as one can be considering this is, after all, a prison. The other bunk would have meant continuous hostility, fighting, and maybe a lot worse.

One of the hardest things to accept about prison is that inmates have no rights. Simple circumstance can mean the difference between happiness and hate, or friends and enemies. Prison is a place where some people come to die because mere circumstance, or just plain bad luck, has worked against them.

In the next cubical I see the eighteen-year-old kid named Billy, who had such a rough time of it in J-3. One of the hardest things to understand about life in prison is that the rules are different here, more so than in any civilized society. Inmates live in a cement jungle where primitive logic rules. The weaker inmates are preyed upon by the bigger and meaner inmates. If an inmate won't fight to protect himself, there can be only one result. He becomes the most scorned and looked down upon individual in the prison. The inmates have a name for that type of person; he is called a punk. A punk is someone whose only hope for safety lies in the questionable protection of another inmate—an inmate who charges dearly for that protection.

Looking over at Billy, I am sad to see that he really is a punk now. He's wearing make-up, his pants are tight, and he moves like a woman as I see him flirting with a biker inmate. Maybe in some misbegotten way he feels that he deserves this punishment for his crimes. Guilt sometimes makes people do the strangest things. Later, Billy is transferred to another institution where he takes his own life. Prison is not easy on the weak. In prison, the weak are often eaten body and soul.

At 5 P.M., the north yard guard unlocks the A Unit door. The rest of the inmates flood toward the chow hall where the dinner line is rapidly forming. I, however, head straight for the south yard, where with great anticipation I intend to watch my first sunset of 1983. Walking the perimeter with the dusk approaching is an extraordinary experience somehow reminiscent of a childhood adventure. The feeling of implied freedom is almost unbearable. I stop to stare at two morning doves pecking for seeds or bugs in the grass. At the southern most fence, a row of eucalyptus trees forms a windbreak. I fill my front pockets with eucalyptus pods under the watchful stare of the guard in the security tower. He probably wonders what I am up to. Actually, I just like the pod's strong scent, which I intend to put in my locker to counteract the dorm's musky smell.

With my front pockets bulging much like a chipmunk's cheeks, I walk over to a date tree, sit down, and lean my back against its trunk. Facing west, I gaze at the sun, which slowly descends behind the rolling hills of San Pedro. As the day fades to dusk, thousands of tiny lights flicker to life on the darkened hillside. The seaport's winding streets come alive with moving ribbons of vehicular light:

flashing yellows, glowing reds, and intense whites. Residential and traffic lights blink or flicker to their own rhythm, while the whole hill for a few minutes is silhouetted in the red halo of the setting sun.

A large white cruise ship sailing gracefully down the narrow channel catches my eye. It's all lit up with festive lights that cast moving shadows of people walking the decks. There is the cheerful clink of glasses, the tinkle of soft music, and the buoyant sound of laughter. I watch the cruise ship as it passes through a group of sailboats heading back toward the harbor mouth. As the fleet of small boats tack from port to starboard, their running lights ripple from red to green.

Looking toward the east, I see a dozen giant freighters and supertankers anchored in pools of light on a darkening sea. Beyond the ships lies the city of Long Beach with its towering skyscrapers. A naval base is at the foot of Long Beach. I can see the outlines of destroyers and other capital ships tied to the piers. From 1966 through 1971, I sailed to Vietnam from those very piers. After fourteen years in the navy, going to sea has become a part of me. Along the active paths of my memory, I go back in time to a stormy night somewhere in the South China Sea.

The giant nuclear-powered aircraft carrier *USS Constellation* plowed into the dark night at over thirty knots. Wind driven rain splattered against my goggles and ran down inside my foul weather gear, wetting my undershirt. Crouching between the number one and two catapults, I watched an F-14 Tomcat prepare for launch. We were having problems with this bird. The pilot had twice failed to line up the nose wheel with the catapult sled. Each failed attempt meant that a gang of us flight deck personnel had to walk the sleek fighter backward by pushing against its wings so the pilot could then taxi it back into position. To prevent excess stress on the wings, the pilot rotated them backward into the supersonic flight configuration.

The catapult officer took a careful look at the plane's alignment. On the bridge, the air boss was getting impatient. "Launch that bird or strike it below decks; I've got aircraft to recover," he grumbled over the loud speaker system. I glanced beyond the pitching deck of the giant carrier where other birds were already entering the pattern. Some of those planes were low on fuel and anxious to land.

The catapult officer, apparently deciding that the F-14 was properly lined up, began to twirl one hand overhead in a circular motion with his index finger pointed skyward. The pilot responded by going to full throttle. Twin funnels of fire over twenty feet long leaped from the rear of the fighter. Under the massive

thrust the aircraft's nose lowered into a crouch as the plane prepared for launch. The catapult officer glanced down the short flight
deck to make sure it was clear then stuck two fingers into the air.
The pilot responded by going to full afterburners. The twin giant
blowtorches flickered in an instant from howling yellow fire to white,
screaming fury. The intense roar of the aircraft caused the deck to
shudder where I crouched just beyond its wingtip. We were but a
moment from launching the straining fighter. That was when I
noticed that the fighter's wings were still locked backward in the
super-sonic flight position.

When launching supersonic aircraft, the wings must be swept
forward to provide maximum lift on take off. I knew instantly that
this plane would stall and fall into the sea as soon as it left the flight
deck. Even if the pilot and gunner ejected immediately, they would
probably be run over by the passage of the aircraft carrier's massive
hull.

I didn't remember standing, let alone running in front of
the crouching fighter. I was just suddenly there with my arms crossed
over my head in the universal signal for fouled deck. I could feel the
straining fighter hovering over my shoulder. The roar of its jet engines filled my consciousness and set my body to trembling.
For a moment I wondered if I was about to die.

The catapult officer took a last careful look toward the bow to
make sure the flight path was clear; then his helmeted head slowly
rotated back toward the straining fighter . . . and to me. His right
hand was still poised to launch the screaming bird as his goggled
eyes, like reflective black mirrors, stared. In slow motion, I saw his
hands cross slowly over his head duplicating my fouled deck signal.
The high-pitched scream of the fighter over my shoulder abruptly
throttled down to a rumbling roar; the vibrating deck stilled. My
breath, which I had been unconsciously holding, flooded out in a
giant exhalation. Vapor temporarily fogged my flight-deck goggles.
Through the misted lenses, I saw the distorted image of the catapult
officer; steam from the sled's firing slot drifted about his boots.
He had both hands inverted and raised in the classic wordless question, "Why?"

I pointed toward the retracted wings, then, sticking my arms
out, I slowly lowered them to my side mimicking the fighter's current supersonic flight configuration.

"Strike that aircraft below deck!" The air bosses' roar was
amplified by the ship's loud speaker system. "Standby to recover
aircraft." Instantly the flight deck was awash in frenzied, but
coordinated, activity as the USS Constellation readied to receive her
returning birds.

I began to walk aft then glanced upward into the cockpit of the F-14 fighter still standing in the number one catapult. The pilot's head turned; the dark face plate followed me. I paused, wondering what he was thinking; then I saw his right hand move slowly upward into a lingering salute. My hand snapped alongside my own helmet. With a spring to my step, happy to be alive, I headed for my assigned position to recover aircraft.

Leaning against the palm tree, I see a bright, white orb slowly rising in the distance. I have forgotten that this is the night of the full moon. I stand up and walk to the east fence. The moon is large and ponderous on the horizon, and for a few moments it silhouettes a sleek navy warship departing from Long Beach harbor. I watch the ship until it disappears beyond the range of my vision. Then I stare at the slowly undulating sea. I stand alone at the fence with my hands in my pockets while in my mind I thank the Lord for my good fortune, to be healthy and so vitally alive, and with a release date that I can live with. Finally, as nine o'clock approaches, I walk slowly back to A Unit for ten o'clock count with the sound of the ocean lapping in my ears.

CHAPTER 16

Over the next couple of weeks, I practically live in the south yard. Each morning I am up early—anxious to go outside. Standing at the security door, eagerly watching for the guard, I feel like a puppy who can't wait for his owner to let him out. Running alone in the early morning darkness is the closest I can come to actually feeling free. Light of heart, I enjoy racing the sunrise, counting off the laps before first light, while the rest of the prison slumbers.

On the morning of September 27, I'm even more anxious than normal as I stand inside the door waiting for the guard—it is my thirty-third birthday. At 6:02 A.M., I hear the guard's shoes crunching on the gravel path that leads to the door, then the sound of a key turning in the heavy lock. I wait until the guard's footsteps fade away before slowly pushing against the door. To push against a door—and have it open—is probably only amazing to inmates and small children. With all the thrill of a child escaping the house, I bolt for the south yard.

A dense sea fog lies heavily on the ground and covers the still surface of the ocean. With each lap around the dirt track, I push the pace a little harder, racing against the dim red glow that is slowly growing on the fog-bound horizon. I sprint the last half mile then climb an old set of wooden bleachers to better see the globe of the rising sun, its blood-red light misted by a shroud of white fog.

From a nearby tree, a bird twitters a greeting to the new day. Inhaling deeply the crisp morning air, I feel totally at peace with the world. The fact that it is my birthday lends a vitality to my sense of well-being and is a convincing argument to do a little weight lifting before breakfast. I am riding on a natural high as I jog toward the open door of the weight room without the slightest suspicion that I'm happily heading towards a terrifying experience.

A light mist floats in the still cold air inside the large weight room. The few windows that haven't been broken out of the old clapboard building are frosted with dew. Iron weights and rusty steel bars are scattered haphazardly about the wooden floor. I stoop to pickup a long steel bar; it's cold and the dew that covers the metal wets my hands. Turning toward the bench press to rack the heavy bar, I smell the pungent musk of marijuana smoke. That's when I see the two men. They're standing just outside the back door getting stoned. Their darkened silhouettes, shrouded in the white fog, have a disconcerting sinister air about them. Slowly the two men begin to walk toward me. The fog drifts from their bodies in long wispy tendrils that cling to their silhouettes in a smoky embrace. The empty room waxes colder at their stealthy approach. I have the intimidating feeling of being openly stalked.

They are only a few feet away when one of them, a broad-chested Samoan, raises a blunt finger to his nose, pinching off one nostril; then he snorts forcefully. A thick wad of mucus lands inches from my feet. The other inmate laughs loudly—the high-pitched laughter of a demented maniac. The maniac, who looks Polish, has a hulking, muscular build. His shaved head looks like a blunt bullet. The exposed skin glistens in the mist. His open mouth has a dark gap where two front teeth are missing. The man looks remarkably like a villain from a James Bond movie. He steps closer then leans his meaty hands on the heavy bar, which I have unfortunately set down. I regret not having the bar in my hands; it would have made a nice weapon. The maniac smiles in a malicious way, the gap in his damaged teeth causing him to lisp as he says in a threatening voice, "Know what we like to do?"

Not waiting for an answer, he moves closer; bad breath tainted with marijuana whiffs into my face. "We like to get young boys alone down here and rape 'em!"

Startled, I straighten up. My happiness of a few moments earlier has already fled before the storm of their threatening approach. Now I desperately try to remain calm, while sudden fear sweeps across me. I have to make an effort to keep my voice even as I answer gruffly, "Well, it's a good thing there's no one down here but us men." The maniac cackles his insane laugh then thumps me solidly in the chest with one of his beefy hands. I almost lose my balance from the unexpected impact.

"Acting tough isn't going to save your butt, cream puff." He is chewing a piece of gum, smacking his lips loudly while eyeing me up and down. I decide to kick him in the groin. It's not an easy decision. After all, who wants to attack someone much bigger than yourself, particularly when he has a giant Samoan friend, but I don't see that I have a choice.

Sudden voices pull our attention to the front door. A couple of biker types are just walking in the open doorway. "Hey, Bad Bill," yells the Maniac. "Lookie what I got me here."

Obviously the Maniac hadn't been paying close attention in his high-school English class; he'd probably been kicked out of the third grade for not being able to play well with other children.

While the Maniac is momentarily distracted, I glance over my shoulder at one of the broken windows. *Maybe I can make my escape by diving through it,* I think hopefully, *because I know I don't stand a chance against four burly inmates.*

The Samoan sees my fugitive look and steps to cover my only apparent escape route. He snickers in anticipation. The maniac swings his bullet head back toward me and grins in an evil way. One of his meaty hands sweeps automatically downward, shielding his groin.

O.K., I thought, he's smart enough to cover his groin, but in a fight almost no one ever thinks to protect their kneecap. A quick snap kick angled into the knee can easily dislocate the joint, making it impossible for the victim to stand. After taking out his knee, I'm planning another snap kick to his groin or face, whichever is the most exposed. The double snap kick should keep my hands free for the Samoan. I hopefully plan a back-spinning, knife-edged strike to his throat. I realize that the blow might crush his wind pipe, but I am past caring. In my mind I see a horrid visual picture of what will happen to me once they get me down. Terror fills my thoughts, goading me to the edge of fury as I subtly shift weight to my rear foot—I am half an instant from striking . . .

"Hey, it's the Fall Guy." I freeze. Bad Bill is holding out his hand in my direction. "Hey, remember me?" he asks hopefully. I am reminded of a sad-eyed hound dog hopeful for attention. He continues, "You autographed the comic strip for me." The memory floods back to me. He is one of the inmate plumbers who slipped into my cell in J-3.

"Hey, Gonzo, this is a right-on dude." While shaking my hand, he smiles brightly, "Gonzo calls me Bad Bill, but my friends call me Sweet William." Gonzo shifts roles instantly, from attacker to want-to-be-best-friends in a heartbeat. He insists on helping with my workout. I've loaded the bar on the bench press to one hundred sixty-five pounds, and with Gonzo spotting me, barely manage to squeeze out ten repetitions.

"Ahh, you can do more than that," he lisps. Then he adds a ten pound plate to each end of the heavy bar. For the next hour I lift iron with Gonzo. Toward the end of the workout I want to work with lighter iron, but Gonzo knuckles me good naturedly in the chest and says, "Ya gotta drive the heavy iron, sugar." Then smiling sweetly, he adds, "If ya wanna stay a virgin in here, ya gonna need bigger muscles, cutie."

Later, while walking back up the breezeway with my arms hanging rubbery at my sides, I think about how the joint has a way of inducing inspired workouts. Several hours later I remember that it's my birthday, but I don't feel like celebrating anymore.

On Thursday evenings the American Indian inmates are allowed to worship in a homemade sweatlodge on the south yard lawn. They begin the ceremony by building a small bonfire in which they place stones. The fire is lit an hour before sunset. Then as the sun begins its descent behind the foothills of San Pedro, they dig the hot stones from the red ashes of the fire with forked sticks and carry them into the hut for their sweatbath.

I regularly enjoy sitting downwind from the fire and its adjacent small hut just to smell the wonderful campfire smell of burning wood. In prison, one learns to take pleasure from the simplest things.

Sitting down upon the grass on a chilly evening in early October, I inhale the smoky fragrance of the fire. Closing my eyes, I allow the Bible I am carrying to open to an arbitrary page. Surprisingly, I find that the unlooked-for text often relates directly to what I'm thinking about. I casually read a sentence—abruptly, the stability of the world about me shifts.

When I sit down, my thoughts are clouded with speculation about my life in prison. I wonder how serving time inside such a callous institution is going to make me a better person. I stare in amazement at the answer that lies beneath my finger, which is pointing at Romans, chapter five, verse three:

"But we also exult in our tribulations, knowing that tribulation brings about perseverance; and perseverance, proven character, and proven character, hope; and hope does not disappoint."

Prison is my tribulation. If viewed as a test, a test of adversity, then the tribulation that is my daily companion will lead me to growth—growth in spirit and in character. Prison, when viewed as a testing ground, takes on a uniqueness not often found in the tameness of a civilized society. I reach for a greater comprehension and am aided in that quest by adversity, which is my guide and teacher.

As I think these thoughts, my eyes wander to the end of the sentence, "And hope does not disappoint." There is the anchor that will get me through prison. I know in my heart that God loves me and with his help I am a good person. My "hope" is to one day be recognized again as that good person. I close my eyes yet see the words plainly, "And hope does not disappoint." I have my watch words for getting through prison. Tucking the Bible under my arm, I return up the breezeway to A Unit much more at peace with myself.

I pass a darkened cubical where three inmates are sitting around a plastic bucket full of pruno getting drunk on the potent homebrew made from brewer's yeast, raisins, and canned fruit. At the television lounge I pause to watch a pinochle game being played by four inmates. Suddenly, one of the inmates, an older man, slams his cards down on the table and glares at one of the other players, a shrewd-looking Italian. "Are you really that stupid?" rages the older inmate.

"Who are you calling stupid?" The Italian is affecting an indignant look.

"You, you stupid idiot. You're cheating and we're not even playing for cigarettes, drugs, or candy."

"So what? That doesn't make me stupid."

"It does when you're upsetting my partner," responds the angry inmate. We all look at the partner in question whose face reddens and bloats with rage. "You're stupid because Smittie's in for murdering his wife, who was also cheating on him," declares the inmate.

Smittie glares at the offending player, "I hate cheats," he scowls then lunges toward the guy's throat. I know this is my cue to split as I head rapidly for the semi-privacy of my cubicle.

Hours later I am lying on my bunk staring out the window. The lights are out. The unit is still and quiet except for the soft breathing of the sleeping inmates. A full moon, the second one since my release from J-3, is just rising over a calm and placid sea, its shimmering light dancing softly on the mirrored surface. Except for the chill of the California evening, it is reminiscent of a winter night in Hawaii where Susan and I were walking on a hotel's beach front in Lanai.

I remember how Susan's silk dress slid softly under my hand as we slowly walked arm in arm under the soft lunar light of an almost full moon. I loved this woman so much that it hurt deep down inside. I was also feeling a touch of fear as we danced—my orders, after four incredible months with Susan, had finally been cut. I was to be leaving in a week.

Holding Susan in my arms, I smelled the fragrance of coconuts in her hair. I nuzzled my face into her thick, blonde mane while thinking what it would be like to spend the rest of my life with this incredible woman. Whispering into her ear, I asked, "Susan, would you like to come to California with me?"

Susan pulled back and stared into my eyes, "Your orders came?" she asked. I nodded, too nervous to speak, she hadn't answered my question. My heart was pounding wildly.

Susan smiled, and in a soft voice that penetrated straight into my soul, said, "Yes, Steve, I will come to California with you."

My joy was a fire that flushed through my entire being. I pulled her very close; my fear of losing her evaporated in the heat of our love.

Much later that night, Susan and I were holding one another close in one another's arms. Puu's snores were clearly audible from inside *Revelstoke*. I was thinking of our rosy future when Susan asked, "What about Puu?"

I shook away sleep's embrace, "What do you mean?"

"Well," Susan words came out slowly. "If two of us were to live in the truck it'll be cramped, with monster dog it's crowded."

I realized that she was right. I knew that she really didn't want to leave Puu behind. It was just that the idea made a lot of sense. After all, in California the leash laws are much more strict, and I would have to find work. In Hawaii, I argued to myself, Puu could enjoy a carefree, unrestricted lifestyle. I also already had a friend who had offered to give Puu a home. He and Puu were good friends. He took care of Puu while I was in the brig.

I sure didn't want to part with my four-legged friend, but *Revelstoke* wasn't that large, particularly as a home for two people and an over-sized dog. I knew that my love for Susan clouded my judgement. Giving away Puu turned out to be a decision I would regret for the rest of my life.

It was an overcast Thursday afternoon when I took Puu over to my friend's house. Puu seemed to know that something was up; he was staying very close to me. My friend had a condominium with a fair-sized backyard. He lived on the side of a hill, and beyond the fence there was plenty of open grass land on which Puu could run. I really hoped that Puu would be happy with his new owner as I passed over the handle to his leash.

I kneeled and ruffled Puu's ears just so he'd know that I loved him, then, with my heart breaking, I turned and left, closing the screen door on Puu who naturally attempted to follow me. He barked once to let me know that I had forgotten him, but I hurried out to *Revelstoke*. As I drove away, I heard him barking anxiously; tears were streaming freely down my face, then rounding the corner, I could hear the barking give way to a long, drawn-out howl that slowly faded away with distance.

Susan had to work that evening, so I spent a rainy night alone on the Northshore. I missed Puu terribly. I realized just how much a part of my life he had been—I felt empty inside. His favorite towel was lying on the floor. I thought about how much fun we had together. Happy, little moments came to mind, like how much he enjoyed wrestling me for that towel after his bi-weekly baths. I vividly remembered all the silly things he had done, and I kept thinking that I should go back and get him.

The next morning I woke feeling miserable. It was such a lonely sight without Puu's wagging tail, the dog dish that needed immediate filling, or sad-eyed friend with his head pillowed on my lap looking for attention.

I called Susan before going to pick her up. As soon as I heard her voice I knew that something was wrong. Stuttering and crying into the phone, her words broken with sobs, she said, "Oh, Steve, I'm so sorry!"

"Susan, what's wrong?" My heart thumped wildly.

"Last night," she continued while gasping for air, "Puu jumped the fence at your friend's house. He ran out into the street and was struck by a car."

"Oh, Puu," I moaned, tears already forming in my eyes.

"Your friend wasn't home—just his girlfriend was there. She said there weren't any visible injuries so she didn't take him to the vet. But later that night he seemed to be having problems walking and was groaning a lot. Then while she was watching television, Puu limped over to her, laid his head on her lap and, with a low groan, he died."

"Susan," I cried, "I have to hang-up. I'll call you back."

I collapsed into the phone booth.

That afternoon, I picked up Puu's sheet-shrouded body at my friend's house. Then I drove to the trail head at Maunawili, which was one of Puu's favorite places. A light drizzle began to fall as I made a sling for Puu out of a beach towel. I placed my friend's body across my back and set off up the trail. I slipped often in the mud and twice had to rest, but finally I made it to a ridge above a spilling waterfall. Using the same folding shovel that I used to fill Puu's dog dish with dry food, I began to dig a grave. When it was deep enough, I cradled my Puu in my arms a last time.

The rain began to fall harder as I laid Puu to rest. The waterfall tinkled softly in the background, wind rustled through the trees, and the rain made a splattering sound as it fell forming shallow puddles in the bottom of the grave. I laid Puu's towel across his body then quickly shoveled the wet earth over him. The showers were beginning to pass as I tamped the soil around the gentle mound. Looking toward the horizon, I saw a full moon emerging from behind the clouds and by its glow I made my friend a final promise. "Puu, listen to me," I called out into the night, "Whenever the moon is full, I will stop and think of this mountain and my friend who sleeps here."

Walking back down the mountain, I felt a terrible rend in my heart where a great loss resided.

Now, staring at the calm sea through the prison bars, I gaze at the lunar light shimmering on the water from the full moon, and the tears silently come. The shimmering water dissolves into a film of tears. Pulling the cover over my head, soundlessly, I cry.

CHAPTER 17

The next day I go after the best job in the prison: movie projectionist. The theater has an antique 35mm, Simplex projection system that is in a worn and abused state. The projection booth is a mess with equipment thrown everywhere. The guy who runs the booth is a slob, but more importantly, he is being released in two weeks. I ask the officer in charge of the Recreation Department for the job.

"Why should I make you the projectionist?" he asks. "Have you ever worked with a 35mm projection system before?"

"No," I reply honestly, "but I've seen the condition of the booth and its equipment. I'm perfect for the job if only because I'm a clean and neat person." Apparently those simple qualifications get me the job.

The next day I stand in the projection booth surveying the incredible mess. I drag a large trash can into the booth and begin to fill it with hundreds of pounds of junk that had been accumulating over several decades. I hand sand the walls before painting them white. It takes a full two days to scrape a thick, crusted coat of yellowed wax from the tile floor. Then I lay down fresh wax and buff the floor till it shines. Next, I attack the antique projector, disassembling it in stages, industriously cleaning its parts. Working on that projector and sprucing up the rest of the booth is a cleansing process that I find I'm also mentally applying to myself. I'm getting rid of a poor self-image and replacing it with a cleaner vision of me as a good person. When I finally finish, I take a lot of personal pride in how neat and tidy the booth looks; then I take a closer look inside myself and like what I see there, too.

The booth becomes my private refuge within the prison. Privacy is rare and treasured in the joint. I also enjoy watching the movie as often as I like. The huge screen becomes a personal giant transporter through which I visit the outside world.

Despite all my best efforts, it is often difficult for me to escape depression. The hardest time descends upon me with the approach of my second Christmas inside. A mid-December storm seems to echo my mood as I lie upon my bunk, unable to sleep. Staring out at the raging ocean, I watch wind-driven waves beating against the rocks at the base of the security fence. The wind is coming directly at my window, hurling sheets of rain against the glass. A third of the glass panes have been broken out by the previous tenant. Normally, I enjoy the fresh air that blows through the empty panes (inmate windows don't open), but tonight, in a vain attempt to keep the rain out, I try taping cardboard over the empty panes. Still, the wind-driven water soon soaks through the paper, allowing the cold, wet wind entrance to my bunk. Next, I try stuffing my old underwear into the empty panes, but it doesn't work either, as water soon begins to run down the wall and onto the corner of my mattress. Wearing two pairs of sweats and wrapped tightly in my worn prison blanket, I can't help shivering as I stare out the dark window. Beyond the glow of the security lights, I see sea gulls flying desperately against the blustery wind. Finally tiring, they land on the turbulent water, until they are swept too close to the rocks. Then, they again take flight in a vain attempt to fly against the raging wind.

It is a powerful night full of energy and lust for life. I mentally strive against the bars that hold me and wish for the future and its promise of freedom. Like a beast in a cage, I rise from my bunk and stalk the dark corridors preying on the electrical flash of lightning and the deep rumble of thunder that shakes the walls. The fury of the storm fuses with my need for life outside this cement quarantine that binds me. I rave for my freedom and silently fight against the society that locks me away from it as I stride the corridors angrily, a human fury running in the eye of the storm.

The next morning finds me sitting red-eyed in the unit lounge. My fury and passion has been washed away with the passing of the storm. A gentle rain is washing the window outside.

I feel a lot better now about the approaching Christmas. I think to myself that there are times when it is best to express the passion of our feelings to help flush away the negative energy that often lurks in all of us.

Standing up, I decide to indulge myself this Christmas by decorating the entire visiting room. After breakfast I track down the Recreation Officer and get him to allow me access to the basement storeroom where they keep the Christmas decorations.

Rooting around in its dank and moldy corners, I dig out a six-foot-tall standard prison-issue, plastic Christmas tree and four cardboard boxes full of chipped colored lights and bright, but rat-chewed, ornaments. It's a little depressing looking at the condition of the mostly cracked and broken ornaments, yet I regret more not being allowed to decorate a real tree. Christmas isn't Christmas minus the wilderness scent of a Douglas Pine, its bark oozing tiny cascades of honey-brown sap.

Placing the Christmas goods on a cart, I imagine that it is a sleigh as I head almost happily for the visiting room. A guard locks me in the large empty room as I quickly go about my task. I string ornaments from the walls and ceiling then erect the plastic tree in the middle of the room. I spend a couple of hours weaving the lights around the tree and suspending the chipped ornaments to present their best side. Then I industriously begin wrapping empty boxes to put under the tree. I'm beginning to tire of my labors when I hear a tiny thump against one of the windows. I go over to the bank of the windows and am surprised to see the sun setting. I think how quickly the day has passed as I look out into the fast approaching winter night.

At first all I see is the ocean beyond the bright security lights; then a tiny movement on the ground attracts my attention. Lying on the cement, fluttering occasionally, is a small brown sparrow. Apparently blinded by the bright lights, it flew into the thick plate glass.

Had I been home I would have gone outside and carefully collected the bird. Even if I couldn't nurse it back to health, I'd have at least given it comfort, like a warm box filled with towels, so it could at least die in peace. Instead, locked inside, I watch it slowly die in the cold chill of the evening under the harsh glare of the lights. It flutters a bit, then once more frantically before it lies still— with its little life went my desire for Christmas.

Reluctantly, with my spirit dragging, I return to the plastic tree and again begin to wrap the empty boxes. I can't help the tears that start to fall. I don't know if I'm crying for the small bird or for myself, but the tears continue to fall freely all the same. They spill upon the fake presents dampening the Christmas paper. The colors begin to soften and run and, in the process, make me more sad by the moment.

The chill of the evening is just beginning to make my hands stiff with cold when I finish wrapping the last of the empty boxes to put under the made-in-Korea tree. Staring at the false tree with its litter of vacant presents, I wonder if its gay deception doesn't really make a statement about the spiritual hollowness of Christmas in prison.

I stand against the cold metal door for over an hour before the guard remembers to come for me. Walking across the chilly and blustery north yard, with my hands in my pockets, I think how sad it is to be living inside a prison—particularly during the holidays.

CHAPTER 18

With the trial behind me, Sam is finally allowed to visit. Sitting next to the Christmas tree, we have a wonderful, laugh-filled conversation. Sam is happily telling me about the events that happened to him the night I was arrested.

"I went back to the Valley Hilton and caught that science fiction movie I told you about. I fell asleep before it ended and didn't wake up until the next morning. That's when I began to wonder where you were. I went out for breakfast, and when I got back, there was still no message from you. So, I hung out in the room for the rest of the day watching cable T.V." Sam pauses dramatically. "Then I decided to catch the five o'clock news and there you were in your *Surfer* magazine team rider T-shirt wearing handcuffs. It totally blew me away."

"I guess," I answer, laughing. "It was quite a shock for me, too."

"Yeah, well, my life got really frantic after seeing that," Sam says seriously. "I snuck back down to San Diego using nothing but back streets and stayed well under the speed limit. It took me over six hours just to go only ninety miles."

"You must have been pretty scared," I offer.

"Scared?" Sam smiles hugely. "Man, I was freaked out! I spent the next couple of days sleeping in my car and hiding."

"Hiding where?"

"Surfing at La Jolla shores," Sam visibly shivers as he remembers. "I darn near froze I spent so much time in the water. I'd sit out in the line-up for hours keeping an eye on the parking lot. Every time I saw a non-descript car cruising the lot, I'd panic. One day I spent almost three hours just sitting out there because a cop car was parked next to my baja bug for a real long time."

"What happened?"

Sam smirks, "Just after sunset a tow truck took it away; it had broken down. I was so cold it was difficult just paddling back in," laughs Sam. "After that I figured 'the heck with this, I'm going home for a hot shower.'"

"And then . . . " I prompt anxiously.

"I still had shampoo in my hair when my mom opened the door and said, 'Sam, you've got visitors.'"

"'Can't it wait until I get out of the shower?' I answered."

"'I don't think so honey', she said sweetly, 'they've got badges.'"

Sam rolls his eyes dramatically. "They were DEA agents. I thought

they were going to take me away for sure, but they said all they wanted
to do was talk." Sam pauses for a moment then continues, "I told
them I didn't know there was cocaine in the car just like you told
me."

"Were they buying it?" I ask.

"No," laughs Sam, "the agent said that if they wanted me, I'd be
on my way to prison right then and there."

"They didn't want you?"

"Nah, he said they decided to let me go after I almost got them
killed the night of your arrest."

"Almost got them killed?" I echo.

"Yeah," laughs Sam, "after leaving you at the Marriott Hotel, I
immediately got lost in downtown Los Angeles. I was in bumper-to-
bumper traffic on a main street when I realized that I should be
going north instead of south." Sam is actively using his hands to
describe the action, "So, I just swung the baja bug over the cement
divider and, after bouncing off the curb, raced in the opposite direction. I didn't have a clue that two car loads of DEA agents were hot
on my tail. According to the agent, only the first car was able to
jump the center divider before traffic cut the second one off. He
said they decided to pull me over and arrest me right then and there,
only that's about the same time that I realized I was going in the
right direction after all . . . so I whipped another fast U-turn jumping
over the curb again. The agent said their car almost got taken out by
a bus when they tried to follow me." Sam grins in delight. "Can you
imagine that, I lost two car loads of federal agents without even knowing that I was being followed."

I remember Sam's unique driving technique when he almost
got us killed in Texas at that left turn into the hotel parking lot.
"Yeah, I can imagine you doing that without thinking." I lean secre-
tively across the table, "I have a big favor to ask you." Sam looks
immediately suspicious. "I want to trade sandals."

"What do you mean, you want to trade sandals?" He pops his
head under the table to eye the decrepit flip-flops I'm wearing. "Is
that green stuff growing on your sandals mold?"

All too soon Sam's visit comes to an end. I sadly watch my friend
heading for the exit, walking rather awkwardly in my worn-out flops.

My next visitor is Michelle, my closest friend, and I have been
anxiously looking forward to her first visit. I need to talk with someone to whom I can open my soul. I see her as soon as I enter the
visiting room, sitting in the sunshine next to a window across the
room where she is trying to ignore the leers from two of the inmates
and one of the guards. Our eyes meet over the crowded room. It
takes me a minute to work my way through the press of humanity,
some of whom are involved in the worst sorts of deviant activity.

A moment later, I'm standing before Michelle. She stands also and smiles at me with eyes that sparkle. In that single instant in time, I realize how much I've missed the tender comfort of a woman friend. Michelle couldn't mask the sad look that momentarily passes across her face as she gazes at her inmate friend. Then she bravely recaptures her smile and steps into my arms.

For the longest time we just stand there holding each other. For a few precious moments, I am at peace with the world. Then it dawns on me. Except for my mother's modest hugs, I have not been touched by another human being since my arrest. In prison, you learn to keep to yourself. You don't encourage anyone to touch you, nor do you make physical contact with others. To accidentally brush up against another inmate is a major insult and can lead directly to being stabbed or, if you're lucky, just some serious pounding on your body. The only acceptable physical contact is in sports, which is usually played with fierce physical abandon. However, even sports carries a serious threat of its own. Inmates love to bet and there is no such thing as a friendly bet in the joint. The wages can be money, cigarettes, someone's body, or practically anything at all. If one of the players makes a foolish error, particularly if it costs the game, serious death threats can be made from the side lines. Realizing this, the only game I play in general population is frisbee. I always throw the plastic saucer very carefully to ensure that I don't hit a gang member.

Standing in Michelle's arms, holding her soft and warm body to mine, I realize how much I've missed simple human contact. There are so many things that prison deprives you of, yet sometimes you don't realize what is missing until you are reminded of their absence. It is as if an empty hollowness in your life is one day brought to your attention, and then you wonder how you could have ever overlooked it before.

After the most unforgettable hug of my life, we sit down. Michelle smiles, her eyes warm in friendship. "How do you cope with this place?" she asks in wonder.

"I just do it," I answer, "it's not like there's a choice." I laugh, "You should see some of the inmates in D Unit, also known as Drug and Drag Unit.

"I thought this was just a men's prison?" asks Michelle.

"It is, but in prison when a man wants to be called by a woman's name, you gotta have enough sense not to argue with him. After all, that kind of inmate isn't exactly stable upstairs."

"I guess!" offers Michelle.

"Not all the gay inmates dress up," I continue, "but the ones that do go all out. They compete with each other as to who is the best-looking girl in the joint."

"You can't be serious?"

"Oh, yeah," I smile and point to a slim Colombian in a peach silk shirt talking intimately with a striking Latin woman.

"So what is so strange about him?" asks Michelle. "At least he is sitting with a girl."

"Well," I grin, "the girl is his sister, and a little while ago she was the one wearing the silk shirt. She brings Juan all her hand-me-downs, including her silk drawers." Michelle's eyes begin to water as she giggles openly.

"We even have a blonde surfer girl inside," I tease. "Her name's Michelle."

"You are kidding me now," complains Michelle.

"No, I'm not. You should have seen the spat she had with Juanita when she wouldn't let Michelle try on a pair of her black silk shorts."

Michelle holds up her hands in mock defense, "Enough about the boys, I want to know about you."

"So ask."

"O.K., what's the best and the worst thing about being in prison?"

Surprisingly, I'm able to answer her question with a single word. "Discipline—I enjoy the discipline I impose upon myself; it helps to strengthen my character and adds focus to my inward journey as I seek to understand myself better. It is through discipline that I hope to turn this prison sentence into a positive experience."

"O.K., what's the negative side of discipline?"

"I hate the regimented, uncaring discipline of the prison system. Logic doesn't apply inside here. As far as the guards are concerned, inmates don't have anything coming. The problem is that a lot of the guards are pretty sadistic and take pleasure in abusing inmates. Think about it, what kind of person in their right mind would ever want a job as a prison guard?"

Despite the joviality of our short time together, I can tell that Michelle is depressed seeing me in such a hostile environment—come to think of it, so am I.

Like all visits this one ends too soon. Michelle gives me a good-bye hug that I know I will treasure for months; then she passes through the visiting room door and out into a world that is alive with change, stimulus, and adventure. I, however, am channeled into a narrow, dirty-walled room for "strip and show," where, standing naked on a cold cement floor, I wait for the guard to finish his search for contraband. While standing, the guard peers diligently with his flashlight, I think of the promise of freedom somewhere in the future. Sometimes I think it is the only thing that keeps me going.

The following week I receive a blank journal in the mail from Michelle. In her flowery script she encourages me to record my thoughts and feelings. It is a book that she one day wants to read. The journal is tall and thin with expensive white bond paper. The cover is bound in fine black cloth. The black outside contrasts the white pages within. The journal of empty pages (like me) is waiting to be filled. In a sense, the blank pages represent a new beginning, an opportunity to establish new goals and commitments. The words that I will write on these empty leaves will be tracks that lead back to myself.

Prison has become my *dojo*, (place of enlightenment). My philosophy is to experience each moment with the fullest of being and awareness. Every action or non-action has meaning and purpose. Joe Hyams expresses it well in his reflection of Zen upon the teachings of karate: "Enlightenment," it has been said, "means to recognize the harmony of ordinary life."

My goal is not an easy one: perfection of accomplishment, no matter how insignificant the task, and total awareness of every act. I think of an old adage, "The wonder of it all, I carry water, I sweep the floor." The answer is realistic appreciation of simplicity in life.

On the stage in the back of the theater I discover a full length mirror hidden behind some props. So far, I have only seen myself in the small bathroom shaving mirror. I dust off the mirror in anxious anticipation and am pleased to recognize an old friend. I have received clothes from home; I no longer look like every other inmate. I see a tall, slim man wearing white high top sneakers, blue jeans, and the blue surfer T-shirt I was wearing when I was arrested. I have a mustache and short brown hair. Many of the stress lines developed in the cell block have gone. Despite being in prison, I'm me again.

Later that day, while relaxing in the privacy of the projection booth, I read in the *Los Angeles Times* that Larry Flint, the publisher of *Hustler* magazine, has been in court again. Flint, who is paralyzed from the waist down after being shot by an unhappy reader, claims to have a copy of a taped conversation between John DeLorean and James Hoffman, the informant. However, he refuses to produce it in court, so is being held in contempt. When Judge Takasugi fines him twenty thousand dollars, Flint shows up in court with all of it in ones, accompanied by two women in bikinis. There is a picture of Flint outside the courtroom. The man is wearing an American flag as a diaper.

Later, the tape is proved to be a figment of Flint's wild imagination. He appeals his contempt charges and takes his case all the way to the Supreme Court, where he makes the mistake of shouting obscenities at Chief Justice Burger. Burger gives him a little time inside the slammer to cool his temper. Flint, not satisfied with the sentence, dares Chief Justice Burger to give him a longer sentence—Burger does.

Flint winds up in the nut ward of the prison hospital above J-3, where he joins the other loonies in what is called "The Thorizin Shuffle." Demented inmates who are a hazard to themselves or others are given Thorizin to make them more manageable. The potent drug all but eliminates clear thought, the result is a shuffling fool. Later, Flint is transferred to Springfield, a prison mental hospital.

Three days before Christmas, I nervously appear before the Parole Board to find out how much of my sentence they are going to require me to serve. The guidelines call for thirty-six months, but they could make me do forty-four months. I await their decision with baited breath. They're considering the longer sentence. My flight to Colombia and error in involving Sam weighs heavily against me. I lack credibility as an honorable person for exposing an innocent youth (Sam was twenty-one) to the dangers of the criminal underworld. But, because of my excellent record at the prison, I am awarded thirty-six months. It means I have less than twenty months to go. I leave the room grinning; the light at the end of the tunnel has just brightened by a few mega-watts.

Jim, my brother, comes to visit, sporting a new winter coat. I note how warm and comfortable it looks then casually mention how cold it gets inside my cubical with the missing window panes and haphazardly working heater. People visiting inmates should only wear old, worn-out clothes. Out in the yard, I show off my new coat to a new inmate friend named Ralph. Life inside the joint is not always without its humorous side.

That night, Christmas Eve, I wander down to the south yard to watch the Christmas parade of boats. Up and down the channel brightly lit yachts all aglow with decorations pass in a line. Some of them have speaker systems that play Christmas music. I'm bewitched by the pageantry. I just can't believe what a good location this is for a prison. If they built condos here, they would go for at least half a million dollars each.

That night I try to fall asleep early so I can get up before the sunrise. Instead, I lay awake far into the night thinking about my last days in the navy.

I arrived at Treasure Island Naval Base in California, on March 15, 1980. Susan and a few friends saw me off from the airport in Honolulu. Susan was going to join me in about three weeks. I wasn't being discharged; rather, I was being released on appellate leave while awaiting final disposition on my Bad Conduct Discharge. My hopes were not high for a favorable ruling from the military court.

I spent two lonely weeks at Treasure Island being processed through the navy's methodical paper machine. Fortunately, since I still retained my rank as a chief petty officer, I wasn't assigned to any work details. My time was my own. I spent most of it just walking around San Francisco or sitting on the beach watching the sun rise and set. It was a time of raw emotions. I hurt desperately from Puu's death. I felt empty and lost. The navy had been my home for almost fourteen years. I had been so proud to be a frogman and a Vietnam vet and now it was all ending in disgrace. The future was an uncertain dilemma. At the end of each day, I stood alone on the cold beach facing toward Hawaii, which happened to lie exactly beyond the sunset, and thought of a woman with golden hair—and a sad-eyed Dane who was no more. At the naval base, the personnel department wasn't exactly aware of my true situation. My orders had simply read "process for discharge," but in the service jacket there was a thick manila envelope; stamped on its cover in bold red letters were the words "TOP SECRET, FOR COMMANDING OFFICER'S EYES ONLY." I assumed it contained the results of the court-martial and orders to initiate my appellate leave.

On March 31, I was told that my papers were ready. I thought it might have been more appropriate if they had waited one more day for April Fools.

The anorexic clerk, wearing over-sized, wire-rimmed glasses, smiled as he pushed the papers across the desk for me to sign. I casually looked down at them . . . my world paused at that moment. I stared, dumbfounded at the colorful and ornate document beneath my hands. In bold, capital script, the words "Honorable Discharge" seared themselves into my mind. "You O.K., Chief?" The clerk stared at me.

"Yes, I'm fine," I answered, wiping a sudden cold sweat from my brow. Someone, I realized, has made a very big mistake.

"Just sign right here." The clerk was beaming through his thick glasses, which greatly magnified his eyes. He looked like a little mouse with his narrow face and big eyes. My hand shook slightly as I signed the precious document.

The clerk slipped the discharge papers into a manila envelope; then he leafed through the remains of my service jacket. He paused encountering the manila envelope stamped "TOP SECRET." I saw that it was unopened. He shrugged, closed the jacket, then pushed the manila envelope across the table and into my hands.

I snatched up the envelope with the honorable discharge papers inside and got halfway to the door when the clerk yelled out to me, "Hey, Chief, hold on."

"Darn," I thought to myself, "has he already realized his mistake?" It took a lot of will power to stop. For a moment, I seriously considered continuing right on out the door. I reluctantly turned around.

"You can't leave yet, Chief," he implored, "your check is still coming over from disbursing."

"Check?" I re-crossed the room and sat down while keeping a firm grip on my envelope. I received my final pay check the day before, so I was curious what this check would be—a day's pay? The check arrived ten minutes later. "Just sign here," beamed the clerk. I signed the cashier's form and received a green-colored check with Department of the Treasury logos stamped across its face. It took a second to be sure I was reading the numbers correctly, "For the sum of five hundred and fifty-two dollars."

I couldn't help the question that leaped from my lips, "What's this for?"

The clerk seemed surprised, "Leave not taken. According to your service record, there are twenty-two days of pay not accounted for. Is there a problem with the sum?"

"Oh, no . . . it's fine," I stuck the check in my wallet while wondering how my command would feel if they knew I had just been paid for the twenty-two days I spent in the brig.

"O.K., Chief." The clerk clapped his hands together, pleased to have been so helpful. "That's it, you're a free man." Staring at the helpful little clerk, I doubted he could ever understand the meaning his last words held for me. I returned to my room to pack.

My elation at being released was soon saddened, however, as I took my uniform off the last time. Never again would I walk with a military swagger to my step or with medals pinned upon my chest. I carefully folded the dress jacket into a suitcase and was slowly closing the lid, when I saw the silver EOD insignia flash once in the sunlight. Then the lid closed with an audible snap.

Lying on the prison bunk, I remember closing that suitcase lid and how it finalized the end of fourteen years of adventure and accomplishment. Back then I had thought my life couldn't fall any further—was I ever wrong.

The next morning is Christmas. I'm standing in the lobby waiting for the north yard guard. He's late. A couple of inmates are complaining bitterly to each other about the delay. I stand at the opposite wall, calm and relaxed. Instead of being angry about the wait, I use the time to harmlessly daydream. When the guard finally comes, the other inmates greet him with complaints and anger. His face hardens as he prepares an angry retort, but then as I pass I wish him a Merry Christmas and mean it. He smiles and waves me out the door.

Nothing special happens on Christmas Day. I have asked my mother not to visit, knowing that the visiting room will be a mad house, crowded and unpleasant. Lying on the grass, I listen to the Beach Boys singing "Surfing USA" on the little box radio.

I remember how I use to do the surf report on San Diego radio while working at La Jolla Surf Systems. I consider the idea of doing one from prison: *Hi, this is Steve Arrington at Terminal Island Federal Prison. The surf today is less than one foot inside the Los Angeles breakwater. No one is paddling out; looks like we're going to be stuck inside for quite a while. If you are selling or doing drugs, you too might consider an extended visit at Club Fed where the social activities include: gang rapes, bare-fisted boxing, fighting with homemade knives; or you can do absolutely nothing at all–for years!* A frisbee lands on my chest stirring me from my thoughts. Eddie, Ralph, and I spend the rest of the afternoon tossing the plastic disk.

Christmas dinner is an inmate delight, though the dry scraps of turkey are strictly rationed. The stuffing sticks together like a ball of goop, and the ice cream has long since melted. I at least enjoy listening to the inmate choir as they roam the tables singing Christmas carols enthusiastically off-key.

After dinner I show the movie. Sitting alone in the darkness, I listen to old songs while the movie plays. Suddenly, I have an uncontrollable urge to dance. Alone, uninhibited, I dance in the dark with tears streaming down my face.

That night I sit upon my bunk plugged into a set of borrowed headphones. The music blots out the noise from the rest of the unit. I stare out the window at the moonlight dancing on the water and wonder where my life is leading me. I have just filled another page in my journal, but the words do not express what I really feel. How can I trust my deepest feelings to mere words, they are too abstract. I look at the next page; it is blank, an emptiness waiting to be filled– just like me.

Today I have given up another lady friend. She just doesn't answer my letters. Right now, women aren't a part of my life; instead, there is just an empty void. There is no one to hold or even to dream about, unless I choose to live in the past with old memories. No loving caresses in the night, no sharing of lovers' secrets or special moments together. The woman I hope for is somewhere in the distant future. She is unnamed with no face to anchor my fantasies on. How can I dream without substance to draw from? I know why I cried in the booth tonight, because I am so terribly lonely. Prison is about loneliness.

Not wanting to think about girls or being alone, I pause to look around the unit. Inmates walk back and forth along the corridor. More than a few of them are rather strange-looking. A Unit is also called Animal House because of all the weird and slightly off-balanced guys who live here. There is one who smears his excrement all over the bathroom walls. Down the hall a couple of druggies are shooting cocaine. They bought the coke with money they extorted from another inmate. Later, they will abuse him in a different way. The television room reeks of the musty smell of marijuana.

The lounge floor is decorated with a composite of trash and food droppings that will lie there until the orderly cleans on Monday morning. Toilet paper lies unrolled on the bathroom floor in a soggy yellow mess that stinks of the urine that didn't quite make it to the toilet bowl.

My bunk is a private oasis from it all. Looking through my window, I see that it is an absolutely beautiful night outside. The skies are clear and there is a freshness in the air. I had spent a lot of the day just walking, and now my legs are tired and a bit sore.

A sudden urge for chocolate causes me to jump down from the bunk as I rummage in my locker for a candy bar. Since I earn only eleven cents an hour, it takes four point one hours of work to buy one candy bar. Unwrapping the chocolate bar, I see three other inmates watching me. My private oasis is apparently not so private, after all.

Back on the bunk, I sit sucking on my quarter of the Hershey bar to make it last longer. Before I am finished, Leroy asks me for some chocolate too. This guy always borrows and never pays back. All his money goes for drugs. I tell him to buzz off. The night passes slowly.

It is morning now. I'm watching a spider stalk a fly on my window. I've noticed that I am more aggressive now. Prison has a way of doing that to you. Inmates must live constantly with violence. In the joint it is the survival instinct that keeps you alive.

Living within these hate-filled walls has awakened instincts I didn't know I had. Until recently these instincts had remained buried in the more primal part of my brain. It's where the cave man inside all of us resides. I find that I assert myself more often now. I know that if I am threatened, it is the cave man who will respond. It is he who is in charge of my survival here. Yet sometimes he comes forth unbidden. He is the one who denied Leroy the Hershey bar. Though the cave man scares me, I appreciate having him awake, knowing he is constantly alert, patiently waiting until he is needed to surface in all his primal savagery. I do, however, wonder about the future when I am released. Will the cave man still be alert and ready inside me? The thought worries me. Is prison slowly twisting me toward the primal side?

CHAPTER 19

I have been in general population for five months now. It is January 20, 1984, and in my hand I am carrying a note that summons me immediately to the unit administrator's office. I wonder what is up as I head across the prison compound to his cubical in A Unit .

Knuckling the door once to announce my presence, I step inside the small dingy office, which is filled with the presence of the huge, fat administrator inside. The obese man, probably the fattest person I have ever seen, is totally engrossed in an empty donut box. He is poking about with one blunt finger in the hopeful pursuit of an elusive crumb or two. Every morning he arrives carefully carrying his dozen glazed donuts, which he swiftly polishes off well before the ten o'clock coffee break.

The Slug, as he is affectionately known by his inmate charges, grunts. It is the kind of a grunt that can only be affected by a really fat man. It wafts into the small enclosure and fills the air with a sweet sour scent. I look forlornly at the firmly closed window and wish for a breath of fresh air. Sucking in his huge gut, the Slug is barely able to open his desk drawer enough to pull out half a pack of gum. His fat fingers quickly unwrap the foil, then wadding the multiple sticks of gum together, he pops the resulting ball into his mouth before speaking. In repulsed fascination, I watch his fat lips slowly form a sentence around the thick wad in his mouth, "Pack up your stuff." The Slug only speaks in abrupt sentences. He is so out of shape that sitting up straight causes him to be short of breath.

I am not really surprised that they are moving me. A Unit serves mostly as a transit dorm. I do, however, wonder where they are moving me to. Each dormitory or unit has its own personality. Some are better than others. The Slug consults his paper work and in the process discovers a donut crumb on his desk blotter. A fat finger quickly jabs at the sugar-coated globule of fat and flour then sticks his treasure-loaded finger between his thick lips. His piggy little eyes squint up in obvious pleasure. "G Unit."

"G Unit! I'm going to G Unit?" I ask excitedly.

The Slug is perturbed, he doesn't like repeating himself. His pig eyes narrow unhappily, "Geee . . . Unit."

"Thanks, Mr. Ryan," I answer honestly. I go quickly to my locker and begin joyously packing up my things. G Unit is the honor dorm, and it's in the south yard. The recreation officer has arranged the transfer as a reward for my enthusiastic work in the projection booth. It takes two trips to carry all of my possessions down to G Unit. I have apparently become a man of substance. Like the prison house expression says, "I be having things."

The south yard dormitories are only eight years old; their modern design more resembles a college dorm than prison units. The front and back doors are never locked and each inmate is issued a key to his own room. The windows are without bars or wire mesh. The bunk beds are made of real wood and even have a thick, clean mattress. I excitedly run my hand over the soft wood grain and then, with a groan of happiness, lie down on the bunk.

It's difficult to describe my pleasure, but imagine the standard prison issue steel bunk painted shades of non-descript gray with a worn mattress barely two inches thick, full of lumps, leaking its stuffing, and covered with brown and yellow stains from dried excrements left by previous inmates. I'm surprised that even the musty smell of mildew is missing. The dormitory actually smells surprisingly clean. It is an unusual situation for a prison dormitory.

I immediately begin moving in. I tape a few pictures of wilderness scenes torn from magazines onto the wood veneer walls then go outside to collect a few small green plants. I carefully put the plants into colorful ceramic pots, which I made in the prison hobby shop. I'm pleasantly surprised to catch myself humming as I happily set about housekeeping in earnest.

Outside again, I appropriate some long-stem roses from the bushes outside the staff office when no one is looking. The velvety flowers fill the room with their soft fragrant bouquet. I also gather two pocketfuls of eucalyptus pods with which I use to spice the clothes drawers.

When the last item is packed away, I place the roses, to which I have added long green ferns for contrast, on the window sill. Then, I pause to stare out the window at the view, which by inmate standards is terrific. I can see the green, manicured lawns of the Coast Guard base with its border of tall palm trees and thick, green hedges. Just beyond is the harbor mouth with its constant parade of tall white cruise ships and exotic freighters headed for open water and distant foreign ports. There are no walls to block my view, just a double row of chain link fences topped with the ever-present razor wire.

Over the next couple of months, I happily watch the green world outside my window. The south-facing window catches the morning light, and often I'm awakened by a sunbeam, which entices me out to run in the California sunshine. Sometimes I volunteer to water the football field and feel a deep inner joy in watching the long jets of water criss-cross the green lawn, casting wandering rainbows of translucent color against a background of green grass and blue sea.

On the first day of spring I'm happily watering the south yard football field when my new best friend Ralph walks up. I met Ralph just after I moved into G Unit. We had a common interest in stealing roses from in front of the staff office.

"What are you doing? he asks.

"I'm watering the lawn," I answer putting words to the obvious.

"I know you're watering the lawn, I heard all about you and your bucket in J-3. I just want to know why you're so into watering the grass?"

"In here, I see ugly everyday, yet the water is so fresh and clean . . . watching the water falling on the grass washing life into it makes me feel good inside. In a sense it's like my inner self is taking a bath along with the grass." I look around to make sure no one is within ear shot, then confidentially motion Ralph closer so I can whisper, "There's something else."

Expectantly, Ralph moves in. The look on his face tells me that he thinks he is about to learn a great secret. "The grass likes it," I whisper.

Ralph isn't amused, "That's it, you do this for hours on end just because the grass likes it?"

"Uh-huh," I nod and smile at Ralph.

Ralph stands still for a minute and watches the wandering jets of water with me. "The rainbows are kind of neat to watch."

"Uh-huh."

Two sea gulls land beside one of the jets. We watch them washing in a puddle. "You know, this is kind of fun," says Ralph.

"Better than watching inmates," I answer.

"Want to go pump some iron?"

"Sure, if you'll help me put the hoses and sprinklers away."

Half an hour later we are in the weight room spotting each other at the bench press when Tiffany arrives. Tiffany is one of our resident homosexuals. He is over six feet tall and weighs close to three hundred pounds. He is sporting a new pair of Dolphin shorts. They are peach-colored. The Tiff has added a few more pounds over the long, cold winter. The shorts don't quite cover his drooping cheeks, which are dotted with angry red pimples. The extra weight tends to make him waddle while doing his flamer routine.

Tiffany has stopped by the weight room to admire all the sweating bodies. He's prancing up and down the weight line ooh-ing and ahh-ing enthusiastically to the general laughter of the inmates. A tall surfer type gets offended when Tiffany stops to admire his bod.

"Stay away from me, you idiot!" shouts the angry surfer.

Pretending to be infatuated, Tiffany put his hands to his face and lisps, "Do you know that when you're mad it brings out the color in your blue eyes?"

The surfer, who finds Tiffany just too offensive to tolerate, makes the serious mistake of sticking his finger into Tiffany's chest as he starts to say something threatening. The surfer doesn't get a chance to voice his warning.

Quick as a striking mongoose, Tiffany spins the surfer around and locks the man's arm behind his back. Then grabbing a handful of long blond hair he pulls the surfer's head vigorously back. The surfer is straining to free himself, but can't, at which time Tiffany very carefully lays a long, wet kiss right on the guy's lips. The distressed surfer renews his struggle with vigor, but can't break away from Tiffany's bruising lip lock.

After playing with the surfer for twenty long seconds, Tiffany lets the totally humiliated guy go. The surfer comes up sputtering and gasping for air. Eyes spread wide in sudden fear, he backs quickly away from Tiffany. Tiffany follows, batting his eyes playfully as he inquires, "Are we playing hard to get?"

The distressed surfer heads rapidly for the door with The Tiff prancing joyfully after him. "I bet he's a moaner; I got goose bumps all over just thinking about it," Tiffany lisps over his shoulder as he goes in hot pursuit of his new found love.

I later see Tiffany still harassing the surfer. Whenever the guy looks over at Tiffany's table, Tiff bats his eyes at him and throws kisses. The surfer has really screwed up by capturing Tiffany's attention. Tiffany is thoroughly enjoying the joke, but the consequences are going to be very real for the surfer if Tiffany follows up on his threats. In prison an inmate never lightly threatens anyone.

On his way out, Tiffany stops at the surfer's table and smiles down at him. The smile isn't reflected in the ice of The Tiff's eyes as he casually says, "I'll see you tonight, sugar." The way Tiffany delivered his threat so casually, casting it even in friendly words, significantly adds to the terror it implies.

As Tiffany slithers toward the door radiating confidence, the surfer cringes in his chair looking wildly about, all but pleading for help, which both he—and Tiffany—know won't be coming. For the young, a men's prison is a harsh place indeed.

The main course today is fried luncheon meat on white toast with stale potato chips. I settle for a lettuce salad. The few tomatoes and carrots that had been in the salad bowl have long since been pilfered by the first guys in line. I roll the fried baloney in a napkin. I stick it into my sock since we are not allowed to take food from the chow hall. I plan to give the meat to the resident cat who lives in the south yard. The cat is under the personal protection of a slightly built, little old man—who absolutely no one messes with.

The old man of the south yard began his sojourn in prison in 1948 after hijacking a truck loaded with cigarettes. He has since been in a constant state of trouble and hasn't been outside prison walls in over thirty-six years. After knifing another inmate from his wheelchair, the old man is no longer even being considered for parole. The parole board refers to him as a hazard to society. He stays inside where he cheerfully glares at the new inmates while mouthing soundless insults at them. It's not considered safe to come close enough to the crazy, old codger to understand what it is he's saying about you.

We all walk lightly around the old man with the wild eyes, who has become much more mobile now that he has given up his wheelchair for a cane.

While heading for the south yard, I unconsciously begin to finger a large and still-growing wart on the knuckle of my right index finger. It bothers me, but the staff refuses to give me any medicine to get rid of it. They probably figure I might drink the acid-based compound or try to feed it to another inmate. I actually understand their reluctance after having seen an inmate gleefully trying with a needle to inject Pepsodent tooth paste into one of the veins in his arm. I would later learn that inmates empty toothpaste tubes then refill them with heroin for a fast fix.

Rounding the corner, I see the old man playing with his cat under a tree. He smiles gratefully when I give him the baloney.

Ralph intercepts me halfway to the dormitory. The rumbling sound of a low flying airplane distracts both of us as we look to the sky in unison. Flying barely a hundred feet above the ocean is a red biplane. It turns abruptly and angles toward the prison and passes directly overhead. I can plainly see the pilot who waves down at us. The antique plane is a two seater. I stare at the empty seat in front of the pilot and wish with all of my heart that I was in that seat. When the plane dips from my sight, beyond the north yard wall, I find that I'm suddenly depressed.

An hour later the depression is still actively with me as I head for the north yard where I have an appointment to begin training a new inmate as second projectionist. We are showing a Mexican film for the Saturday matinee. After I get the complex projector running, I leave the new guy alone in the booth while I head for the north yard telephone. I hope that the line at the pay phone will be short and am pleased to see only two people ahead of me. I am planning on calling Michelle; I need to hear her voice and to air my depression.

The inmate on the phone, a huge biker with heavy black boots, is muttering into the mouthpiece. Then the soft muttering becomes loud curses. The next thing I know he is attacking the phone like a rabid pit bull. He rips the receiver from its cord and kicks the pay box repeatedly until it hangs awkwardly from the wall. Turning from the abused phone, he hurls the handset against a brick wall then goes storming past us. The guy in front of me turns and says, "I think I'll make my call later."

I nod in agreement, "I guess the guy didn't get very good news?"

"What news?" quips the inmate. "That dude was upset because no one was home."

Putting my hands in my pocket, and still saddled with my depression, I return to the projection booth to find my new assistant in a complete panic. The film has broken and is spilling onto the floor at the rate of twenty-four frames a second. He is standing ankle deep in black celluloid and is all but crying. I quickly shut the projector down then begin the slow process of re-winding the film by hand so I can splice the break. Meanwhile the inmates in the theater are screaming bloody murder about the delay. Soon debris is being hurled at the projection booth's small window. A paper cup splats wetly against the wall. When I finally reach the break, I turn to ask my assistant for some celluloid tape, but I notice that the door is open and the booth empty. I guess the death threats being directed toward us from below has unnerved him.

I re-start the movie and slowly the death threats and promises of bodily punishment diminish. Soon the inmates are laughing. The movie is a comedy, but up in the booth, I sit alone in the dark with my depression hovering over me like a cloud.

The loneliness and depression I'm feeling reminds me of my sorrowful state when I got out of the navy. Back then I had no idea what direction my life would be taking. For two weeks I lived in perpetual sadness while secretly wondering if Susan would really join me in California. Then her plane landed at L.A. airport. As I stood in the terminal, a complete change came over me. It was as if my heart had been residing in a dark shadowy place. Seeing her running down the ramp, my world brightened like a light flooding a dark cavern. She threw herself into my arms. Holding her tight, I felt her heart beating against my own, and suddenly I felt as if I had finally come home.

For the next three months, we were complete nomads, travelling little-used roads and highways. We began by driving north to Sequoia National Park at the base of the Sierra Nevada Mountain Range. The sun was just setting when we stopped to camp in a small, hidden mountain valley called Wolverton. The visibility was restricted by wisps of clouds that drifted lightly about the tall trees. That night it snowed heavily even though spring was almost upon us. Yet, inside *Revelstoke* we were warm and toasty because I fired up the furnace, which I installed four years earlier but never used. Susan had never seen snow before—having grown up in the tropical Pacific. For most of the evening, she kept her nose pressed against the frosted window watching the flakes tumbling down while making excited noises about the morning.

At first light, Susan bounced out of the truck. I was right behind her, anxious to share in her joy. Stepping out the door, I couldn't help but pause as I momentarily thought of Puu, who should have been here with us. But my sad thoughts were immediately driven away by the impact of Susan's first ever snowball.

We were like a couple of kids, indulging in a snow ball fight, then together we built a snowman with pinecone eyes. Behind us *Revelstoke*, buried beyond its hubcaps in fresh snow, was surrounded by giant sequoia trees; each was mantled in twinkling snow crystals. Walking hand-in-hand, I shared Susan's excitement as we wandered beneath the towering evergreen trees into a winter wonderland.

Wildly in love, we drove slowly toward the coast then headed south to the savage wilderness beauty of the Big Sur coastline. Our first night there we weathered a Pacific storm while camped on the sheer cliffs of a rocky promontory, which overlooked a raging ocean. *Revelstoke* was half-sheltered from the storm behind a small grove of wind-swept Monterey pines, each uniquely sculpted by the Pacific tradewinds that buffeted the truck through the long night.

In the morning the ocean had worked itself into a surging, stormy froth. Wrapped together in a blanket, we drank hot chocolate and watched the waves surge among the seaweed-laced rocks. A maze of driftwood had been cast onto the beach by the raging sea, so we went down to the seashore to scavenge. We wandered along an overgrown trail that led into a small forest where we played hide-and-seek among the moss-covered trees. The cool air was fragrant with the earthy smell of moldy leaves and wet moss. A light fog made the small forest mystical with a hobbit-like quality, which was probably why I didn't notice that I was hiding in poison oak.

Spring was a time of discovery as we wandered the California coastline, searching out its nooks and crannies and finding contentment in each other's arms.

Living the gypsy life of continuous quest and discovery became an enchanting journey that led us unfettered beyond the commonplace. We laughed together while driving past suburban homes in the evening, each patterned after the other, and saw reflected in their windows immobile people gathered about the glaring orb of their television sets. Outside we ran with the mysteries of the night, questing for adventure under the stars and following the primal lure of the changing phases of the moon. Our lives, patterned by wind and tide, danced in sync with the rhythms of nature. With the revolution of the planet as our alarm clock, we usually awoke before the sunrise to watch the morning light an-

nounce the beginning of each day. Every dinner came wrapped
in a scenic sunset and with the night comes the intriguing question of whether to camp in the mountains or at the beach; to
sleep to the rippling sound of a babbling brook or the rhythmic
crash of pounding ocean waves.

The Fourth of July found us camped in Toualuome Meadows in
the upper Yosemite valley. There were still small patches of snow
on the ground where the shadows dwelt most of the day. The
campground had few facilities, just cold running water and portable
chemical toilets. Most of the other campers were shivering in their
tents or trying to huddle close to smoking campfires. In *Revelstoke*,
Susan and I were in the lap of nomadic luxury.

On July 7, after a long day hiking among the giant redwood
trees, we decided to bathe in a fast-flowing mountain stream just for
the sheer fun and adventure of it. The water was ice cold snow
run-off. We found a secluded spot where there was a bend in the
stream and quickly stripped down to our swimsuits. Susan yelped
when she placed her foot into the frigid water, then laughing gaily,
went splashing through the shallows. I waded out to join her, wondering how many women would brave icy waters just because it was
fun.

Susan was standing in mid-stream where the running water was
the coldest. She was splashing the icy water onto her arms and shoulders and squealing in delight. My heart began to hammer against
my chest as I considered the words I was about to speak. I unconsciously moved closer to her, then said her name, which sounded
like music to me, "Susan." She stopped washing her legs to look at
me. Shivers ran up and down her body. I thought she sensed what
was coming because she suddenly stood very straight and still as she
gazed into my eyes with a questioning look. I was not sure if it was
the icy chill of the water or her stunning beauty that took my breath
away. I knew that the scene which lay before me—this incredible
woman poised in the mountain stream and surrounded by tall
redwood pines—would haunt my dreams until the day I die. I called
the sleek wood nymph's name again, the tremble of my voice left
visible wisps of vapor in the still cold air, "Susan . . . will you marry
me?"

For a moment all was still. It was very quiet except for the gurgle
of the water flowing over the rocks and the chirping of a bird in a
nearby tree.

Susan smiled, her face radiant in the late afternoon light. "Oh,
yes, Steve," she said—her voice like a song, "I will."

I took her into my arms; she shivered in the cold. Staring into
her liquid brown eyes, I promised her that I would never let her go.

I meant that promise with all of my heart and soul, not knowing that we had less than a week before we would be separated forever.

Susan wanted to get married right away by a justice of the peace. Yet for some foolish reason, I wanted the blessing of her parents. They had never approved of my being almost twelve years her senior. Susan was scheduled to return to Hawaii in seven days. She had one of those inexpensive airline tickets where we couldn't alter the schedule.

Our last seven days together seemed to fly by. Then, while driving Susan to the airport, I suddenly became very nervous, but didn't voice my thoughts—not even to myself. I couldn't fill my eyes enough with her. She waited until the very last minute before turning away to board the plane. I watched her walking backward down the ramp. With a wave, she disappeared around the corner. I knew that I would never see Susan again.

In Hawaii, her parents argued against our marriage. Friends counseled that she should give it more thought. By not being together, we drifted apart. I should have gone to Hawaii, yet I had reservations of my own. Marriage was such a scary proposition as I sought to begin my life from scratch. Then she wrote that she was seeing someone else.

Six months passed, then I received a letter. Before even opening it, I knew something was wrong. Through a mist of tears, I read that Susan was married the week before to one of my Northshore surfer friends.

In the booth, my depression deepens. When the movie ends, I wait for the Mexican inmates to shuffle out. I dim the lights and sit alone in the dark with my depression in close attendance.

CHAPTER 20

Terminal Island has the reputation of being the best prison in the federal correctional system. It is often referred to as "Club Fed." Lying on my bunk watching a crescent moon descend over the lights in the harbor, I realize that I don't have it too bad for an inmate. I have made a few good friends, and because of my job in the recreation department, I have plenty of time each day for exercising, reading, and just plain thinking. I shudder to consider what kind of life I could be living in a different prison. Places like El Reo and Texarkana had horrible reputations for violence, over-crowding, and harsh living conditions. When inmates are packed too tightly into already overcrowded cells, the violence goes up astronomically.

Pulling the warm covers up a bit, I snuggle deeper into my comfortable bed. I don't even want to imagine what it would be like to move back into a jail cell again. As I reach to turn off the light, I briefly glance about the small room and smile in quiet satisfaction. The pictures of mountain and ocean scenes I cut from magazines and taped to the walls lend a peaceful ambiance to the room. The ivy plants are thriving in their colorful ceramic pots. Their questing vines are beginning to wind around a bookcase I made in the hobby shop.

On the window sill, a half-dozen roses stand in an empty jelly jar now half-filled with water. I inhale deeply the rich fragrance of the cut flowers along with the subtler woodsy scent of the Eucalyptus pods stashed in the dresser drawers. I smile in quiet contentment then flip off the light switch, casting the room in darkness. After saying a quiet prayer, I settle myself for sleep without the slightest hint that drastic change lurks but hours away.

At five in the morning, the door flies open with a loud crack as it slams into the opposite wall. A guard flashes the bright beam of his flashlight into my eyes then yells, "Arrington, get out of bed and pack up your stuff. You're out of here, buddy."

I sit up, my mind still groggy with sleep. "What's going on?" I ask rubbing my eyes against the bright beam of glaring light.

"You're moving," snaps the guard.

"Moving . . . where?" I ask.

"Boron Prison Camp," he answers tossing an empty cardboard box at my bunk, "you've got twenty minutes to pack up."

I look at the small box. "Hey, all my stuff isn't going to fit into this box."

"Tough, it's all you get," shrugs the guard. "Who do you think you are anyway, Howard Hughes?"

In an instant, my world has been turned upside down. I scurry about the room jamming my most important possessions into the box. I quickly pull a few of my favorite pictures off the wall then carefully pad a ceramic coffee cup and a flower pot that I made in the hobby shop with clothes. The journal from Michelle goes on top, along with the little radio. The rest of my things will be grabbed by inmates who will scavenge the room as soon as I am gone.

Tucking the box under one arm, I hesitate at the door to survey the small room one last time then quietly close the door and hurry toward the control office.

In the morning darkness, I pass rapidly through the north yard. While waiting for the hack to open the door to the control building, I pause to look at J-3. The lights are on in the television room. I can see the orderlies preparing the room for breakfast. A flood of cellblock memories washes through my mind. For a moment I wonder about the little patch of grass. Surely no other inmate is taking the time to water it. Then the control door opens. I leave the north yard and all of its memories behind me.

Inside the control office my cardboard box is taken away. It will go to the mailroom for forwarding. With just the clothes on my back and a twist of dental floss in my pocket (floss is hard to get inside), I'm locked into the same holding cell where they put me when I arrived eighteen months ago. I feel very alone and a bit depressed to be leaving so abruptly, without even the time to say good-bye to my few friends.

The guards call us out one at a time to check our names off the transfer list and to chain us in groups of three. The hacks are angry because one of the inmates scheduled for transfer is late. A moment later Ralph is pushed through the door clutching a small box, which is immediately taken away from him. While the guards curse and prod us into line, Ralph and I grin at each other. The transfer to Camp Boron already seems a lot less depressing with Ralph chained at my side.

On the freeway north, I'm all but pasted to the window of the marshal's van staring at the wonderful sights of freedom. The route we take passes within a hundred yards of my mother's house on the same freeway that I had driven with Sam when we brought that load of cocaine into California. I think about all that has happened since that fateful day . . . was it only eighteen months ago? It seems like *deja vu* to once again be leaving the ocean that I love for the dry heat of the Mojave Desert. I'm a water-oriented person, which is why I never thought I'd ever willingly move to the Mojave Desert—but that was before Morgan barged back into my life.

I think back to that time in my life, of the terrible sadness that filled me as I fought against the reality of losing Susan. After dropping her off at the airport I drove down to San Diego where I enrolled at the state university as a photojournalism major. I got a job at La Jolla Surf Systems selling surfboards for not much more than minimum wage. One of the side benefits of the job was that it gave me a place to park *Revelstoke*. The truck was beginning to get old and the numerous repairs that it needed rapidly began to eat up my meager savings account. Times were beginning to get tough. I could no longer afford to drive the truck to school, so I began taking the bus instead. Despite being broke, I always seemed to have enough money to buy a small bag of marijuana.

The fall waxed to winter. I spent most of my nights alone, locked inside *Revelstoke*. I still desperately hurt over losing Susan and Puu. Then, in the spring, my father passed away after a long, wasting illness. Losing my father was a heavy blow. After returning from his mountain funeral, it became difficult to focus on my studies. My bank account measured in just a two digit figure. I didn't think my life could get much worse, and that's when Morgan called.

I had met Morgan Hetrick in 1975 when his secretary, who was in my scuba class, told me her employer wanted private lessons. Morgan was an aspiring multi-millionaire who was making a bundle of money designing inventions for the aviation industry. He had an energetic company that re-manufactured French military training aircraft into small commercial jets. He called them the Morgan Paris II, and they sold for a cool $300,000 each. Though I was still in the navy, I found the time to work for Morgan on the side. I helped him run his cabin cruiser, which we often took out to the California Channel Islands to scuba dive. We had a lot of good times together. Back then, I admired Morgan Hetrick. I looked up to and respected him. I remember wishing that I had been as close to my father as I was to Morgan.

As such, when Morgan called, I was surprised and quite pleased to hear his voice. My surprise increased when he said he wanted me to meet him at the airport. An hour later, while driving to San Diego's North County airport, I wondered what was so important that he was willing to fly down to meet with me in person?

Morgan was sitting at a table in the airport restaurant when I walked in. He stood and smiled warmly in open pleasure. Morgan looked like the confident millionaire that he was.

"Steve, it's good to see you again," he said jovially, placing a reassuring hand on my shoulder. The physical contact felt good—like a father greeting his son. After we sat down he got right to the point. "I need your help." I leaned forward, anxious to please, wondering what help my rich friend needed.

He waited while the waitress brought us both a grilled cheese sandwich and a cup of coffee, then continued. "I've been real busy these last five years. I now have nine domestic corporations and two offshore businesses to run and not enough time in the day to enjoy the fruits of my success." Morgan leaned forward anxiously. "Steve, I need someone to help me run things, and I find that my sons are just not up to it."

He paused, almost as if he was weighing the value of the words he was about to utter then continued with a sense of drama surrounding his words. "I want you to know that I've thought long and hard on what I'm going to say next. I want you to be my right-hand man. I'll teach you my business and in five years I will turn it all over for you to manage. I'll start you off at fifty thousand dollars a year, but understand," he leaned farther across the table, his face only inches from my own, "I intend to make you a multi-millionaire."

His offer came so fast that for a moment I was too shocked to answer. Melted cheese dripped in a long, yellow string from the sandwich held forgotten in my hands. Into the stunned silence, Morgan asked eagerly, "Well, what do you say?"

"Are you kidding?" I exclaimed. "Morgan, it's like you just answered my prayers."

"My pleasure," smiled Morgan, spreading his hands expansively. "It's going to be good to have you back. I've missed our easy friendship."

Having bitten into the sandwich, I nodded enthusiastically. As if wanting to celebrate the moment, I poured a thick dollop of catsup onto my plate then dunked the sandwich into it.

"Hey, are you still doing any flying?" he asked.

"No," I replied, wiping catsup from the corners of my lip with a paper napkin, "I can't afford it." I had earned my pilot's license just after meeting Morgan in 1975.

Morgan shrugged my answer off, "Well, you're in the aviation business now, my friend, and you're going to be needing a commercial license with a multi-engine and instrument rating. I know just the school. It's in Louisiana." Morgan's eyes took on a sudden glitter behind his thick glasses. "That's after we set you up with your own plane."

"My own plane?" I echoed, inhaling some of the spicy tomato sauce, which set me to choking.

Morgan smiled and rubbed his hands together. "Hey, Steve, if you thought I was rich before . . . well, wait until you see me now."

Though hungry before, my sandwich now lay forgotten in a puddle of catsup as Morgan enthusiastically described the life we would be living in the Mojave Desert.

An hour later, I walked with Morgan out to his airplane. It was a sleek, baby blue Mooney 231. Opening the cockpit door, he turned and we shook hands. "Get up to Mojave as soon as you can. Life is about to get real busy, my boy."

Standing at the flight line, I felt the warmth of his words wrapping around me while watching him take-off. The way he said "my boy" seemed so fatherly. I stood gazing after his plane until it disappeared into the distant clouds, then turned to look about me. The staggered rows of shiny airplanes took on a whole new meaning. I was about to become a commercial pilot. It was such a new and amazing thought. I stared into the limitless sky and thought about the adventures that waited beyond the blue horizon.

Two weeks later, I left San Diego heading for Morgan Aviation with only twenty dollars in my pocket and half a tank of gas in *Revelstoke*. When I passed a sign that said, "Welcome to the Mojave Desert," I tossed my bag of marijuana out the window. I knew that this was my chance to begin a whole new life, and I darn sure wasn't going to screw it up.

Sitting in the marshal's van, I see that same sign again. I shake my head and think how naive I had been. I can't help chuckling as I realize what a great job Morgan had done of setting me up.

Turning off highway 395 onto a narrow side road, I see another sign. This one reads: RESTRICTED ACCESS, BORON PRISON CAMP, NO ENTRY EXCEPT ON OFFICIAL BUSINESS. Mentally, I imagine Morgan patting me on the shoulder and saying, "Well, Steve, welcome to your new life."

Boron Prison Camp sprawls on the side of a hill just a half-mile off Highway 395 in the middle of a broad desert valley. It had been built by the air force in the late forties as a small radar station. The old wooden buildings have since been converted into inmate dormitories. Each of the rooms houses four inmates, that is, except for the honor dorm, which has spacious two man rooms. Yet as a "new fish," I know there is no chance of my winding up over there. I arrive with no possessions and knowing no one but Ralph. Again I must start from the bottom, find a niche, and begin to fit in.

Ralph, apparently sensitive to the stress reflected in my face, says, "Don't worry, Steve, you are so lucky that you will probably get the best job and the best room in the whole place." A week later, both of us are surprised at how quickly he is proven right.

After the check-in process, we walk the hill for the first time, following a paved road that leads up to the top. A thousand feet above the desert floor we stand side by side, astounded at the uninterrupted view. We are used to seeing just glimpses of the real world through wire and bars. Yet here we can see at least thirty miles in every direction. It's early April, and a thin coat of snow covers most of the desert terrain. We stay on the hill to watch the sun set beyond a jagged mountain range. Slowly, the pale white desert landscape bleeds to pink then brilliant red. Long walking shadows of cacti and Joshua trees leaning away from the descending sun march in unison across the broad desert valley. Then the vast landscape quickly fades as darkness settles upon the land.

Above the horizon, the last glimmer of red light dims like a receding tide; then a rolling wave of darkness spreads across the sky. A vast array of stars emerge from the heavens, twinkling brightly in the clear desert air. Staring at the incredible beauty of the desert night sky, I no longer feel sorry about leaving the confines of Terminal Island and my fixed routine.

Over the next couple of days, we discover that the camp is alive with wild creatures. Small chipmunks and rabbits scurry about the dorms, while in the air and on the ground there are large crows, desert quail, owls, starlings, and roadrunners. An over-sized badger lives under the honor dorm. At night it sometimes wanders about the dark halls, until some unlucky fellow heading bleary-eyed for the john surprises the thirty-pound-plus rodent.

Our first morning there we discover one of the wonders of Boron. Edwards Air Force Base is only twenty miles away. Ralph and I hear a double sonic boom while we're jogging. Then, the space shuttle *Challenger* passes directly overhead on its way to touch down at Edwards. Throughout the rest of the day, fighter jets make their own sonic booms while they practice low-level flying and engage in supersonic dogfights. In the late afternoon a B-1 bomber flies over the camp. As the day waxes toward dusk, Ralph and I climb the Boron Hill to watch another sunset. Staring at the descending red orb, we abruptly feel the ground begin to vibrate, then, out of the west, a giant B-52 Flying Fortress flashes across the desert floor with its eight jet engines screaming at full throttle. It seems odd to have such exciting sights as a part of our daily life.

We spend the next week getting processed. While awaiting permanent job assignments, we're assigned to the rock patrol. It's one of those nonsense jobs designed to keep inmates from being too idle. Everyday we rake the ground into smooth patterns around the dormitories. Then in the afternoon, the wind blows forcefully, disrupting the intricate designs—great job satisfaction.

Our second week there, as per Ralph's prediction, I score the best job in the campfire crew. Boron has an agreement with the San Bernardino County Fire Department to provide a fire crew (Engine Company #52) for emergency response within a fifty-mile radius of the camp. Because of my military experience in damage control, first aid, fire fighting, and bomb disposal, I'm perfectly qualified for the job. Being an inmate fireman also means moving to dormitory number seven, the honor dorm.

When Ralph and I see the news on the assignment sheet, all he can do is mumble and shake his head. He's been assigned to the plumbing shop. Ralph eyes the assignment sheet carefully to ensure that there isn't some mistake, then grumbles, "So, you get to go offbase with the fire crew and see girls on the highway while I'm stuck working on the camp toilets chasing turd bombs."

"Turd bombs?" I ask.

"Yeah," Ralph says sadly, "I heard about them last night. It seems there's some demented joker here who entertains himself by jamming rolls of toilet paper into the bowl before relieving himself; then after flushing the toilet repeatedly, causing a foul mess to spread over the floor, he gleefully calls the plumbing shop to complain about the faulty pipes."

Ralph isn't pleased with his bunk assignment either. He is rooming with two druggies and an alcoholic who has a severe flatulence problem. The alcoholic's bunk is directly above Ralph's, who claims he can see visible vapor trails descending upon him throughout most of the night.

Ralph and I go over to check out the honor dormitory, which used to be the officers' quarters back when Camp Boron was still an air force base. The two-man rooms are almost spacious by inmate standards, and, astonishingly, they have a private bathroom—talk about inmate luxury! A private bath is all but unheard of in the prison system. Behind the dorm there is a fenced patio with a very artistic rock garden.

Boron is into rocks in a big way. The camp is littered with waist-high rock walls. Whenever a guard can't think of an imaginative work assignment, he simply puts the inmates to work stacking stones. One particularly inept guard earned the nick name "Box of Rocks," referring to his general lack of functional brain matter.

I join the fire crew on a Thursday afternoon. Walking into the shade of the garage, I pause to stare at the fire truck. It is a big red Ford with its paint burnished to a mirrored finish. The numerous chrome and brass fittings gleam in the shaded light. I run a hand along the wood-handled axes and telescoping ladders that are mounted on each side of the truck. The engineer's panel is a maze of chrome switches, brass handles, and glass-covered gauges. My excitement is hard to contain as I stand there visualizing what it is going to be like to ride on the back of a fire truck.

I spend the rest of the day with the chief engineer getting acquainted with all the equipment. Just before we break for dinner, I pause to look at the fire fighting turnouts (protective clothes) hanging from the wall.

"Don't worry," says the chief engineer looking at the coveralls, jackets, boots and helmets, "we'll issue you your turnouts tomorrow. We don't really get that many calls and it'll probably be just another quiet evening in boring Boron."

Dinner that night is baked macaroni with fake industrial strength cheese made from a yellow powder that comes in twenty-five pound bags. The drink is green Kool-aid—the dessert, red jello. Though the meal lacks nutrition, I think it certainly is colorful. I'm halfway through the macaroni and cheese when Ralph's eyes widen in horror. He is staring at his plate. "What's wrong?" I ask anxiously.

"Worms, there're dead worms in the macaroni!"

"Naa," I shake my head, knowing he is funning me.

"I'm not kidding," says Ralph as he scrapes something off his plate with his fork then offers it up for me to see. I peer at the white, cylindrical shape in horror, then look intently down at my own plate. There is only a scrap of macaroni, cheese, and worms left.

"Arrgh!" I drain my green Kool-aid.

Ralph unhappily pushes his plate away as he says, "Well, so much for eating dinner tonight."

"Missing dinner isn't anywhere as bad as having had dinner," I answer weakly.

Later that night I'm enjoying moving into the honor dorm. Walking through the television room, I note that the dormitory houses a better class of inmate, mostly older, kick-back types. The evenings will be mellower here without the noise and ruckus of the other dorms. In Ralph's dormitory, the favorite television programming revolves around cartoons and karate movies. There's nothing like a good Kung Fu flick to get the boneheads excited. They'll be yelling loud "Ki's" and karate chopping everything in sight for half the night.

I'm just settling back in my new room with a good book when unexpectedly the fire siren wails. I leap from the bunk and promptly jam my foot through the crotch of my trousers ripping the seams out. Throwing the torn trousers onto the floor, I pull on my shoes and sprint for the fire house in my Skivvies.

The chief engineer, who is rolling out the fire truck, does a double-take when he sees me running up in my shorts. I quickly grab a set of turnouts off the wall, half throwing them on; then, I leap onto the back of the truck. The engineer floors the gas peddle, forcing me to hold on tightly as the big truck, spraying gravel from its big, black, spinning tires, leaps forward. The guard at the gate raises the barrier just seconds before we speed through.

I have anticipated wild joy and excitement as we race down the highway. Instead, I'm having some rather embarrassing problems. My pants are about four sizes too big and, to make matters worse, the suspenders are broken. The crotch is hanging somewhere down around my knees. The helmet is way too large and threatening to blow off. I have to use one hand to hold onto the truck and the other to keep my helmet on, which means that holding up my trousers is a lost cause; they're gathered somewhere down around my ankles. The cold wind is blowing through my white boxer shorts causing them to flap vigorously in the night air like a white flag of surrender.

Henry, an ex-CIA agent turned politician who developed a taste for bribes is riding next to me belly-laughing. A car pulls in behind us and flicks on its high beams. The driver leans on the horn, and faintly I can hear a girl hooting.

Six miles down the road the wild ride comes to a thankful end. A Volkswagon beetle stands just off the road completely engulfed in flames. The woman driver has managed to get out safely and is now frantically watching her car burn. We slide to a stop in the soft gravel, raising a cloud of dust, then quickly unravel the attack hoses. Henry runs to one side of the burning car, while I run to the other just in time to get knocked down by a solid blast of water from Henry's hose. My firehose flies from my hands and lands on the wet ground where it whips about madly like an enraged snake. I pounce on it then spend a few seconds trying to get the spewing hose back under control. In the process the woman takes a blast of water right in the face. It knocks her down and momentarily plays havoc with her skirt. I regain control of the hose. Then, with my pants bagged around my ankles like a soggy diaper, I crawl awkwardly toward the burning car—spewing water on the fire. We soon smother the aggressive flames, but the car is totaled.

On the way back to the camp Henry leans over and quips, "Hey, Arrington, you sure looked funny with that big hose whipping madly about. The water pressure really knocked that lady down. Can you imagine the story she is going to tell to her friends?"

The next day, Saturday, I went to my favorite place in the camp, the swimming pool. The government doesn't normally provide inmates with such luxury. We had a swimming pool only because it had been built while Boron was still an air force base. In any case, I wasn't long getting into the small pool. It had been too long, over eighteen months, since I had been immersed in water. The bottom of the pool felt safe for me. I enjoyed sitting underwater with a rock in my lap to hold me down while I practiced holding my breath for several minutes at a time. It was one of only two places in prison where I could really relax my guard. The other place was the inmate church.

The Chapel on the Hill is a peaceful place. It's a small building standing at a solitary site near the top of Boron Hill. A stone wall raised by inmates during their spare time protects the church from the seasonal sand storms. Ralph and I usually begin our trek up the hill while most of the inmates are watching the girls dance on Soul Train.

We enjoy arriving at the church early because we like to sit against the wall and feed bread crumbs to the wild animals while staring out at the vast desert. We watch cars driving on the distant highway and talk. Mostly our conversations are about what we hope to do when we get out. Our Christian faith gives us the confidence that we will be able to make it on the outside. Surviving the prison experience mentally intact is all but an impossibility.

Both of us are changed, not only from the effects of incarceration, but from the implication that we are misfits in a society that deems us better locked away. Ralph and I are in need of whatever help we can get. I am still confident that I am a good person, but questions keep creeping into my mind that need sustaining answers. Fortunately, we have found hope for the future through Christian fellowship.

Hope is a very big word with inmates. Not just the hopeful wish to be free, but a true wondering question about our future lives. Will we be easily accepted back into society? How are our friends, loved ones, and future acquaintances going to react to us? Prison is only part of the punishment. Later, we will have to face social indictment on a daily basis. I hate to imagine having to tell a potential employer or, even worse, a girl's parents that I am an ex-felon.

Yet, all these questions have indeed found a simple answer in the fellowship of worship. In church, we are slowly healing our personal scars of crime and guilt. The purging process is going to take a long time, but at least there is now something real to cling to: "And hope does not disappoint."

CHAPTER 21

Outside my dormitory window, I watch a winter sand storm raging. The winter winds can blow intensely cold in the high desert of the Mojave. It is the frigid and abrasive fury of the seasonal sandstorms that add such dimension to the weather. Across the compound I see an inmate struggling to open a dormitory door held shut by the gusting wind, which momentarily shifts. The door swings swiftly open with a loud crack, casting the inmate down the steps where he falls heavily onto the ground. It takes him a few moments to rise unsteadily to his feet; then leaning into the blowing sand, he sets off for the chow hall with his head down, which is probably why he doesn't see the hurling trash can that takes him out at chest level several seconds later.

Judging by the fury of the storm, I decide it just isn't worth going to chow on a day like this, particularly when the Sunday brunch special is creamed beef on white toast, grits, stewed prunes, and yellow Kool-aid; actually, I might have enjoyed the stewed prunes.

Inside the room it is desperately cold as I lie shivering upon my bunk all but cocooned in two threadbare blankets. A thin, gray cloud of dust particles hangs suspended in the room, while more dust, with its baggage of frigid air, continues to seep in through the weathered frame of the window sill. From one corner of the window, a tiny cascade of sand leaks in a steady stream to the floor, where it's busily building itself into a small mound. The falling grains remind me of the slow relentless passage of prison time. I want to flee back into the Vietnam paperback I've been reading, but my cold and stiff fingers are currently jammed knuckle deep into the reluctant warmth of my armpits.

I figure nothing could lure me out of the room on a day like this—then, over the mournful howl of the wind, I hear the wail of the fire siren and bolt from the room.

Sprinting into the fury of the windstorm, I see the chief engineer driving the fire truck out of the huge, double doors of the fire house. The truck's head lamps, dimmed yellow by blowing sand, resemble two enormous, angry eyes. For an instant the long red truck, with the side aluminum ladders resembling wings, looks like a raging dragon furiously exiting its lair.

Rapidly donning yellow turnouts, I leap onto the back of the carriage. We are off in an instant with the rear of the vehicle fishtailing wildly into a high speed turn. Our mechanical beast flies into the storm, the roar of its siren a primal scream that clears lesser vehicles from its path.

Clinging to the back of the truck, I revel in the excitement of the moment as the sand-laden wind whips past my face at eighty miles an hour. The wild ride after weeks of institutional boredom rivals the thrill of a prison escape. My life inside prison walls has been slow and much too dreary; the prison sentence seems overly long. My spirit yearns for adventure, passion, and excitement.

Rounding an abrupt turn ten miles down the road, we arrive at the site of a nasty wreck. A Datsun pickup truck lies smashed on the side of the road after a high-speed, head-on collision with a Dodge van. The van has a severely crumpled front end. The driver, though badly injured, will recover. It's an entirely different situation in the Datsun—inside the little red truck the young driver is dying.

While the rest of the crew frantically tries to pry and cut away the damaged driver's door, I stand at the front of the truck with a charged water hose in case of fire. The shattered windshield has been thrown from the smashed vehicle, apparently part of the force was supplied by the impact of the driver's head because broken shards of glass are embedded in the young man's face. From five feet away, I look into the youth's dazed and unfocused eyes. One of the inmate firemen yells that the driver's pulse is weak and getting thready. I know without a doubt that we are losing him. The gaping wounds on his face hardly bleed, a sure sign that his vital functions are rapidly failing. As the door is frantically torn from the frame and even as anxious hands reach for the youth, I watch the light of life fade from his drooping eyes. The head slowly lowers as the now lifeless body slumps to one side.

Despite attempts at CPR, he is lost. We gently lay him on the desert ground next to a mesquite bush; his blood leaves weeping streaks of red upon the coarse brown sand. One of the firemen carefully closes the youth's staring eyes then covers him with a brown rescue blanket. We are all profoundly moved by the moment. It is a very sober and subdued crew that rides back to the camp on that lonely desert highway.

That night, after the winds have subsided, the stars stand out clearly in the dark sky. Staring into the black void of the heavens, I listen to two Mexican inmates playing guitars while singing outside on the dormitory steps. Their melancholy songs lead me down paths of love and tragedy. I think about the vibrance of life and how quickly it can be extinguished.

In my hand I hold a ripe peach. It is my first peach in over two years. I purchased it several days ago at the camp store and have been patiently waiting for it to ripen. Turning the peach in my hand, I inhale its fragrance and look at the soft, subtle colors of the fuzz-covered skin. I realize how perfect a creation a peach is while sinking my teeth into its succulent flesh. On this sorrowful day it feels good to be alive . . . the peach's flesh tastes uncommonly delicious.

I think that life is expressed well in a peach. When it is ripe, we harvest the fruit and eat of the flesh. A peach fulfills its purpose by being eaten. The seed is hopefully spit upon the ground, and maybe from it a tree will grow. I wonder if it is the same with man? Death is always stalking us, hovering closely even as we frantically pursue our short lives. Through our individual experiences of love and tragedy, we grow. Then one day we surely wither and die, unless, like the young man, our lives are cut short. I wonder if, when the Lord harvests our souls, he doesn't pause to savor the fruits of our brief, yet intense lives.

Thoughts of death make me think about life. I know that I want to feel good about myself; I want to know happiness in my life. Two simple goals—by pursuing one the other is found. It is as simple as that. By dedicating myself to good I will know happiness. Likewise, the opposite is true. To court evil is to invite bitter sadness into your life. The criminal waltz I danced with Morgan was a downward spiraling vortex that was pulling me into corruption—being arrested had set me free again. Sitting under the desert night sky, I think what a startling discovery it is to realize that going to prison is my first step toward freedom.

Another month idly passes as the cold desert winds of winter give way to the dry Santa Ana winds of spring and summer.

Standing in the shade of the fire house, the firemen form an awkward line. It is a moment of excitement and sadness combined. The chief engineer, having completed his sentence, is departing to an uncertain future out in the real world. This man, who doesn't fear to run into a burning building, is horribly afraid of beginning life anew on the outside. Here he has friends and an established routine. His life is ordered with rules, regulations, and schedules. We who are to stay envy his release yet understand his fears, for we secretly harbor the same reservations. We truly understand this inmate's fear of freedom. Prison scars run deep. Institutional conditioning is a fearsome mental state.

In the fire house, the chief engineer shakes each of our hands and smiles sadly. He pauses to run his hand over the bonnet of the fire truck then walks alone down the road to the control building. Without him, our team seems unusually smaller. We have lost our leader and a friend.

One of the older firemen turns to the others, "Are we agreed?" he inquires. The rest of the men nod, but I have no idea what is going on as I look from face to face. The fireman who had spoken walks over to the fire fighting turnouts and removes the chief engineer's helmet. Then he walks to where my turnouts are hanging and removes my helmet from the hook. Then he hangs the chief engineer's helmet in its place.

While I stare in awe at the helmet, the rest of the firemen silently walk out of the fire house toward the chow hall. Just before they are beyond hearing distance one of them quips, "You know, that's the first time I've ever seen Arrington at a loss for words."

Standing alone in the shaded fire house, I turn to stare at the big truck. The polished red paint glistens wetly in the low light. I step a little closer to the fire truck and peer at my reflection in the bonnet. For a moment, in my mind, I see the departing chief engineer and remember how he lovingly caressed the truck as he walked reluctantly out the door. Suddenly I understand his feelings for this magnificent machine. A machine that is mine.

The fire truck looms inside its stall. I slowly walk around it. The engineer's panel is a maze of precision machining. I touch the shiny brass gauges and finger the chrome levers and knobs. Then, unable to resist the temptation, I climb into the cab and start the engine.

Slowly, I ease the fire truck out of its stall and drive it to the top of the hill. Parking next to the chapel on the hill, I sit in the cab and stare out over the vast desert below. With the radio on, I listen to other fire trucks responding to emergency calls and daydream that they are calling Engine Company 52.

"Hey, what are you doing?" inquires Ralph, who is standing outside the door.

I look at my friend and grin, "I'm the new chief engineer."

"No kidding?" answers Ralph as he climbs up on the running board. In his hand he is carrying a toilet plunger. I eye the plunger, which is dripping a suspicious fluid on the running board. "Any chance of going for a ride?" Ralph asks hopefully.

"Sure, hop in," I answer cheerfully, "but leave that wet plunger outside."

"Why," Ralph asks, "it's only got water on it."

"Yeah, toilet water," I answer.

"No, it's water from the sprinklers."

"You used a plunger on clogged sprinklers?" I'm confused.

"Nah," Ralph grins, "I just find that if I'm carrying around a wet plunger, the guards tend to leave me alone."

Ralph climbs into the cab, plunger in hand. As we are driving slowly down the hill, we are both struck by the same thought. After being at the island for so long, where you walk everywhere, it seems odd to be riding in a vehicle, particularly without the supervision of a guard. With no real destination, we cruise the camp, like a couple of kids out on the town in their father's car.

A week later the siren finally makes its wailing call. I sprint for the fire house. In mere moments I'm dressed in turnouts and am easing the big truck out of the fire house. Stopping on the driveway threshold, I anxiously wait for the other inmate firemen to climb aboard. My heart races as I key the radio microphone, "San Bernardino Command; this is Engine Company 52 standing by."

"Roger 52, respond code three (red light and siren), single car accident involving injuries, Route 395, six miles south of four corners."

I unconsciously revive the engine in eager anticipation.

"Roger command, 52 responding code three." I am so excited that I'm on the verge of drooling.

A buzzer in the cab announces that the last fireman is aboard. Instantly, I floor the accelerator. The spinning back tires leave twin smoking skid marks as the truck leaps out onto the road. I'm already shifting into third gear before the gate guard even has the barrier up. We fly down the road, red lights flashing and siren wailing. The inmates riding on the back clearly hear a loud continuous surfer hoot coming from the front of the cab over the howl of the engine as I peg the rpm. I am ecstatic. In my excitement, my right foot begins to tremble from keeping the gas pedal jammed against the floor board.

Eleven miles down the highway, we come upon a white station wagon with its front end embedded in a sand bank fifty feet from the pavement. A weaving, broken path of torn desert brush tells of a speeding car out of control. It had blown a tire and the elderly gentleman driving it had almost rolled the car. His wife sits beside the car with an injured leg. The rest of the crew quickly renders first aid while I confirm that an ambulance has already been dispatched.

I had just hung up the radio when the loud, thumping sound of rotor blades draws my attention to the sky. A sheriff's helicopter is coming in low over the desert terrain. It settles in a cloud of dust not thirty yards from the fire truck. The pilot leaps out and, leaving the engine running, runs toward the accident. Passing me he shouts over his shoulder, "Watch my chopper."

I grin at him wondering how long it will take for him to discover that he has just left his ride in the care of an inmate.

It doesn't take long. He comes running back for all he is worth, his fat stomach shaking with the exertion of his short sprint across the soft sand. He stops between me and the helicopter, huffing and puffing. He tries to talk but is just too winded.

Finally he exclaims, "I just found out that you guys are an inmate fire crew."

"Really," I grin.

"Hey, it isn't funny," he complains. "If the guys at the station ever found out that I left my helicopter running in the hands of a bunch of inmates, I'd never live it down."

I am prepared to leave it alone, but then he insults me. "Not that any of you turds could operate such a complicated machine."

"Oh, really. Have you heard of the DeLorean case?" I ask.

"Of course, so what?"

"Well, I'm the pilot you may have read about, and if I tried escaping, even unsuccessfully in your copter, it would have made the front page of tomorrow's paper." I didn't see any point in telling him that I have no idea how to fly a helicopter.

Instead I add thoughtfully, "You know, the *Los Angeles Times* is doing a follow up story about how I'm getting on in prison. This is exactly the kind of blunder they'd love to write about. I can see the headlines: 'DeLorean co-defendant chooses not to flee in sheriff's helicopter.'"

The fat sheriff's weathered face begins to pale.

"How do you spell your name anyhow?" I ask, stepping closer to better read his name tag.

He quickly shields the name plate with one pudgy hand, "I guess I shouldn't have been so insulting, huh?"

"Ah," I quip, "I'm just teasing you." Remembering that I'm going to try to live my life truthfully, I even admit that I don't know how to fly a helicopter.

He brightens visibly, "Hey, are you really the pilot from the DeLorean case?"

"Yeah," I shrug.

He runs over to his helicopter and comes back with a ticket book. "Would you mind autographing this?" A few minutes later after he lifts off, I watch the disappearing helicopter and wonder what kind of story he is going to be telling back at the sheriff's station.

Returning to the camp, I realize we have missed lunch. The cooks take the time to whip us up a couple of steaks. I appreciate the kindness of the act and don't let on that I'm a vegetarian as I pass my steak to another fireman. It seems that I never get enough to eat in prison. The meals are strictly rationed. Only so much food is allotted per inmate. No one is allowed to take food from the chow hall. So I've taken to smuggling out small boxes of cereal and fruit in my socks. On occasion I have even wrapped peanut butter in paper napkins and then walk nonchalantly out the door with the oily wad bulging grotesquely at my ankle. I have to be careful because they often search inmates leaving the chow hall. A friend of mine was caught smuggling donuts out the Sunday before last. He had to see the unit manager over the petty offense and forfeited one month of his good time—a tough price to pay for a couple of donuts.

CHAPTER 22

I'm sitting on the cement bottom of the Boron swimming pool with a large rock in my lap while holding my breath. I'm trying for a new personal record. So far I've been able to hold my breath underwater for two minutes and forty-two seconds. I find it best if I distract my mind from thinking about breathing, so instead I'm remembering another swimming pool. This one was much larger than the tiny Boron pool. The pool at the Explosive Ordnance Disposal School in Indianhead, Maryland, was seventy feet long and a whopping twenty-four feet deep. I was standing at the pool's side unhappily wondering if the goosebumps on my arms were brought on by the winter chill that hung frigidly in the air or whether the real culprit was fear.

"What are you looking at?" shouted Chicken McNair, one of the less-friendly instructors.

"The goosebumps on my arm, instructor." I was not pleased to have attracted McNair's attention. His scrutiny was usually followed by physical pain.

"Are you scared, Arrington? Do I make you nervous?" he leered from inches away.

"Yes, instructor, you make me nervous," I nodded vigorously.

"Don't screw up, Arrington," cautioned McNair, "I'm going to be riding your butt down there boy."

Today was to be our final diving test, called pool harassment. McNair was grinning, "I guarantee that at least one fourth of you creeps are not going to pass this little exercise." *Well, so much for the pep talk*, I thought to myself.

"The rules are quite simple," yelled McNair, "all you worms have to do is stay on the bottom of the pool until your tanks run out of air. Anyone who surfaces before their scuba tanks are completely empty will be unconditionally dropped from training." Our twin tanks held 180 cubic feet of air, which meant we could look forward to spending almost two hours underwater while being attacked by Chicken McNair and his enthusiastic cohorts.

"The purpose of pool harassment is to weed out the weak," snarled McNair, then glaring at me he roared, "Arrington, drop and do push-ups until your goosebumps go away." I started to remove my heavy diving tanks.

"Did I say you could take your tanks off?" he angrily inquired, while standing on my flippers.

After twenty push-ups under the added ballast of the ninety pound scuba tanks, I felt my arms begin to go rubbery.

"You wimp," McNair hovered directly over me. "Get your butt into the water, Arrington." I awkwardly began to get to my feet. "Did I say you could stand? Worms don't stand, slime ball; they crawl." I slithered to the side of the pool and thankfully slid into the cool embrace of the water.

I didn't waste any time swimming to the deepest end of the pool where I hovered just above the bottom . . . waiting. I promised myself that I wouldn't let McNair drive me to the surface because I wanted to be a frogman more than anything else in the world. I consciously forced my rushed breathing to settle to a more normal pace. Then I saw McNair swimming toward me with broad strokes of his UDT fins. He was grinning. It was not a pleasant sight.

My breathing accelerated as I saw his large hand reaching out. He grabbed my mask and pulled it vigorously away from my face. When it seemed that the rubber strap must surely break under the strain, McNair let go.

The mask exploded back into my face with its cargo of chlorinated water. I quickly cleared the flooded mask, but then to my great surprise, I saw only empty water before me. Where was McNair? I had my answer a moment later while attempting to take a breath of air off the regulator, which was rapidly filling with water. McNair, having turned off my air valve, was now busy releasing my tank straps. Then he jerked the fins from my feet and, just before flooding my mask again, showed me my regulator, which he had just diligently removed from the tanks. Through the now blurred vision of the flooded mask, and with my nose filling with water, I saw him let the regulator slide from his fingers, letting it drift slowly to the bottom.

I no longer had enough air in my lungs to risk clearing the mask again, so I was forced to reattach the regulator by feel. I was frenzied for air by the time I got the tank valve open again. A cascade of bubbles began to escape from the mouthpiece, which I quickly raised to my lips, and got almost half a breath of air before it was violently ripped away. At first I thought it was McNair screwing with me again, but after clearing my mask I saw that it was another student—his dive gear hanging about him in disarray. I gave the regulator a little tug so the guy would know that I needed it back, but the crumb clamped down on the mouthpiece with his teeth.

By the look of panic in his eyes, I knew he wasn't going to share that regulator with me any time in the near future. I placed a finned foot against his chest and pushed. Successively, the regulator came free with a flush of bubbles, the other student disappeared for the surface with a rapid fluttering of his fins, and, as I placed the hard-earned regulator back into my mouth, McNair shut off my air again.

Over an hour later, there were only a dozen of us left on the bottom of the pool. McNair signaled the end of the exercise. The five students who were driven to the surface would be dropped from training, but I now knew that I would go on to realize my dream of becoming a frogman.

Sitting at the bottom of the Boron prison pool, I release a long exhalation of bubbles and watch them rise in a bobbing stream toward the surface. They cause the surface water to ripple, which distorts the reflective image of two inmates standing at the side of the pool staring down at me. Sadly, I realize that no matter how far I stray with my thoughts, it is always but a few moments before I'm forced to return to the grim reality of prison. Having held my breath for two minutes and thirty-five seconds, I leave my rock on the pool bottom and follow the last of the bubbles to the surface. Once again, I am back in an inmate world.

CHAPTER 23

With fourteen months left to serve, I am about to go on my first furlough—a thirty-six hour pass. At 8 A.M., I'm standing just inside the prison gate anxiously watching the highway. Then, in the distance, I see a white baja bug with two surfboards strapped on top. The speeding Volkswagon wildly passes two cars and a lumbering truck. Instantly recognizing Sam's unique driving technique, my heart leaps in sudden joy. Moments later he whips into the parking lot and pulls into one of the slots reserved for the prison guards. Sam jumps out of the car wearing a red surfer T-shirt, green shorts, and yellow sandals; Sam is into clashing colors.

Inside the control building, I wait impatiently as Sam signs the necessary papers accepting responsibility for my custody. I feel like a puppy in a pet store anxiously watching his new owner arrange for its purchase. The papers signed, I literally dance out the door behind Sam and into the parking lot, which is on the freedom side of the control building.

At the Volkswagon, I stop to run my hand over my favorite surfboard then leap happily inside. Sam's smile is radiant as he asks, "Ready to go surfing?"

The implications of that simple question boggle my mind. *Ready to go surfing?* I look at my young friend and think how he cannot imagine the importance of those few words to my battered soul. I know these few precious hours on the outside are going to pass quickly. *So, yes, let us go surfing,* I say to myself, *let there be dolphins to share the waves with us and pretty girls lying on the beach. But most of all, my friend, let us be as we were before—before the crime, the drugs, and the incarceration. Let us go back in time to when we were just two friends riding the waves and enjoying the simplicity of life.* Then, out loud in sudden inspiration, I shout, "To the beach!"

The tires squeal as Sam floors the accelerator. The baja bug leaps out of the parking lot, narrowly missing a sign warning of the strict five mph speed limit. For the barest moment I cringe, thinking that the guards will be upset when I return because of Sam's flagrant disregard for their rules. Then, Boron Prison Camp fades in the dust behind us. I glance at Sam, who as a free soul is totally unintimidated by the prison keepers who rule almost every aspect of my daily life. I wonder whether he has any idea just how far apart we have grown.

Before us the open road beckons, allowing me to shed the

worrisome burden of an inmate mentality like a wet overcoat while standing before the roaring fire of freedom. There are no guards or other inmates to contend with. For the first time in over two years I don't have to watch my back or what I do or say. Sam and I chatter joyously while he continues his assault upon the highway and against other cars, passing everyone in our mad dash toward the ocean. Freedom has a wonderful taste and feel to it. It rushes through my open window with the wind as I fill myself with the flavor of it.

Several hours later, nearing the beach, I smell the scent of the ocean in the air. I revel in seeing the common place people just being people, unhindered. The streets are alive with bright colors. My senses soak up the rainbow stimuli of real life after enduring the boring, drab gray of prison routine for so darn long. Sam wants to stop for a burger, but I hunger for the sea. Soon we pull into the beach parking lot. I am pleased beyond comprehension to see long lines of overhead waves rolling in, crashing against the pier, and throwing frothy white water onto the beach. We quickly wax up our surfboards and run down to the water.

I outpaddle Sam to the line up and sit gleefully splashing water while waiting for him. The young kids around us think I'm stone nuts. Together Sam and I rip and slash the waves for hours. Between sets I bounce on my board occasionally spitting columns of water at Sam. When a pod of dolphins swims past, I all but lose control. Abandoning my board, I swim underwater mimicking their undulating swimming style. Without a mask I can only see the dim shadows of their streamline bodies shooting past me, but my ears clearly hear the high-pitched squeaks and chatters of these happy, intelligent creatures.

We surf until our arms hang wearily at our sides. I am insane with happiness. Finally we take a last wave together hooting and hollering all the way to the beach.

Lying on the hot sand, we bask under the summer sun, which soon warms our chilled bodies. There are girls everywhere. Concealed behind my sun glasses, I watch everyone and everything. I see people flying kites, throwing frisbees, jogging on the beach, riding bicycles on the boardwalk, fishing from the pier, waxing up surfboards, and swimming in the surf zone . . . and I'm in the center of it all. Like a sponge I soak up the happiness and the vitality, storing up the memories of this glorious day to fend off the dreariness that awaits me tomorrow inside prison's stone walls.

All too soon it is time to leave the beach for my mother's house. Riding in the Volkswagon, I merrily stick my sand-covered feet out the window while plucking pieces of surfboard wax from my chest hairs.

Sam honks his horn twice as we drive up my mother's driveway.

The front door swings open, and I see my mother running toward me. Before I'm fully out of the car she is in my arms asking continuous questions most of which relate directly to whether I am hungry or not. Soon she is busy in the kitchen making my favorite dishes. She is pleased to have me home, even if only for a little while. At least it implies that I will soon be leaving prison for good.

At 8 P.M., a few of my friends arrive. It isn't long before we decide to go out dancing. Just as we're about to leave, a yellow Porsche screeches to a stop in front of the house. A beautiful blonde with thick, wavy hair and wearing a red dress steps out. It is Jessica, the girl who wrote that she wouldn't be sending anymore letters because of her father's disapproval. She throws herself into my arms, which are quite pleased to be suddenly holding such an exciting woman.

Snuggling a bit closer she whispers into my ear, her breathy words sending a tremor up my spine. "I was so afraid I might miss you," she says, "my father didn't want me to come but at the last minute I knew I had to."

"Your timing is perfect," I grin, "we're going dancing."

"Good, then I claim the first dance." She takes my hand and pulling me toward her car, says, "want to drive my Porsche?"

It turns out that all of my dances belong to Jessica. When the band plays a slow song, she slides into my arms and holds me close. My hand resting on the silken swell of her hip begins to tremble. Jessica pulls away to look at me. I have been alone so long, I'm sure that the wounds I carry are betrayed in my eyes. She stares, then covers my trembling hand with hers. She leans closer again and whispers softly into my ear, "It's O.K., Steve." Her breath against my neck is as soft as a bird's flutter.

Back at the house, Sam and a couple of other friends who've also driven long distances camp out in the front room. Unwilling to sleep through any part of my temporary freedom, I stand in the backyard and stare at the stars with Jessica beside me.

After a few moments of silence, she asks, "What is it really like inside?"

"Mostly it is about being alone," I answer. "It is also a deep wondering about yourself as a person. And sometimes it is about terror." I turn to face her. "You cannot imagine the hate and the deviant criminal activities that stalk prison halls."

"How can you exist in that horrible place?" There is concern in her voice.

"I just do it. It's not like I have a choice." I pause to stare at the stars for a moment. "You know, Jessica, it's my own fault that I am there. Realizing that makes coping just a little bit easier."

Jessica's hand tentatively touches my cheek. Then a moment later she is in my arms. Much later we go inside together.

I awake with sunlight in my eyes.

"I thought you weren't going to sleep?" laughs Jessica, who is standing in the doorway. Her golden hair sparkles in the bright morning light. "You better get out of bed, sleepy head. Your mom and I almost have your breakfast on the table." After breakfast I walk Jessica out to her car. She takes my hand in hers and smiles brightly. "I'll write," she offers.

"So will I." We stand still, silently staring into each other's eyes. She lowers her head and gets into the car.

The engine snarls to life. Jessica revs the engine once then quickly drives away. I step out into the middle of the street to watch. Jessica keeps one arm waving out the window until the sleek, yellow Porsche disappears around a distant corner.

Sam takes me back to the camp later that morning. After dropping me off, I watch him drive away, too. Standing alone in the parking lot, I stare after him until his car fades from sight down the desert highway. Then, slowly turning around, I look upon the desert camp. I watch the inmates, mostly dressed in khaki drab, going drearily about the day's dismal routine. The rich vitality of life I have just been so immersed in is completely missing here. The pace is depressed, in slow motion. No one is in a hurry because they simply have no where to go. On the inside the goal is simply to make it through another day. Here, accomplishment is measured as just another black checkmark on the inmate calendar.

I shake off the depression that seeks to bind me. Another fourteen months is nothing compared to what I've already been through. In the control building, the guard doesn't notice my flagrant violation of prison rules. I'm smuggling in a new pair of running shoes, which I've scuffed and rubbed with dirt to give them the required aged look. I also carry a picture of Jessica hidden in the back pocket of my new 501 jeans. The jeans underwent a special aging process invented by Sam. He tied them to the back of his baja bug and took them for a short ride.

Leaving the control building and stepping out into the yard, I remember an old Charlie Chaplin movie where the little tramp is walking sadly down a dirt road, apparently without a friend in the world, then suddenly overcome with the vibrance of life about him, and from within, he kicks up his heels then goes whistling into an unknown future that is yet filled with hope and promise. I didn't exactly leap into the air, but I find it isn't hard to put a lop-sided grin on my face and scuff the dirt a bit as I walk towards dorm 7.

Another month quietly passes while I break-in my new running shoes. As my release date approaches, I've become more active in the Christian programs offered at the chapel on the hill. On Thursday evenings I attend an inmate fellowship where our main effort is helping the newer inmates to cope. I am talking with an older Mexican man who is worrying about how his family is ever going to financially survive without him, when the minister calls me aside.

"Steve," he asks, "the Chuck Colson Prison Fellowship has requested seven inmates for their program in San Francisco next week. How would you like go?"

Chuck Colson was one of President Nixon's men who did time because of his involvement in the Watergate fiasco. In prison he found comfort in Christian fellowship and had since founded a program where inmates went out into the community on church-sponsored furloughs to do civic service.

The following Friday the seven of us inmates board a PSA jet to San Francisco. We will be gone for two weeks. A robust black minister meets us at the airport. Our first stop is at a small community church, where we are fed a home-cooked breakfast and introduced to our host families. The congregation had taken the time to learn a little about each inmate. Having discovered that I am a surfer, they assign me to a family that has a house by the ocean in Pacifica Beach.

Riding in the car with my new host family, I think about these Christian people who are knowingly taking an inmate into their home. I fully realize that I'm being exposed to a very special kind of Christian love. It's one thing to put a little money in the offering plate; it is an entirely different situation to reach out and touch an inmate by inviting him to share your home.

I happily sit in the back of the car and visit with the two young children who have never seen a real inmate before. Looking at their friendly eyes, I think back to the night in J-3 when I found my way back to Christianity rather suddenly. I had been lying on my bunk wide awake, thinking about the criminal bent my life had taken. I wondered whether I would ever be able to look honest people in the eye again. Some of the cocaine I'd smuggled into California had undoubtedly filtered its way down into young hands. I wondered how I could ever atone for that?

I was feeling pretty emotional when I asked the Lord if he was still there for me. I've asked the Lord questions before, but had never gotten, nor expected, an answer. Well, I got one that night. I didn't exactly hear anything; it was more like being suddenly filled with a word. The word was "ALWAYS." I felt it flow through my body and soul; it instantly brought me complete and sudden peace.

There is a Christian story about a man walking on the beach with Christ. Looking back upon their footsteps in the sand he saw that in the periods when his life had been the toughest there was only one set of foot prints in the sand. He asked the Son of God why he hadn't been with him during the times of his greatest need. Christ replied, "My son, there is only one set of prints in the sand during your times of hardship because that is when I was carrying you." Well, that's how I feel about the Lord. He isn't a God who sits up in heaven handing out burdens for man. No, he is a God who is down here at our side helping us to carry them. When I need his help, he lets me know he is there, lending a shoulder to lift away the burden that is threatening to crush me.

In San Francisco, we spend our days working at a Christian elementary school: painting, cleaning, and doing repairs. At night, I often walk down to the beach to stare out at the ocean. I have a lot of thinking to do. I am trying to decide what to do with the rest of my life—freedom is rushing toward me. I'm not sure how I am going to begin again from scratch and with the stigma of a criminal record.

On our final day in San Francisco, we are taken to a large, majestic church for a last service together. Each of us inmates are asked to stand and speak before the congregation. When my turn comes, I'm not sure what to say, so I tell them what I was feeling in my heart about Christianity. It's not easy to stand before a congregation as an inmate and an ex-felon. I take several deep breaths to settle my nerves before I begin:

"When I was a young man growing up, my family didn't go to church very often. Though I believed in God, my belief was small, quiet, and very reserved. When I fell under the corrupting influence of criminals, I knew I needed help, but I couldn't hear the teachings of my small, quiet, and very reserved faith. It wasn't until I landed in a prison cell that I thought to ask the Lord for his help. My question was a simple one, 'Are you there for me Lord?' I hadn't expected an answer, and was thoroughly surprised when I felt his presence with a word. The word was, 'Always.'

"I knew I needed to understand myself better to know why I had fallen. I best understood when I viewed myself as a living vessel, a cup that is suppose to be full of love, but instead I had been busy filling my cup with greed and corruption. Trying to understand myself better was the first step toward cleansing this vessel that is me. Peeling away the corruption enabled me to see the surface of my cup, which I sadly noted was full of cracks and flaws. One of the cracks was so big I gave it a name, I called it Greed.

"By reading the Bible, I was learning to deal with my flaws, but I could only go so far alone. Many of my questions were going unanswered, then I came on this fellowship. The ministers and lay fathers of this church have taught me how to go about patching those cracks in my cup and together we have begun to wash away some of the guilt that caked it. The Christian love of my host family, which so willingly took an ex-felon into their home, is like the intense fire of a kiln that has tempered and strengthened the fragile repairs.

"I have learned a lot being here with this congregation. Now as I prepare to return to prison, I hope that the new strength I have found in my cup, and in myself, will be of aid to other inmates who have lost track of their possibly small, quiet, and reserved faith."

It is a sad moment when our Christian friends drop us off at the airport. For the rest of my life I know that I will always try to live by the Lord's way. It is through the Bible's teachings that I hope to find peace and contentment within myself.

Back at the camp, I do not push what I have learned on the other inmates. Instead, I follow the teachings of Ecclesiastes: to seek happiness through truth and honesty in life. When others ask how I can be happy inside of prison then I freely share what I have. I am continuing to learn that happiness is easiest found in pursuit of the good.

The next day the *Los Angeles Times* carries the headline, "DeLorean Acquitted." Reading the article, I still couldn't believe that Gerald Scotti, having resigned from the DEA, is now a witness for the defense. He gave incriminating evidence of an overly active effort by the DEA and FBI to involve an apparently reluctant man.

With DeLorean's trial out of the way, the government is finally free to sentence Hetrick. Despite his cooperation, and even though the government recommended a light sentence, Judge Takasugi nails Morgan with a full ten year prison term. He has since disappeared somewhere into the prison system. No doubt he will later be put into a witness protection program. I wonder if he will one day wind up like Hoffman, working as an informant?

This is one of my complaints about our legal system. Mr. Hoffman was guilty of some very serious smuggling charges, yet he is a free man, able to walk the streets and (unbelievably) is even being paid by the government for his cooperation. I sometimes wonder about the government's "Let's Make a Deal" attitude about prosecuting certain criminals.

Yet, I can't get too upset with the government today. Rick Barnett, my attorney, calls. He says that the government has decided to release *Revelstoke*, which has been rusting in a federal impound yard. I can't believe that my home is going to be returned to me. Suddenly, the future looks a whole lot brighter.

CHAPTER 24

We are attending a first-aid class in the education building on the hill when the big plane goes down in the desert. The call comes over the guard's radio, "Fire crew, respond code three, a large jet aircraft has crashed approximately six miles east of the camp!"

We run for our vehicles.

Climbing up into the cab of the fire truck, I pause for an instant to stare at a towering cloud of thick, black smoke billowing into the blue sky on the horizon. I hope it isn't one of the giant B-52s. Even when only on training missions, the flying fortress is crammed with all kinds of explosives: the ejection seats are mounted on small rockets; there are shape charges to blow away emergency hatches; and sometimes the B-52s carry cruise missiles under their wings. Even the aircraft's sophisticated metal parts can be a serious hazard; certain metal alloys, when burning, emit highly toxic gases and if struck by water while on fire, they can explode!

There is no doubt in my mind that we are about to face a very dangerous situation as I reach for the ignition key. The big engine roars to life. I revive the engine to two thousand rpm, switch on all three radios, then hit the red light and siren. The high low wail of the siren precedes the fire truck out of the parking lot. Double clutching, I jam the shift lever into second even as a tracer of doubt flashes though my mind. I realize that if we aren't careful, an inmate fireman could die today.

The pickup truck, with a small water pumper on its back, leads the way down the narrow road at forty miles an hour. I'm right on his tail with the big fire truck. The pickup slows and turns sharply at the chow hall. I try to down shift, but miss the gear. I'm going much too fast. The firemen on the back lean outward and to the right in worried anticipation of a high speed turn, but I continue straight instead. On the narrow road ahead, surprised inmates scatter from the path of the hurling truck. I desperately ride the brakes trying to slow the heavy machine as the control building fills the windshield. I feel the shift lever finally slip into second and quickly pop the clutch while stomping harder on the brakes. The heavy truck's bumper comes to a stop just yards from the large pane glass window of the control building—much to the relief of the wide-eyed guard inside. Backing the truck rapidly, running over two metal trash cans in the process, I turn toward the open gate and floor the gas peddle; gravel flies from the back tires, spraying several inmates who have taken shelter behind a telephone pole. The pickup truck is a quarter of a mile down the road and accelerating. In the rear view mirror, I see our four-wheel drive carryall and prison ambulance fall in behind us. Pegging the rpm in third gear, I shift to fourth; only then do I have a free hand to radio the San Bernardino command center: "Command, this is Engine Company 52 responding code three to a downed aircraft of unknown origin. Be advised we are heading for a thick column of black smoke rising six miles east of Boron Prison Camp in open desert terrain. Engine Company 52 urgently requests multiple engine and helicopter backup."

"Roger Engine Company fifty-two, advise possible size and type of aircraft."

Down-shifting for a stop sign and breaking hard before accelerating onto the main highway, I'm forced to speak in a rapid stutter. "The smoke column has reached one thousand feet, and it is still climbing. Judging by the size of the cloud that has already formed I believe it has to be a very large aircraft, maybe a B-52 flying fortress with possible explosives on board."

"Roger Engine Company 52, keep us posted on your progress."

The squelch on the radio hisses loudly; then the call goes out, "All engine companies, all engine companies, this is a four-alarm action alert, companies 24 and 18 respond with all engines to assist 52 currently northbound on 395 adjacent to Boron Prison Camp. Be advised that a large aircraft is down, and explosives may be involved. San Bernardino airport, scramble rescue choppers 7 and 8. All other engine companies are ordered to stand-by."

A mile down the desert highway, I see a dust cloud where the pickup truck has turned onto a dirt firebreak. I slow and down-shift to second, then accelerate into the turn. The back of the fire truck fishtails wildly before it regains traction, throwing a broad swath of dirt and gravel. The ambulance hits the turn going too fast and slides off the fire break and into a shallow ditch. A moment later the driver radios that he is O.K. but out of action. I shift into third but keep the rpm down. The firebreak isn't well-maintained. There are cuts and pot holes in the narrow track. The carryall is riding in the thick dust cloud trailing my fire truck, which is probably why he doesn't see a large pot hole in the middle of the firebreak. The carryall hits the hole solidly, weaves sharply from one side of the firebreak to the other then slows to a stop. It won't be until later that I learn his battery had broken free and slammed against the hot engine. I follow the spreading dust cloud of the pickup truck ahead of me.

I have to continuously change gears, down-shifting for dips and accelerating up small hills. The guys on the back are having a rough time of it. One of the side compartments springs open and dumps all its contents onto the dirt road, yet I don't dare stop for fear of getting stuck in the soft sand. While driving, I am operating two radios, directing other emergency vehicles to the scene on one radio, and keeping the camp advised of our location on the other. The guard riding next to me is all but useless. He has acute motion sickness. He throws himself at the open window and spews his guts. When he pulls his head back inside, panic fills his eyes. He yells at me to slow down, but I ignore him completely.

From the intercom speaker over my head, I hear a sudden plaintive cry from the back of the truck, "Hey, did someone just puke up there? I've got wet spray all over me and it smells like vomit. Please tell me that the guard didn't just up-chuck all over me."

I push the intercom button, "Roger, Fred, it's puke; better duck, I think the guard is about to blow lunch again."

The hack lurches for the window, hanging desperately onto the door, his stomach convulses repeatedly.

"Ahh, man," comes the cry over the intercom. "Can't the dude ride in the pickup next time?" A moment later, I strike a deep pot hole with the right front tire, the guard's head bangs solidly off the ceiling.

He clutches the top of his head and glares at me. His lips are moving but I can barely hear his words. "I hate inmates; I hate inmates," he curses repeatedly.

Three miles into the firebreak the pickup truck swings left into the open desert terrain following a more direct line toward the smoke column. I follow—employing skills learned in the navy operating four-wheel drive vehicles on beaches and in the jungle. I keep remembering that this big truck was meant for highways, not rough off-road conditions. Ahead of us the pickup truck strikes a sudden bump. All four wheels leave the ground. It crashes heavily into a thick clump of desert shrubbery. It continues fifty feet plowing plants from the ground and knocking over cactus before rolling slowly to a complete stop. The right front tire has gone flat and is bent at an impossible angle. Three rattled firemen climb awkwardly out of the cab and jump onto the big Ford as I drive by slowing but not stopping. The big fire truck is now crowded with bodies: the useless guard rides at my side as he bounces about the cab. Three firemen are holding on desperately to the hand rail at the back of the truck. Two others are hanging dangerously off the driver's side of the hurling Ford, and the last one is unhappily standing on the passenger side running board looking from the vomit-covered door to the sick guard. The guard begins to lurch for the window, the inmate's eyes widen in horror, then the hack spews all over the inmate's jacket and trousers. The guard flops back into his seat while the inmate outside curses mightily.

In the distance I see a jet fighter circling the huge black plume of smoke. We are now only two miles away. We have to make it, I think to myself. Lives could be lost if we fail to get to the accident site on time. I know it is up to me to get the big fire truck there, and I can only pray that I won't fail them. When the rough terrain gets even worse, I send one of the firemen running ahead to help me pick a clear path. I can not afford to stop or dare risk backing up. Soon the running fireman begins to visibly lag in his heavy turnouts. I honk my horn and beckon for him to jump back onto the truck as I drive past. Meanwhile, another fireman has already leaped off the truck to take his place, running against time, running to save the lives that might hang in the balance of our timely arrival.

I have to carefully weave our way between large boulders, over sharp-edge ridges and through soft sand gullies, knocking down heavy desert shrubbery along the way. When we are only three hundred yards from the burning wreckage, two air force helicopters flash directly over us, the heavy thump of their rotors is clearly audible inside the cab. Ahead of us a glint of reflected light splashes off a shiny silver capsule. The helicopters quickly settle to the ground, creating twin clouds of swirling dust to one side of an ejection pod.

The desert brush at one end of the capsule is aflame in a crackling and rapidly expanding fire. Two parachutes draped over the escape pod are beginning to smolder and burn. We knock down the flames with shovels and streams of water then help to force open the emergency hatch on the ejection pod. Two of the firemen, assisted by air force personnel from the helicopters, reach inside and begin to drag out three bodies. The pilot is already dead, but two other badly injured air crewmen are quickly pulled free—still alive.

I leave two firemen to help attend to the injured men. There is still a major fire raging where the rest of the aircraft has impacted. An area half the size of a football field is burning fiercely. The blackened metal wings of the aircraft are a crumpled mass of semi-molten metal awash in angry red flames that are erupting forty feet into the air fed by tons of jet fuel. The aircraft's huge tires are burning furiously, spewing heavy clouds of thick, rolling, black smoke. We quickly suppress the flames with foam, water, and shovels, carefully staying upwind of the toxic gas emitted by the burning metal alloys.

When it is obvious that we have the main fire under control and that the brush fire will burn itself out, I pick up the microphone, "San Bernardino County, this is Engine Company 52, the fire is under control. I repeat, the fire is under control. Be advised aircraft type is B-l bomber. I have one dead on the scene and two major trauma being evacuated by military helicopter."

Multiple dust clouds begin erupting all around us as more and more helicopters settle to the ground. The accident site is beginning to look like a Vietnam airhead as several security teams, running with rifles at the ready, dash from the landing choppers to set up a protective perimeter at the outskirts of the crash site. Soon, land vehicles begin arriving trailing clouds of dust, among them a big, yellow crash truck which quickly moves to pour foam onto the smoldering wreckage with its top-mounted water cannon.

Our job finished, the inmate firemen return in ones and twos to sprawl in the shade of the fire truck; their blackened faces are creased with white smiles of satisfaction for a job well-done. We were in time. We helped to save two lives that might have been lost.

A young air force officer, wearing a .45 automatic at his hip, walks self-importantly up to our fire truck. He stops to look at the fire truck's door insignia. His lips move as he reads, "Boron Prison Camp, Engine Company 52." Shocked, he looks at me with surprise, "You guys are inmates?"

"That's right," I answer proudly, "Engine Company 52 at your service."

"This site is classified top secret; inmates can't be here."

"If we weren't here, you'd still have a nasty fire to deal with, and maybe a few baked air crewmen from the B-1," I say, stating the obvious.

"What makes you think it's the B-1?" The young officer's panic is plain to see.

"Come on, it's the only plane that's got an ejection pod."

"Well, pretend you don't know that it's the B-1, O.K.? This has got to be kept totally under wraps, and that's directly from the White House as of fifteen minutes ago."

"Oh? Ah . . . I'm afraid it's not exactly under wraps anymore," I meekly hold up the microphone. The young officer cringes. We are politely asked to leave.

Following my tracks back out, I'm surprised at the number of air force vehicles that had accidents of their own while rushing to the crash site. The desert is littered with vehicles, some of them canted into ditches, others with their tires dug into the soft sand.

When we hit the paved highway, both sides of the tarmac are lined with numerous press vehicles. I learn later that they have monitored my radio calls, within five minutes of which San Bernardino command was receiving inquiries from as far away as New York City asking them to confirm that it was indeed a B-1 bomber that had crashed. The firemen hanging on the sides of the truck wave and give a little cheer as a film team pans us with their camera, but judging by the general lack of reaction from the news people, I don't think they recognize us as the heroes we know ourselves to be. In less than twenty-four hours, I will learn that it's tough to get recognition as an inmate, that is unless the inmate is doing something illegal or horrendous.

That evening and the next day the major networks run the crash of the B-1 bomber at the top of their news headlines, but there isn't any mention that it was an inmate fire crew that responded first to the accident and saved the lives of the airmen. The *Los Angeles Times*, however, did give us one sentence from the feature story that was splashed over most of the front page, "An inmate fire crew from Boron was the first on the scene; they quickly put the fire out."

That's it, nothing more. Some of the guys are more than a little upset. Sure, we are just a bunch of inmates, but we are real life firemen, too. Just like other firemen, we risk our lives in dangerous situations. Is it too much to ask that just once inmates get some kind of recognition for doing something good like saving a few lives?

Since I have the ear of the press, the guys wonder if I might be able to stir things up a bit. Big mistake, because I have no idea just how much trouble I'm about to stir up. I put in a phone call to Casey Cohen, my legal consultant, who doesn't waste any time getting a feature reporter from the *Los Angeles Times* on his conference phone. The reporter asks for details on the crash, but instead, I want to tell him about our wild ride across the rugged desert and how we helped rescue the air crewmen from being roasted alive inside their silver ejection capsule. I try to explain that the Boron fire crew regularly responds to all kinds of emergency accidents, that there are inmate firemen standing guard in the desert and that we have already saved dozens of people from death and injury—sometimes at serious risk to ourselves.

Unfortunately the reporter can care less about inmates' good deeds and doesn't think the paper will want to advertise that an inmate fire crew does anything but fight brush fires with shovels and hoes. However, my phone call does get the complete attention of the unit manager (the pay phones are always monitored).

I find myself standing in front of his desk less than ten minutes after the reporter hangs up on me. "Why were you talking with the press, idiot?" When a prison staff member begins a conversation by calling the prisoner names, most inmates know to keep their mouths shut. In any case, I am not allowed to answer as the unit manager continues in a raging voice, "Well, I've got news for you, buddy, you're off the fire crew! I'm sending you to the plumbing shop."

Stunned, I stare not quite believing that this is really happening to me. I start to say something in my defense, "But . . . "

"Shut up!" he yells from six inches away, spittle spraying my face. "Get your butt up the hill and report to the plumbing shop supervisor."

Stepping outside his office I want to release my anger. Instead, I stalk up the hill. My fury slowly dissipates to be replaced by frustration. It isn't a question of whether I broke any prison rules—I didn't. What I did do is accidently make an enemy of a prison staff member, and now I'm going to have to pay the price.

I, of course, hate my new job. The plumbing shop is at the top of the hill, far away from the pay phones. To make sure they know right where I'm at, the plumbing shop supervisor locks me inside the tool bin. The inmate I'm replacing is ecstatic. "You're going to hate this job," he says sagely. "It really sucks." On the wall of the tool bin there is a sign listing the rules for issuing tools. Someone has crudely lettered their own set of rules at the bottom:

Rule one—Inmates have nothing coming.

Rule two—For all other situations, refer to rule one.

The next two months pass ever so slowly; the days seem longer while I whittle away the hours in my lonely tool bin. Motivation is hard to find as I stare at the rusted tools about me. The worst part is hearing the fire siren wail and knowing that the fire truck is responding and that they could be doing a better job if I was there.

Being a fireman had meant a lot to me. My prison time seemed so much more constructive knowing that I was doing something important—like saving lives. As chief engineer I had dedicated myself to learning everything I could about fighting fires. Yet my most important contribution to the fire crew involved maintenance and training. The guys knew how much effort I put into making sure that everything on that truck worked, which meant they could press their fire attack knowing that they weren't going to lose water right in the middle of a critical situation. After each fire response, I got the crew together to go over the incident. Together we brain stormed how we could do it better the next time. We were a motivated fire crew. Things have since changed. Suspiciously, I am replaced on the crew by the unit manager's clerk. One of the inmate firemen writes "I spy," on the clerk's helmet. Moral is low among the fire crew; training is non-existent.

When the crew returns from their second fire response without me, they tell how they lost an entire motorhome to an out-of-control fire because the new chief engineer doesn't know how to prime the water pump. Without its prime, the pump can't deliver water. I wonder what kind of story they would have had to tell if children's lives had been at stake. Locked in the tool bin, my depression deepens.

Finally I become eligible for another furlough, a full five-day pass. Sam picks me up, and we drive all the way down to San Diego. Our first stop is La Jolla shores to surf. I see many of my old friends on the beach. They are surprised to see me. A teen-age surfer airs his thoughts, "What are you doing here? I thought they had you crushing rocks in the desert."

I spend most of the day in the water and on the beach. In the afternoon I decide to abandon Sam for a while so I can walk alone on the shoreline to ponder my future. I have no idea what direction my life will soon be taking. My approaching release date is, in a sense, a source of worry for me. I can't wait to be free, but the future is so uncertain, full of self-doubt and ill-defined.

At sunset we head for Sam's mother's house. Though I already know it's there, it's still startling to see *Revelstoke* again. Sam flips me the keys as he runs to the house. He's going to work at a restaurant where he's a waiter captain. Unlocking *Revelstoke*'s back door, I step inside with great anticipation. It's an incredible feeling being back in my old familiar home. Outside, a California winter rain begins to fall. Parked under a broad tree, I listen to the wind stirring among its leafy branches; then, looking through the forward porthole, I see a street light glowing in the dark at the end of the block. There are clear crystal rain droplets suspended in the wire screen of the porthole. They are catching the shimmering light from down the street and refracting it into hundreds of tiny rainbows. I remember another rainy night when staring out of this porthole I saw these same wondrous rainbows.

Mentally, I transport myself back to Hawaii. Back to a time when I wasn't so lonely. I was parked outside the restaurant where Susan worked. Looking through the port hole at the street outside, I saw that the pavement was a wet, black slickness. The headlamps of passing cars were mirrored in dark puddles where raindrops danced upon their rippled surface. Then I saw Susan stepping out the restaurant's door. For a moment she stood under the protective awning while I stared at her through a star burst of tiny twinkling rainbows. She looked toward *Revelstoke* then ran lightly across the wet street, dodging the mirrored puddles of black water. A few seconds later she came in through the back door, collecting a lick from Puu and a kiss from me. "How was work?" I asked.

"Too long." Susan was brushing raindrops from her long, blonde hair, "let's drive up to Pali Lookout to watch the lightning and listen to the thunder."

We drove up a steep narrow pass to the top of the volcanic mountains. The windshield wipers were beating a happy cadence to our laughter. We were in the nova of our love.

Soon, we were pulling into the Pali Lookout parking lot. The truck's headlights illuminated the volcanic rock that bordered each side of the high mountain pass. Backing *Revelstoke* up to the retaining wall, I stopped and set the brake while Susan cast the double back doors wide open. She stood in a halo of warm, yellow light from the truck's interior; before her the cliffs fell away in a sheer drop of several thousand feet.

Perched high on the mountain top, *Revelstoke* stood at the threshold of the sky. Lightning cut the night, and deep, rolling thunder reverberated up the mountain side. I put some Hawaiian slack key music on the stereo then glanced at Susan just as a lightning bolt silhouetted her in the door way. She stepped into my arms and kissed me—kissing Susan was never boring. Puu moved to the back door and barked happily at the rain then nudged his empty dog dish.

A bolt of lightning cuts the darkness of Sam's street; the resulting thunder clap shakes *Revelstoke* ever so slightly. The living shadows of Susan and Puu begin to fade away. I'm instantly saddened but deny the tears that threaten to spill. Instead of indulging in the tragedy of my loss, I will myself to remember the beauty of that rain-shrouded night in Hawaii.

Outside, I listen to the sound of the California rain as it drums on the metal roof of *Revelstoke*. I light a few candles and burn a stick of sandalwood incense. The truck shakes now and then to the beat of thunder and to the sudden gusting of the wind. Much later that night I fall asleep and dream of Susan and Puu. They are running along a hazardous trail ahead of me, and I can't quite catch up to warn them of an uncertain danger that lurks somewhere down the trail. They keep disappearing around bends in the trail. I can hear Susan's laughter and Puu's excited bark. Slowly, their happy voices fade, and I find myself lost and alone.

I wake the next morning and go in search of Sam. He's sleeping in his room, but a swift kick in the butt quickly cures him of that. I want to go surfing.

I spend every day in the water and my nights in *Revelstoke*. Jessica is away at college in Santa Barbara. Despite Sam's company, when he isn't working, it is a vacation of sadness. All too soon, my five-day pass ends, and I take the Greyhound bus back to Boron.

My third Christmas comes and goes uneventfully. I spend my time writing, putting my depression on paper.

In late January I'm called to the unit for my bi-annual counseling. There are four staff members on the board. The unit manager, my enemy, sits at one end of the table. He stares sternly in my direction, which makes me nervous. The unit counselor begins the meeting with a surprise statement, "Mr. Arrington, we've decided to send you to a five-month halfway house."

I'm shocked. It means I will be leaving the camp in less than three months. "Thank you," I stand, anxious to go and tell Ralph the news.

"Ah, Mr. Arrington, there's something else." The Counselor looks at the unit manager who is glaring angrily at me.

What have I done now? I wonder to myself.

The unit manager wipes his mouth as if removing a bad taste, then says, "How would you feel about going back on the fire crew?"

Stunned, I sit back down in my seat, "What?"

"We need you back on the fire crew." He isn't happy to be saying this.

The safety officer comes to his rescue, "Steve, we had a rather embarrassing event happen this morning." I turn in my seat to look at the safety officer.

"You know that there's a couple of congressmen visiting the camp right now, don't you?" I nod. "Well, this morning they wanted to see the now-famous Boron inmate fire crew in action. So I put a forty-four gallon trash can in my driveway and set it on fire. The fire burned itself out while the chief engineer was still trying to prime the pump." I clench my jaw in a determined effort not to laugh.

"The warden is a bit upset," continues the safety officer. I look at the unit manager and grin.

"Your job is to re-train the crew and get the chief engineer up to speed before you leave in three months." The safety officer also looks at the unit manager and grins. My enemy slams his notebook closed and stalks from the room.

At the plumbing shop I excitedly tell Ralph the news. Ralph looks a little unhappy. "So, why didn't you ask to have me put on the fire crew, too?"

I grin at my friend. "I did."

"What?"

"Yeah, you're coming with me." I glance at his plunger, which is dripping on the floor. "But you've got to leave that here."

"Certainly," grins Ralph. With a double overhand stab, he sticks the wet rubber plunger to the sign.

My first job at the fire house is to show the guys the proper procedure for priming the water pump. During the next week we go over each and every piece of fire fighting equipment; then I lay out fire attacks for all the buildings in the prison camp.

On the night of the new moon, three weeks after I rejoined the crew, we get our first call. It is quite a drive, over twenty-five miles with only the lights of the truck glowing on the dark highway. I carefully follow the interrupted white line down the center of the black tarmac while all about, the truck's flashing lights throw a pulsating red strobe intermittently illuminating the sparse desert landscape. With the pedal to the metal I'm having the time of my life as we hurl toward excitement and adventure. How I hated working in that boring plumbing shop.

Rounding an abrupt turn, I see a compact car lying shattered on its side just off the highway. A young couple with a crying baby is trapped inside. The driver had lost control in a skid. We aren't long getting them out. The baby and mother are O.K., but the driver has all but lost a foot. It hangs from the ankle by a single thread of flesh and tendon.

I've already called for a helicopter, and soon I see its approaching lights. Having recently repaired the small generator that powers our two huge spotlights, I am able to illuminate the nearby power lines for the rapidly descending helicopter. After seeing the helicopter safely off, I return to Boron feeling the satisfaction of a job well done.

The next morning I'm called to the unit manager's office. He glares at me from across his desk, "Who said you could leave the base without authorization?" he yells in a loud, blaring voice.

"What authorization are you talking about?" I ask, genuinely confused.

"You were put back on the crew to train them," he rages. "Nobody said anything about you going off base."

"What is the point of my being the chief engineer if I don't lead the crew on fire response?" I ask thinking it's a fair question.

"Listen to me, inmate," he snarls, "I don't give a damn about fighting fires outside this camp. You go through that gate again and you're going to have me to contend with."

Five days later the fire siren wails. Despite the threats of the unit manager I don't even consider not going. The new engineer I have been training isn't nearly ready to lead a fire attack. In fact he's a bit of a bonehead. He sits unhappily next to me while I drive the truck out the gate.

Not far from the camp a Toyota pickup truck has collided head-on with an 18-wheeler at a combined speed of over 130 miles an hour. The driver of the big commercial truck has a broken arm, but the driver of the pickup is totaled.

The red Toyota is a flattened mess. The steaming engine has been driven with tremendous force into the cab impaling the driver on the broken drive shaft. We spend an hour just cutting the ravaged body out of the mass of rubble and torn metal. Disemboweled by the force of the horrendous impact, his legs are almost torn from his mangled body. A stream of blood, mixed in a horrible collage with oil and gasoline, runs in a broad slick across the tarmac. It's a horribly depressing sight, and I flush the wet mess from the road with a firehose. The high pressure jet chases the hideous collage of body and engine fluids into a swirling maze glistening with dark hued rainbows. We spend hours cleaning up the sickening crash site.

Driving back into the camp, I see the unit manager glaring angrily at me through his office window.

Of course he pulls me off the fire crew again. I expected it. Yet, I couldn't let the truck roll and not go along. Sometimes you make a decision and just have to stick with it. Though they can lock up my body, they cannot own my soul as well. I do, after all, answer to a higher Source than a prison guard.

CHAPTER 25

I'm surprised to find that my new job is in the Education Department. Apparently I am the new science teacher. It is an unexpected assignment as my only college degree is an Associate of Arts. Somehow this qualifies me for the job. I understand better when I meet my class for the first time.

They are a sullen lot. I doubt if many teachers have ever had a more reluctant mob of students. They have earned their admittance by failing the prison system's general education exam, which is equated to an eighth grade level. None of them are pleased to be in the classroom. Their time, as far as they're concerned, would have been much better spent doing drugs and terrorizing the newer inmates.

I spend a few moments surveying the hostile class of eleven. My oldest student, a white-haired black man, who has to be at least seventy-five years old, sleeps soundly on his desk. His slight snores could hardly have disturbed the rest of the boisterous class, who are talking loudly and totally ignoring me in the process.

No one really expects me to teach anything—least of all the students. We're just supposed to go through the motions of fulfilling the prison standards of inmate education, which means the inmates are only required to occupy the classroom. The training director has already cautioned me not to administer any tests. "They just use the paper to scribble profanity on," he cautions. I wonder how best to get their attention.

"Would anyone like to discuss weight lifting?" I inquire hopefully. Since most of them consider themselves experts on the subject, I instantly have their reluctant attention. They are a leery lot, ready to ignore me again if this proves to be a ruse to distract them from their far more important interests like shooting the bull about crime and what they're going to do to various people when they get out.

Taking a deep breath, I continue, "Have you ever wondered why some people like the Hulk sitting here in the front row get such exceptional response from their workouts, while other people, despite intense commitment, show little development at all?"

The hostile class stares silently, only vaguely interested in my answer, which they're now sure is just a cheap trick on my part to lure their attention.

"Well, the answer is education. Igor here," I point at the weight

lifter who hurriedly removes his finger from his nose, "assisted somewhat by genetics, has stumbled upon a routine that apparently works
for him." The weight lifter is beaming at me; I guess he likes being
called Igor. Somewhat encouraged, I continue.

"If your workouts are not resulting in the build you aspire to,
we might be able to do something about that through simple
science and basic physics." With that inauspicious beginning I launch
into a simple explanation about the difference between fast-twitch
and slow-twitch muscle groups, the advantages of negative weight
training, why steroids are bad for you, and the value of cross-train-
ing. Recognizing the limitations of my class, I'm careful to avoid
words with more than two syllables.

Using body-building as a vehicle, we are able to discuss such
subjects as: physics, physiology, human chemistry, and nutrition. One
of our inmate doctors, who is in for insurance fraud, agrees to come
into the class to answer questions about vitamins and the questionable value of force-feeding yourself protein powder.

Somehow my class unexpectedly grows to twenty odd students.
"Odd" is such an accurate word because it adequately describes my
drop-in students. Many of them are the animals that hang out around
the weight pile with little on their minds except pumping iron, sex,
and drugs. All of which are easily found in the prison camp, except
that the sex part might involve a less-than-enthusiastic partner.

I don't really have much to complain about in these final days at
Boron. I have most of the day to myself since I only teach classes at
night. Usually I'm up well before first light to stretch and do yoga
exercises followed by some vigorous solitary karate. At 6 A.M., I continue to be the first one out of the dormitory—off for a secluded
run around the hill or a quiet workout at the weight pile. The desert
in the early morning hours before sunrise has a lonely beauty that
washes away the mindless chatter of my brain while encouraging a
certain purity of inspirational thought. I do some of my best thinking in the open air weight pile while listening to wild birds in the
nearby mesquite bushes singing in anticipation of the dawn.

In early May we have an unexpected snowfall. Alone in the crisp
morning air at the weight pile I stare in awe at the winter-like beauty
of the icy wonderland that has fallen during the night. Under the
bright security lights the ice crystals on the iron weights sparkle magnificently. Scooping a handful of frost into my gloved hand, I peer
closely at the flakes that glitter like a handful of diamond chips. In
disciplined silence, I go about my routine, wondering whether I'm a
bit nuts pumping iron alone in the snow.

Lately, I've again taken to making ceramic cups in the hobby
shop. I enjoy painting colorful scenes on them. Some, I will take
home. Others are to be given away to inmate friends.

As I put the finishing touches to a fire truck I am painting on a large mug, I hear heavy breathing just over my shoulder. A huge brute of a guy is staring at my work. With an awkward smile he silently asks to hold the mug. He carefully picks it up, handling it gently in his oversized hands. He isn't very bright. Many of the inmates enjoy making fun of him—but only from a safe distance. Actually he is quite harmless in his simple state. His favorite activity is carrying Crackers, the prison cat, around the camp cradled in his huge arms. The cat is his one and only friend.

After a moment he hands the mug back. "I like fire trucks," he grunts with a lop-sided grin. Turning the cup over, I label the bottom—number 142. It will be my last piece. Later that night, I leave the mug on his bunk while noting that he has few possessions. It reminds me of my early days in J-3 when I owned so little—and felt so terribly lost and alone.

Whenever an inmate is being released, the whole dormitory is liable to get together to throw him a guacamole party. Friends pitch in what they can: avocados, Jalapeno peppers, chips, and soda pop purchased from the prison store, and garlic, onions, and salsa pilfered from the chow hall. Smuggling the garlic out has added a toxic odor to my old socks.

For my party, a cocaine smuggler from Florida breaks out his guitar and sings, in a voice made raspy by whiskey and cigarettes, "The Smuggler's Blues."

There is a custom in prison that when an inmate is being released he takes nothing with him. Everything is given to others; even old, frayed jeans are appreciated. As I prepare to start my life from scratch, I mentally count my possessions: *Revelstoke* (a bit older for wear), two surfboards, a wetsuit, and the clothes on my back. I also have a student loan that I owe three thousand dollars on—making the two hundred dollars in my prison account look pitifully small. I still don't want to consider the six and a half million dollar tax lien that the government has imposed, which voids any chance I might have of getting any kind of credit.

I have just finished a book by Ruth Bebe Snow, called, *Hanta Yo*. The main character is a young Lacota Indian. The son of a chief, no matter what he does or how well he does it, he can't please his father or the tribe. The people always expect more from him than the other young men. Finally in desperation he seeks advice from the medicine man. "Why is it that no matter how hard I try to please my father, or anyone else, it is never good enough?" he pleads.

The stern medicine man simply tells him that he must give away everything that he owns, cautioning him not to keep a single trinket. Only then will he find the answer he seeks.

The following morning, standing naked in a meadow under a

glorious morning sun he gives away his last possession, a buffalo robe to an ancient warrior. Solitarily he looks toward the sky. He is man alone owning nothing, yet he suddenly realizes nothing owns him. For the first time in his life he is completely free. He is man in his essence, and all paths are open to him. The meadow turns a golden color as a cloud passes, letting in the warmth of the sun. Life has suddenly taken on new meaning. Walking tall, self-possessed, he returns to take his place among his people.

I feel like that Indian, eager to tackle life from a fresh new beginning. In great anticipation I lace up my running shoes for a final run around the Boron Hill. Running in the morning light, I listen to the rhythm of my feet pounding on the road; the cadence is like the ticking of a clock counting off time. Each step carries me closer to 8 A.M.—my projected release time. Returning to Dorm 7, I see that Ralph is waiting for me. I remove the running shoes from my feet and hand them to him, along with my extra socks even if they do still carry the toxic odor of crushed garlic. Then reaching into a drawer, I take out and hand him my treasured radio. Its plastic box is scarred from wear. Ralph is as excited as I was when I first took it from its plastic wrapper in J-3. *Has thirty-one months of my life slipped away already?* I wonder to myself.

After a shower, I dress in a pair of old, worn-out jeans, a T-shirt, and white high-top sneakers. I then wander casually down to control to pick up my release papers. At the barrier I stop to look at the camp one last time. I have learned so many things about myself here, yet I will not miss Camp Boron in any way.

Soon, coming up the long, straight highway, I see my brother's BMW approaching. Jim stops alongside and reaches across to open the door for me. Suddenly, I hear the wail of a fire siren. The camp fire truck is coming rapidly across the dirt baseball field trailing clouds of dust with its emergency lights flashing. The truck comes to an abrupt halt on the other side of the gate while the dust cloud settles about it. The fire crew is hanging off the back and sides. They are waving vigorously. Then in the cab I see Ralph, the friend I so desperately needed and found in general population so long ago. Ralph waves slowly. A sad smile begins to play across his face, but then he brightens and signals happily with two thumbs up.

My brother Jim smiles knowingly from the driver's seat of his car, understanding that this is a special moment between parting friends. He reaches out and touches my shoulder. Silently, I climb into the car with tears clouding my eyes. As Jim drives away, I turn in the seat to stare at the fire truck and the waving inmates until we round a distant bend in the highway.

THE BEGINNING

CHAPTER 26

Sitting quietly on a cement bench, I stare at my reflection in the curved warp of a sheet of stainless steel that is wrapped around a thick cement column. My image, like the huge and empty parking lot that surrounds me, is ill-defined and oddly distorted. I look exceedingly small and very alone in the vast emptiness of black tarmac that fills the metal mirror's curved horizon.

I think that the malformed reflection aptly mimics what I'm feeling inside, which is lost and quite out of place in a world grown uncertain. It's my first day of freedom, and the future is clouded and full of doubt.

I'm returning from my first visit with a parole officer. Between buses I await the connection that will take me back to the halfway house. I have no idea what the future holds for me, nor what kind of job I hope to find. Ill at ease, I plan to commence the search for employment tomorrow. A grossly distorted yellow bus appears in the warp of the metal mirror, passing from left to right the image accordions outward, then squishes in the center, and then lengthens again as it stops with an ear piercing screech of brakes directly behind the bench. A slim, black youth in an old army jacket steps off the bus to the sharp hiss of the sliding pneumatic door. With a loud grinding of gears, the bus drives away noisily trailing a cloud of thick black smoke that lingers acidly in the air long after its departure.

Reaching into a wrinkled paper bag on the bench beside me, I withdraw a hard-boiled egg and crack its white shell on the bench. The black youth standing at the edge of the mirror's reflection turns at the sound and appears to be eyeing my egg enviously. The distortion of the warped mirror makes his eyes look unusually large, like a starving child. I take a second egg from the paper bag and hold it up wordlessly. The youth quickly joins me on the bench.

We peel our eggs together in silence.

Out of the corner of my eye, I notice that his finger nails are chewed to the quick and black with grime. They sharply contrast the clean white flesh of the egg. "So, where are you coming from?" the youth asks politely while munching hungrily on his egg.

"Today from my parole officer . . . yesterday from prison," I reply unemotionally. "Would you like some salt?"

Salting the remaining half of his egg, he somewhat nervously asks, "What were you in for?"

"Poisoning people," I answer flatly.

White chunks of egg and bits of yellow yoke splatter the curved sheet of stainless steel as the youth spews the half-chewed egg from his mouth. "What?" he chokes.

"Just kidding," I laugh, morbidly pleased that my sense of humor has apparently survived the prison experience intact. Looking at my young companion, I can't help but feel bad about my little joke. He is obviously quite shaken. A small piece of egg dribbles from his lower lip down onto his pant's leg, which hasn't been washed anytime recently. He dusts it off looking quite forlorn about the wasted egg.

"Would a peanut butter and jelly sandwich make you feel any better about spewing your egg all over the parking lot?" I ask. He brightens visibly.

We both look at the crinkled brown paper sack that sits between us with its promise of more food. I remove both of the peanut butter sandwiches I made earlier that morning. Chunky peanut butter and thick raspberry jelly leaks grossly from between the semi-flattened slices of brown bread. I offer him the least damaged one, which he opens and eyes suspiciously. He clamps the gooey mess back together then waits until I've bitten into mine before he risks a tentative bite himself.

"So what does it feel like your first day out of prison?" he mumbles around a thick mouthful of sandwich.

"It's wonderful to be out. It's hard to explain. I don't feel like I'm really a part of society anymore. It's like I'm on the outside trying to find my way back while not being sure that I am wanted or even belong here anymore."

"But if you served your sentence doesn't that mean you've paid your debt to society?" The youth inquires, wiping a glob of peanut butter from his cheek with the frayed sleeve of his olive-drab jacket.

"It's not that simple to shed an inmate mentality," I reply. "Institutional conditioning runs too deeply; prison and all its experiences are inside me now. It's something I have to live with for the rest of my life." A vision of Bruno pounding the cell wall flashes through my mind as if to prove he is still with me.

A few moments later the squeal of hot brakes announces that my bus has arrived. I wad the now empty paper bag into a ball and toss it into a trash can before stepping onto the nearly empty bus. The youth waves in an unsure manner as the bus drives away. He shuffles toward the trash can to inspect the paper bag. I have no idea what clues it might hold for him.

Selecting a seat near the back, far away from anyone else, I sit down and close my eyes to shut out an insecure world that lacks the luster I dreamed about from my prison cell. Being around people makes me feel as skittish as an abused pup in the city pound. It isn't the comfort of a home to which I am heading. The halfway house is just another part of the institutional system that still owns my body.

The following day I board another bus. I've decided to make my first stop the College of Oceaneering in Los Angeles harbor, where they teach commercial deep-sea diving. Maybe they would have a lead on where an ex-con diver could find a job. My hopes aren't very high. I'm just hoping I won't have to start out pumping gasoline at some out-of-the-way service station or wind up sweeping floors at a 7/11 in east Los Angeles. I certainly don't expect any employers to be overly enthusiastic about hiring an ex-felon. Even in my mind, the tag "drug smuggler" has an ugly ring to it.

An hour later, standing at the entrance to the school, I mentally tuck my tail between my legs and go inside. The receptionist, after hearing that I am looking for a job as a diver, calls the training supervisor on the telephone. "He'll see you in his office. It's the third door on the right," she says over her shoulder already dismissing me from her thoughts to return to work.

Tom Mix stands as I open his door. He motions me into a hard-backed chair before his desk. "Are you here to sign up for a class?" he asks hopefully.

"Actually I'm looking for a diving job," I answer just as hopefully.

Tom Mix sighs, "We're not looking for anyone right now, but what are your qualifications anyhow?" He puts his legs up on his desk like he is a man who has time to burn.

"Well, I'm an ex-navy diver and an ex-felon. You see, I just got out of prison the day before yesterday."

The coffee Tom is drinking spills into his lap. He leaps to his feet, but it's too late. His pants are thoroughly soaked. "You sure know how to surprise a fellow don't you," he says while wiping the spreading wet spot.

"Sorry," I offer, looking at the mess I caused. "I just didn't want to waste your time and thought it would be better if you knew right off."

Tom pauses for a moment, then says thoughtfully, "I think I need some more coffee. Would you like a cup?"

Over the next hour we discuss my diving background. Tom's attention quickens when I tell him that I am a scuba instructor. Then his next question takes me totally off guard.

"Can you draw?"

"Ah . . . well I do a certain amount of drawing on chalkboards when I'm teaching," I answer, unsure where his question is leading.

Tom shakes his head, "No, I mean can you draw cartoons?"

Seeing the surprised look on my face, he explains, "I have an idea for a really tricky T-shirt. Imagine a large human being sitting on a bench. Around him smaller deep sea divers are working to remove his helmet, which is actually his head. As the head lifts off we see that the body encases one of the little deep sea divers . . ." Tom smiles expectantly like he has told me a great joke.

Totally confused, I stare blankly back at him.

Tom smiles weakly, "You get it don't you?"

I laugh politely. "No, but I could do it," I answer enthusiastically without any idea what he is talking about. "Ah . . . what about the job?" I ask trying to jar him back to the purpose for my visit.

"Oh, you got that," he says off-handedly, "come on we'll get you a set of keys and I'll give you a tour of the school."

I'm floored and for a few seconds just sit there open-mouthed like a fish out of water.

"Close your mouth," laughs Tom. "You look like a fish out of water."

As we walk down the hall together, Tom asks casually, "Do you know that there are a lot of ex-felons working in the commercial diving industry? Actually you guys do quite well. Ex-felons are the best for handling the isolation of living offshore on the big rigs."

That afternoon, riding on the bus back to the halfway house, I keep fingering the keys in my pocket. I'm amazed that the college is willing to trust an ex-felon with access to millions of dollars worth of commercial diving equipment. I decide right then that I will be the best instructor the College of Oceaneering ever had.

CHAPTER 27

I thoroughly enjoy working at the College of Oceaneering. The only bad part is its proximity to Terminal Island Prison. I am deeply disturbed by the prison's foreboding presence, which lurks but a mile away. Sometimes school business takes me dangerously close to the institution's gray walls, which always causes me to tremble deep down inside. The guard towers, with their dark mirrored windows, have a foreboding air about them that is quite intimidating even when viewed from outside prison walls.

Part of the student's three-month training program involves night diving in the harbor. While the divers work on their many underwater projects, I often pace the rusting deck of the diving barge for hours on end staring at the dark hills of San Pedro. The view recalls too many memories of the south yard. I can see the same city lights on the hills and hear the same harbor sounds of passing ships. In my mind I can all but hear the prison's siren call and know it is seeking to pull me back into its walls.

Inmate memories linger about me and haunt my sleep. I don't rest well at night as phantom DEA agents, prison guards, and inmates stalk my dreams. Often I wake up in a cold sweat. Time passes slowly as I live a desolate fantasy lifestyle that twists the reality I am living. It is almost like I am dreaming my freedom. I daily live with the secret terror that I might accidentally be dragged back inside prison because of a simple parole violation, like missing daily count at the halfway house or fighting with one of the other inmates, some of whom are usually spoiling for trouble.

On a hot summer night in July, I'm a little late getting back to the halfway house because of problems at the college. I casually step into the staff office to check-in and am shocked to see my few possessions in a box on the counselor's desk.

I stand there at a total loss. Are they sending me back for being a few hours late? My heart collapses into itself as I vividly remember the cold and dank Terminal Island holding cell. "About time you got here, Arrington," grumbles the counselor. "Here, sign these release papers."

"Release papers?" I'm not sure I am hearing him right.

"Yeah, they arrived with today's mail. The judge has commuted your sentence from five to three years."

Grabbing the papers, I read that Judge Takasugi has finally ruled on an appeal I submitted over two years ago. I thought it unrealistic that the judge hadn't acted on the appeal sooner, considering that I had been released from prison several months ago. But I'm not complaining. I now only have the three years special parole to serve before I can truly count myself a free man.

"You know you can't spend the night here tonight," says the counselor, breaking my line of thought.

"What do you mean?" I ask, looking up from the court paper.

"Now that you've served your sentence, the halfway house cannot be responsible for your safety around sentenced inmates," the counselor answers quite frankly.

"Don't expect any arguments from me," I quip happily. I sign the release papers, grab my box of clothes, and exit through the door. Outside I quickly walk away from the halfway house without looking back.

That night I drive *Revelstoke* to Huntington Beach and park it in an approved camping slot. Later, walking along the water's edge, I stare out to sea and wonder if prison will ever truly be behind me. I still have the three years special parole to do, which means monthly visits to see the parole officer. The threat of being sent back to prison for a parole violation is still very much a worry for me, particularly when I consider that 70 percent of all ex-felons are re-incarcerated. It's a very sobering thought knowing that the odds are over two-to-one against my being able to stay out of prison. I feel a tremble rush up my spine and know it isn't from the crashing waves breaking at my feet.

The next day I begin the search for a place to live. I'm lucky to have *Revelstoke*, but I need a place to park it on a long-term basis. I can't afford a trailer park and end up renting half of a Mexican family's driveway in the town of Wilmington on the poorer side of Los Angeles harbor. Across the street an oil well dips and pulls with a reciprocating squeal twenty-four hours a day. Wilmington is such a rough town that when the police have to go into the alleys they prefer to back their patrol cars in so they can be assured of a fast exit.

Revelstoke becomes the one anchor that I can really latch onto. It is a refuge of good memories, and I use it as a place to hide. I flee the social life that I fear for my own self-induced cage. I can't help but think that the interior of the *Stoker* is smaller than my J-3 cell. I seriously wonder whether I can ever cleanse myself of my felon past.

Though I long for female companionship, I am much too shy and ashamed to ask anyone out. My nightly companion is a six pack of beer in which I try to lose myself in an alcoholic daze. The months pass. Ever so slowly I begin to heal while I learn to cope with my mental scarring.

Because of my emergency first aid and hyperbaric medicine

background, I'm assigned the collateral duty of being the college medic. On a cold, gray day in December, a frantic student barges into my physics classroom yelling, "Mr. Arrington, they need you down at the harbor—hurry, a student is drowning!" I grab my first-aid kit and run after the frantic student.

On the diving barge, panic has already begun to set in. Five minutes earlier the student diver screamed into the radio-telephone that he couldn't leave the bottom. Then from the surface speaker came the dreadful gurgling sound of water filling his helmet—just before the line went dead!

From the deck speaker I hear the standby diver reporting the situation, "The diver's fouled; we can't get him off the bottom."

"What about his helmet?" the instructor yells into the radio- telephone."

"It's off—he looks dead," came the reply.

Glancing at the log keeper, I shout anxiously, "How long has it been since you heard water flooding his helmet?" After four to six minutes without oxygen irreversible brain damage usually begins to occur.

The shaken student looks at his log then the clock. "Coming up on seven minutes," he stutters.

"Mr. Arrington . . . " the student's chin quivers, "is Chris going to die?"

I turn away not wanting to echo what he has guessed. Seven minutes is just too long. I feel helpless while a young life is ebbing away in the mud at the bottom of the harbor. Standing at the edge of the diving barge, I peer anxiously at the mass of bubbles that surface in a large foreboding boil from the divers working desperately below.

"We got him." The words erupt from the surface speaker. "We're coming up."

The diameter of the bursting bubbles increases like a pot of water that has been left boiling too long on the stove. It is a sign that the divers are nearing the surface. Between them they support an inert, seemingly lifeless body. I quickly reach down and grab the shoulder straps of the unconscious student and begin to haul him aboard the barge. Other hands are quick to help as we drag the limp student onto the rusting metal deck. I know that we are losing a desperate race against time. Chris' skin is a ghastly shade of purple from a complete lack of oxygen and an excessive amount of carbon dioxide. The black pupils of his eyes are dilated, fixed, and staring—as if he has already passed from this world.

Placing one hand under Chris' neck and the other on his forehead, I quickly tilt his head back to establish an airway. Chris' skin is cold and clammy under my hands; it's like touching a cadaver. Taking a deep breath, I forcefully blow air into his lungs. I see his chest rise while in my mind I ask the Lord for his help, "Father, let us not be too late."

With each breath, Chris gushes water from his grossly distended stomach. I give him a total of four rapid breaths, then begin full cardiopulmonary resuscitation (CPR).

I'm surprised at how easy it is to do CPR on a person. I have actively taught CPR for over fifteen years. After all those late night classes working with plastic mannequins, I'm suddenly doing CPR for real. I see his chest convulse inward a full two inches under the driving force of my clenched hands. Though his dark purplish skin waxes to a deathly shade of white, I know his chances of recovery aren't very good. He has been down for too long. I continue with my efforts to revive him despite being convinced that he is already gone. In my mind I see Chris, the vibrant young student, who just hours earlier wished me an enthusiastic "Good morning" as he hurried to the diving locker. I continue the compressions on his chest while another instructor helps with the breathing.

It is a full twenty minutes before the fire department arrives on the scene. They immediately hook Chris to a portable EKG machine that measures the body's vital functions. The meter reflects a total flat line indicating clinical death. The two paramedics glance knowingly at each other. Chris was too long in the water without oxygen. There isn't a chance of his recovering; however, since the young student carries a donor's card, the organs might be worth saving. The firemen continue the CPR en route to the hospital.

Along the way, a routine check is made for any vital functions. The paramedic is quite surprised when he detects a weak and thready pulse, which is rapidly followed by spontaneous breathing. The hospital is advised and special arrangements are made to transfer Chris to an ultra-modern hyperbaric unit at Northridge hospital. He is going to be treated in a high-pressure oxygen environment inside a recompression chamber. Still, no one's hopes are very high. The odds are that irreversible brain damage has already occurred. Throughout the treatment, the young diver remains in a deep coma as expected.

The following day the young man is moved to intensive care; his condition is considered critical. His mother sat weeping at the side of his bed throughout most of the night. The situation looks completely hopeless. The doctors have warned her to expect the worse. Then, without any prior warning, Chris' eyes flicker open. He turns to look at his mother and, as his eyes focus on her, weakly asks, "Mom, what are you doing here?"

Incredibly, Chris fully recovers with no apparent brain damage. He even remembers his drowning. When he fouled himself on the bottom, instead of waiting for help, he recalls his panic and how he foolishly removed his helmet in a vain attempt to free himself.

Chris returns to the college and completes his diver training with high grades. He even dives on the same underwater project that almost cost him his life. I stand ready on the diving barge . . . just in case. When he finally surfaces, I stop my anxious pacing of the barge's rusty deck and smile in quiet satisfaction. As he walks past me he grins and, referring to the project, says, "You know, it's smaller than how I remember it." Chris remains on campus over the next couple of months completing his advanced commercial diver training.

Because so much time had elapsed while he had been trapped underwater, the fire department and the Red Cross credits me for saving Chris' life. The Red Cross presents me with their highest award for lifesaving, the Certificate of Merit signed by President Ronald Reagan. When they pin that medal to my chest at the Red Cross headquarters my heart swells with pride.

In the audience sits James Walsh, the prosecutor in my case. He now seems almost like an old friend. I feel that I have been treated very fairly by the judicial system. I fully deserved the sentence I received. He later wrote the letter recommending that I be paroled over a year early.

Looking out at all the applauding people in the audience, I remember the terrible sadness I felt when I removed my naval uniform for the last time. I think about my tragic state six years ago when I placed my medals and chief's insignia into a little wooden box and sadly closed the lid. Receiving this honor for life saving washes away all that old sadness, but, more importantly, it makes me realize that I really can step into a new future and put prison and its awful memories behind me.

Saving Chris' life winds up being the turning point in my own life. I feel good about myself and even find the courage to start lecturing at high schools about drugs, crime, and prison—one so often follows the other. The principal at Woodrow Wilson High School in Long Beach, California, is astounded that his students—there are over three thousand of them in the audience—actually enjoy the presentation. I keep the kids' interest because I don't lecture them.

I begin with the basic facts of my story; then I quickly open the floor to questions. We talk mostly about life in prison and what it's like living inside the drug underworld. The kids relate their own negative drug experiences. By actively participating, the students become more engrossed in the answers. At the conclusion, the principal comes on stage and says, "I would have to call that the 'Miami Vice' presentation of the anti-drug lecture circuit." Then, looking out into the audience he asks, "What do you think?"

It is my first standing ovation.

I know that I am well on my way toward recovery and becoming a contributing member of society again. The world has indeed taken on the golden glow that I had so hopefully envisioned from my prison cell. There is, however, one more thing I have to do before I can truly put my past behind me. It's time to sell *Revelstoke*.

After ten years, the *Stoker* is getting old, and I am ready to find a real place of my own. The "For Sale" sign isn't on it very long before I get a buyer. Surprisingly, it is an older man, alone and single. He wants to retire to Mexico and build a house alongside a river. He figures that *Revelstoke* can be his temporary home while he builds a more permanent structure. The day he drives it away is sad and charged with positive energy at the same time. I watch *Revelstoke* being driven down the street by a stranger. Slowing at an intersection, it makes a right turn and disappears into my memory where Puu and Susan reside.

CHAPTER 28

I have been working at the college for almost two years. I enjoy my job but yearn for the adventure I had known in the navy. When you are young, teaching is seldom as satisfying as doing. I lust for travel to exotic places and chafe to get back into an active diving career. Little do I know that my life is about to be altered in a radical way. The change is unexpectedly linked to a potted house plant that is growing by leaps and bounds directly behind my desk. I purchased the broad-leafed plant at a Mexican supermarket along with a frozen pizza and a six pack of Pacifico beer. Barely a foot tall at the time, it has since sprouted numerous long vines that are threatening to take over the entire wall behind me. A few months earlier one of the other instructors had asked, "What are you going to do when that thing reaches the ceiling?"

After a moment's consideration, I carelessly replied, "Move on to another job."

Now as I sit at my desk admiring the morning light coming through the office window with the gargantuan plant looming behind me—it likes sunshine too—I hear Doug abruptly say, "So, tell me about your new job."

Confused, I ask, "What are you talking about?"

"Your plant," Doug points to the giant growth behind me. "It just reached the ceiling."

Spinning around in my chair, I see that the plant has indeed sprouted yet another leaf. It is on the verge of opening. The delicate green tip is slightly bent as it brushes against a white ceiling tile. "Maybe I spoke a little too carelessly," I answer, shrugging my shoulders.

I pour the rest of my coffee, which has grown cold, into monster plant's pot. I think it likes the caffeine; maybe that is why it has grown so quickly. Collecting the diving log for my class, I head for the door. I'm scheduled to teach in the harbor this morning. Letting the door swing shut behind me, I can still hear Doug laughing good naturedly as I walk down the hall.

It is one of those beautifully clear spring days in mid-May. The bright morning sunshine is dancing in a sparkling tapestry upon the smooth sea water that laps ever so gently against the barnacle-encrusted wooden pilings of the inner harbor.

Down at the barge, I wipe black oil from my hands with a red cloth. I'm teaching the students how to hand-crank start the diesel air compressor without hitting their head with the thick metal crank. Over the heavy pant of the diesel engine, I faintly hear the pier phone ringing. It is a distance away, and I just barely catch it on the sixth ring. While trying to blot out the sound of the diesel engine, which rumbles loudly in the background, I hear Don Santee, expedition leader and chief diver for the Cousteau Society, saying, "Steve, how would you like to come and work with us?"

Earlier in the year Don had sat in on my diving medicine class just to brush up on any new changes that had occurred in treating diver's maladies. Like almost every other diver that Don met, I offered him my services should he ever need a diver. I sincerely meant it when I made the offer, but I never actually expected him to call. I was just giving voice to a dream, a dream that I thought was too incredible to ever come true.

While growing up in Southern California, I never missed an opportunity to watch "The Undersea World of Jacques Cousteau." I fantasized about diving with the Cousteau team ever since donning my first pair of flippers, but it had always been just an idle daydream.

Listening to Don on the phone, I can't believe that my childhood dream is suddenly putting down roots. "Don, it would be my absolute pleasure to come work for you," I say enthusiastically.

"Great! You better give notice to the college right away. I need you as soon as possible."

"Oh, one more thing," Don adds casually like it is just an afterthought, "your title is going to be chief diver. I've more expedition work than I can handle, and my wife is going to kill me if I don't start spending a little more time at home." Don laughs; then the line goes dead.

Chief diver? For the Cousteau Society? My happiness is hard to contain as I hoot and holler while dancing about the barge's rusty old deck. Meanwhile the students are standing open-mouthed at the top of the pier wondering if their instructor has just lost his marbles.

Finishing a flying spin with a two-footed stomp that lands me in the middle of a puddle of rusty water, I leap from the barge and bolt up the pier scattering the confused students from my path. At the top of the walkway, I pause to yell down at them to finish setting up dive stations, but not to get into the water until I return. Dive students are a shifty lot, usually looking to drown themselves when not watched carefully.

I find Doug in the recompression chamber room where he is conducting oxygen tolerance tests on a junior class. I dance about him waving my arms shrieking, "Guess what, guess what?"

"Whoa . . . slow down," implores Doug, "you look like a hovering helicopter trying to take off with a heavy load."

"I just got a job offer over the pier phone," I gasp between pants. "Shake hands with the newest chief diver for the Cousteau Society."

"Nah," laughs Doug, trying to free his hand from my grasp, "you're kidding me!"

"Oh, yeah? Well, watch how fast I give two weeks notice," I yell over my shoulder as I race out the door for the training supervisor's office.

The day I leave the college, I bring Doug a potted plant and leave it on his desk with this note: "When this plant reaches the ceiling, you're out of here."

It was a miniature cactus. Much later he told me that in its first year the small cactus had grown less than a quarter inch—despite over-fertilization by Doug.

CHAPTER 29

Several months later, Jean-Michel Cousteau sends me to Costa Rica in Central America on my first expedition. My excitement knows no bounds as I anxiously meet the French team for the first time. Fortunately, most of the French men speak English. With a basic French language book tucked under one arm, I eagerly board an eighty-five foot Swedish schooner named *Victoria*, which the Cousteau Society has chartered specifically for this expedition.

At sunrise on the following day, we hoist *Victoria*'s tall sails and, with the outgoing tide, leave the small port town of Punta Arenas on the West coast of Costa Rica. Our destination is the solitary island of Cocos in the warm Pacific waters three hundred miles due west. This beautiful volcanic island, lush in tropical foliage and sheathed in spectacular waterfalls, is also known as Treasure Island. Fable and historical record point to tiny Cocos as the hidden burial ground for vast amounts of lost pirate treasure. In my cabin at night during the three-day passage, I lie on my bunk feeling the gentle rocking of the schooner and dream of treasure chests filled with gold doubloons, pieces-of-eight, pearl necklaces, and jewel-encrusted cutlasses.

At sunset on the third day of our voyage, I find myself at the plunging bow of *Victoria* watching dolphins riding the bow wave. The setting sun paints beautiful iridescent patterns of passionate color on the dolphin's slick backs. A couple of the divers climb out on the plunging bow sprint then hang from the rope stays in an attempt to touch the leaping dolphins as they surface for air. Glancing toward the horizon, I'm surprised to see the sharp volcanic tip of Treasure Island caught in the blood-red orb of the setting sun. For a few moments, the island's jagged features are silhouetted in the bright glow of the descending globe. At the bow of the schooner I look in awe at the surrealistic beauty of Treasure Island. I can only wonder about the adventures that await us in this tropical paradise.

Over the next couple of weeks we make numerous dives in the virgin splendor of Cocos. We swim with large schools of jacks and barracuda that part before us as if they are a living metallic curtain, flashing like burnished silver as we venture into their midst. There are schools of hammerhead sharks, some of them over twelve feet long. From the relative safety of the sea bed, 150 feet down, we watch the large sharks swimming overhead like ghostly squadrons of death.

At the end of the day, with our skins taut from exposure to sun and sea, we bathe under the spilling coolness of a waterfall that cascades directly into the sea. It requires a bit of finesse by our driver to nudge the inflatable boat's bow against the moss-slick rocks at the base of the waterfall. Then he has to hold it gently in place with the engine at low rpm while the rest of us soap up. It takes a lot of skill to keep the small boat from slipping away while the waterfall pours heavily into the Zodiac and the small ocean waves sweep us to and fro.

Towels are not necessary. After the shower we drive rapidly across the protected bay with the Zodiac just skimming the surface while the wind quickly dries our hair and skin.

Back aboard the *Victoria*, in the warmth of the tropical night, we dine topside at a large communal table. Laughter leads us into the night. We toast the glorious sunsets and listen to the music of the wind as it rustles through the furled sails and sings lightly in the rope rigging.

At the end of the expedition, three of us descend with underwater scooters. We fly in tight formation. Mimicking acrobatic pilots, we do synchronized loops and rolls then dive down to a depth of 130 feet where there is an awesome underwater cavern. Trailing buoyant streams of iridescent bubbles, we fly through the spacious cavern, its walls alive with vibrant living corals. Suspended in the cavern are numerous schools of fish, each patterned differently in bright colors that part before our passage like successive shimmering veils as we traverse the length of the two hundred foot submarine passage before exiting into the blue water on the other side. It is without doubt the prettiest dive I have ever made.

Returning to Los Angeles, I spend a frantic month readying the equipment for our next expedition. We are going to Hawaii to film humpback whales in Maui and molten lava flowing underwater on the big island.

As the chief diver, it is my responsibility to make sure the small mountain of gear we're taking on expedition is working properly before our departure. In many ways it's a lot like when I was with the teams in the navy. Diving equipment has to be checked and repaired. The portable generators and compressors need to be run under a load to ensure that they won't fail at the worst possible moment. However, unlike the frogman teams, we are taking cameras and underwater lights instead of guns and explosives. Ours are expeditions of discovery. I love every aspect of our work. As explorers, our fare is incredible adventure spiced with the knowledge that we are actively involved in improving the quality of life for all of us and for the generations of people that will follow.

While working late on a Sunday night, I think about our upcoming departure scheduled in three weeks for Hawaii. I can't wait to return to the Hawaiian Islands where so many of my favorite memories reside. I idly wonder if Susan still lives on Oahu. As I put the finishing touches on a scuba regulator I'm repairing, I hear unexpected voices upstairs. A moment later two sets of legs descend the circular staircase into the basement. The second pair of legs are long, feminine, and very interesting; they have my complete attention.

Bruce Hamren, one of our divers, eyes me suspiciously while introducing me to his sister. I guess I look a little too enthusiastic about meeting her. All my thoughts of Susan quickly flee before the friendly radiance of Cindy. She has a captivating smile and an open, easy manner that is refreshing. We talk about diving and other harmless subjects while her brother hovers worriedly at our sides. It seems that Bruce only brings his kid sister by the office after hours because he fears she might take up with one of the Cousteau divers.

He is right to worry; for both of us it is love at first sight. I soon become lost in her playful brown eyes, which are almost on a level with my own. She stands almost six feet tall.

Bruce looks unhappily from Cindy's face to mine then back at Cindy. Reluctantly he leaves us alone to pack a dive bag. However, the way he is rapidly throwing his gear into the bag, I know that if I want to ask Cindy out, it will have to be done quickly. "Would you like to go out with me next weekend?" I blurt.

Cindy's eyes crinkle as she smiles, "Certainly, do you know I live in northern California?" Bruce is having problems stuffing his wetsuit into the bag as he glances anxiously in our direction.

I make my mind up in an instant, "I'll buy you an airplane ticket."

Bruce has the bag half-closed and is industriously dragging it over toward us.

"O.K.," laughs Cindy.

"O.K.?" Bruce doesn't like the implications of that word as he looks from one of us to the other, "O.K., what?"

"Just O.K.," Cindy glares at her brother, "can't I even talk with a guy without your overbearing protectiveness?"

"He's not just a guy," Bruce argues lamely, "he's a diver."

The following Friday I arrive at the airport almost an hour early. I'm carrying a hundred and one long-stem red roses. I hope to make a good impression. I have no intention of telling her that I purchased the bundle of flowers on sale.

Cindy is easy to spot as she walks off the plane. She is taller than most everyone else. I'm not sure whether I should shake her hand or kiss her, so I give her the flowers instead. Cindy loves the flowers. "You shouldn't have," she says in a voice that ensures that I should have. "They must have cost you a fortune."

"Nah," I say with a sweeping gesture, "I got them on sale."

"You're not supposed to tell me that."

While Cindy has her face buried to the nose in the roses, I take the opportunity to have a closer look at the lady who will become my wife. She is wearing a khaki jacket with a matching skirt, which accents her light brown hair. She looks very outdoorsy, despite the high heels. According to her brother, Cindy is into skydiving, mountain climbing, kayaking, scuba diving, and all the various types of skiing. Bruce also warned me that she tends to pack quite a punch when upset. Cindy certainly doesn't look violent as she smiles at me over the roses.

Our first stop is at one of the more expensive French restaurants in town where I soon discover that mountain women have big appetites, particularly in reference to rich chocolate desserts.

We then drive up Molhuland Drive and park on a turnout above Beverly Hills. We hike to a ridge overlooking the vast Los Angeles basin. The sprawling city with its dense carpet of glowing lights glitters magnificently beneath the dark sky. It is here that I kiss Cindy for the first time.

For our second date I fly north to Sacramento where Cindy picks me up at the airport. Then we drive to the quaint mountain town of Paradise where she lives with her parents. The ride up is very exciting since she drives her MR2 sports car in a very aggressive way. She affectionately refers to the little speeding machine as her pocket rocket. Cindy considers every turn a challenge and by the time we pull into her parent's driveway I am a nervous wreck.

We don't spend very much time in the house before Cindy leads me outside and innocently asks if I would like to go for a hike in the canyon.

Her parents' house stands at the top of a high ridge, which quickly drops away into a deep gorge. Pine trees line both sides of the gorge for as far as the eye can see. A swift moving river snakes a windy course along the bottom. I gladly accept her offer, having no idea that I'm about to undergo a test that has become a family tradition. As a young girl Cindy determined that she wouldn't get stuck with a guy who couldn't keep up with her in the canyon. A few minutes later, while lacing up my hiking shoes, I wonder why the rest of Cindy's family has come outside to see us off. "Ready?" beams Cindy.

"Sure," I reply.

Cindy is off in an instant, her long legs literally flying down the steep path.

Taken completely by surprise, I'm a little slow chasing after her. I can't close the distance but do manage to keep her in sight. When the trail gets rather steep, Cindy slides down on one boot, her arms held out like wings to maintain her balance. Sliding on one foot turned out to be easier than I thought . . . until I begin picking up speed. Cindy glances over her shoulder and sees that I'm rapidly gaining on her, but by my prolonged scream, she realizes that I am also out of control. Cindy comes to a stop before some dense bushes; I slide through them going full speed. As I pass her, Cindy shouts, "Do you know that's poison oak?"

Cindy doesn't slow her pace when a couple of minutes later we get to a very steep part of the path known as the goat trail. She has a way of leaping downwards that requires landing on the edges of her boots before she leaps again. My technique involves sliding almost out of control and grasping desperately at passing branches. She reaches the canyon floor and quickly checks her watch, "Darn, we're a minute behind schedule."

I arrive at her side huffing and puffing, "What do you mean we're behind schedule? We just ran down the side of a thousand foot mountain."

Cindy grins, "Well, we'll just have to make up the time on the way back up." I think she is kidding—she isn't. As I chase her back up the steep slope of the gorge, I know that this is one challenge I don't dare lose.

I'm a little light-headed when we break out of the brush at the base of her parents' house. We are side by side when her father yells down, "How did he do?"

Cindy looks up into the bright afternoon light and announces, "I think I'm going to keep this one." One week later when it comes time for me to depart on an expedition, I don't want to leave her behind. So, for our third date, I take Cindy to Hawaii.

The expedition begins on the island of Maui, where we have a permit to dive with humpback whales. Cindy, who has a lot of experience operating small boats, helps out by skippering our support vessel, a thirty-two-foot sport fisher.

When actually approaching the whales, we have Cindy standoff in the support boat while the cinema team slowly moves in with our inflatable Zodiacs. The small rubber boats are a lot less intrusive for the whales. The humpbacks use the warm tropical waters of the Hawaiian islands as a breeding and calving ground. The males often hang vertically in the water, suspended at a depth of about sixty- to eighty-feet. With their heads in a slightly downward position, they commence to sing in the hopes of attracting a female. The bulls' songs are lovely whale melodies that range from very deep rumbling lows to shrill peaking highs that fill the water with their deep musical resonance. Approaching a large singing male at depth, with rays of sunlight radiating into the blue water as though through stained glass, is like being in the proximity of a majestic cathedral organ. We could feel the penetrating sound reverberating off of our fins and echoing through our bodies.

The highlight of the expedition occurs on a stormy day. The choppy sea is covered with white caps, and the trade winds are blowing twenty knots or more. The Zodiac, momentarily airborne, slams into an oncoming wave and then another. Wiping the sea spray from our faces, we see in the near distance a huge humpback whale breaching three times in rapid succession. The Zodiac races well ahead of the whale pod; then, two of us roll backward into the frothy sea. We dive quickly downward with rapid strokes of our fins. We're free diving (without tanks). Scuba bubbles can be distracting for whales, sometimes leaving underwater bubble wakes of their own as a warning to intruders.

Daisy is leading the pod of seven whales. She is a cow named for her white-spotted tail. The encounter we hope for is totally dependent on her. If she shies away, we'll abandon the pod so as not to stress her week-old calf. The calf (swimming shyly at her side) is already over fifteen feet in length and weighs over two tons.

Luckily, Daisy angles toward us and passes just twenty feet away. The calf swimming at her shoulder is very inquisitive of us small dolphin-like creatures and swims closer to investigate. Hovering in the water, I am stunned that the calf so willingly approaches. I almost forget to take pictures in my excitement. Swimming alongside the calf, separated by only a few feet, I shoot full-frame pictures with a wide-angle lens while my lungs labor for air. When I can no longer deny my need to breathe, I begin to kick upward but pause when a large shadow passes overhead. Directly above me, a large bull momentarily blots out the light of the sun with its freight train passage. I stare in awe at the immensity of this gentle giant. Its dimensions, when seen from below, stagger my mind. With my lungs frantic for air, I have to wait for the huge mammal to pass overhead before swimming desperately to the surface.

We spend a full month diving with these wonderful creatures. Often pods of dolphins accompany the whales. They always make several close, high speed passes on the strange silvery creatures that so closely resemble themselves, yet are so alien.

From our little inflatable boats, we watch humpbacks repeatedly launching their massive bodies completely out of the water, then twisting in the sunlight as they slam back into the ocean with a gigantic splash. It is a wondrous event, forever treasured, to watch a cow encouraging her calf to breach for the first time as she teaches it the ways of the sea. One calf, slightly longer than our fourteen-foot Zodiac, circles our small inflatable boat breaching eleven times in rapid succession as I shoot an entire roll of film in a matter of thirty seconds.

The second part of our mission finds us off the south coast of the big island of Hawaii. A volcano has been erupting on the Kilauea ridge off and on since 1984. The lava is flowing into the sea at the rate of 350,000 cubic meters per day. That's the equivalent of over seventy thousand cement truck loads. Our job is to try to film the lava as it flows underwater.

This undoubtedly is going to be the most dangerous diving I have ever been involved in. As chief diver I am responsible for the safety of the team. Often, we must tread in dangerous situations if we are to get the exciting footage we all hope for. I'm pleased that Cindy has flown home because danger is such a lure for her, but I am sorry that she is going to miss all of the excitement. For this mission I charter a swift twin-engine, Hawaiian fishing boat. If we have to move suddenly, I want a boat that can get us out of harm's way fast.

Cruising the shoreline from two hundred yards out, I nervously note that the situation looks to be completely out of control. The liquid lava is pouring into the water in broad fiery sheets across a wide rolling front. The sea water boils vigorously at the base of the lava falls while throwing off thick clouds of sulfur-laced steam. The steam is rising thousands of feet into the blue Hawaiian sky. The conflict of liquid stone and boiling sea water results in explosions of terrible magnitude that hurl globs of molten rock up to fifty feet into the air. The fiery globules leave visible tracers of steam in the humid air before arching back into the boiling ocean. Upon impacting the turbulent water, they bubble hotly and spin about emitting whiffs of white and yellow smoke before slowly sinking beneath the frothy surface. Our guide, a veteran of many lava dives, turns and says with worried eyes, "I don't think I've ever seen it this far out of control before."

We can't get any closer than a hundred yards without the water temperature going well over a hundred degrees. While looking for a patch of water that isn't scalding so we can enter the water in relative safety, I have the startling realization that this is going to be the first time I have ever worn a wet suit to keep cool.

Two hundred yards from shore the surface temperature drops to ninety-eight degrees Fahrenheit. We quickly leap into the hot water; it's like diving into a giant Jacuzzi. The team of five swims rapidly downward through the creamy white froth that covers the surface to the deeper depths where the water is significantly cooler. Using compasses, we navigate toward the flow. The direction, however, is easy to determine by listening to the intensity of the noise generated by the exploding and imploding lava. We are continuously bombarded with ripping, tearing, and crackling sounds that send sharp, bone-rattling shock waves right through our bodies. We know we are getting close when the frightful noise actually increases in magnitude.

The water visibility keeps changing as we approach the shoreline—from eight to two feet then back to eight. It is incredibly scary playing hide and seek with over two thousand degree lava in limited-visibility water. To make matters even worse there is a heavy swell running. The surge is hurling us up to fifteen feet in opposing directions. It's like we've entered an underwater war zone. I'm thinking about canceling the dive when I see a glimmer of glowing red in the dirty water ahead of us.

Bob Talbot, of whale poster fame, moves in with the underwater camera to film. He is having a lot of difficulty trying to stay in one place with the surging water throwing him from side to side. He manages to get within one foot of the red hot, seething lava that creeps ever downward at the rate of about half a foot per second. The liquid rock resembles angry red worms that surge abruptly forward then slow as a black, cooling crust forms about the molten rock. The lava tube momentarily halts; then, the leading edge begins to bulge from the tremendous pressure pushing it downward. The tube's black crust splits into a spider's web of angry red cracks that glow brightly from the intense liquid fire within. The molten rock bursts forth pouring freely in a glorious fountain of thick, molten fire. It's fascinating beyond comprehension to watch this island-constructing process from a few feet away.

We can't touch bottom, not only because of the hot lava flowing haphazardly across the whole shelf, but because the bottom is continuously shifting from the extremely dangerous rock slides that are occurring all around us. The hardened lava rubble is settling into an unstable mass precariously pitched on a forty-five degree incline that is regularly shifting and tumbling. With no warning, the entire bottom slides away and falls in a massive submarine avalanche toward the dark depths thousands of feet below us.

It's very disorienting. This becomes even more dangerous when the slide creates strong underwater currents that tend to suck the unsuspecting diver toward the unseeable bottom. This happened to a diver several months earlier. It pulled him down to a depth of three hundred feet before he barely managed to escape. It almost cost him his life. Now he doesn't dive with volcanoes anymore.

It doesn't help matters that the moving rock influences our compasses making underwater navigation extremely tricky—if not totally impossible. Following the weaving lava tubes downward, we have to stop at a depth of ninety feet as the concussion from the imploding and exploding lava beats against our face plates, causing us to get massive sinus headaches. The sound is so intense that the shock waves force our dive masks to move visibly inward against our faces.

While swimming just several feet above the continuously sliding slope, a smoking boulder, almost two meters in diameter, comes tumbling down between Bob and me, narrowly missing us. We both pause to stare at the large rock. The fast tumbling rock looks like a falling meteorite burning its way through a liquid atmosphere as it bounces downward and disappears into the blackness below.

Late in the day we film an active lava tube at a depth of eighty feet. There is a sudden, loud avalanche of sound heavily punctuated by a sharp concussion. Our bodies vibrate to a rolling thunder of repeated shock waves announcing that the earth is moving in a really big way. A huge, black cloud thick with ash rises rapidly from the bottom. Instinctively, Bob and I reach out and grab for each other just as the dim light of day disappears into an engulfing wave of darkness, intense heat, and floating debris.

Lost in total blackness, we can only imagine what is happening around us. In my mind I see us suspended over a hellish image of Dante's inferno. Using the changing sense of pressure against our face plates as our only guide, we slowly swim upward, fearing that we may encounter a downward flowing lava tube or be buried in another avalanche.

We emerge from the dense cloud of suspended debris into the somewhat clearer water nearer the surface. We remain at a depth of about thirty feet as we swim underwater following our semi-functional compasses away from the hellish shore. Knowing that a fiery tempest is raging at the surface, I think how this is definitely not the kind of place where one would ever want to run out of air.

Finally back on the boat and while staring at the angry red fingers of lava flowing into the ocean, we can only wonder at what we have just experienced. It feels like having been present at the dawn of creation. In a way, geologically speaking, we had.

It seems improbable that only five days later I am standing outside the small airport in Madang, Papua New Guinea, wiping the sweat from my brow. In the Cousteau Society, travel and adventure are often hurled at you at an unbelievable rate. I am en route to join the *Alcyone* for my first expedition aboard the Cousteau Society's new wind ship. I am so excited that I almost don't mind lugging around the twenty-two pieces of excess baggage Don Santee has saddled me with prior to my leaving Los Angeles.

Standing in the empty parking lot, I wonder if anyone is planning on picking me up, when a rusty old truck comes rocking down the dirt road trailing smoke and dust. It pulls alongside as the native driver switches off the engine, but the smoking machine refuses to die as it continues to cough and pant. The driver shrugs then pops the clutch, which causes the truck to lurch forward before it stalls with a sharp backfire from the corroded muffler. The driver leers at me from the front seat. He is a dark-skinned New Guinean, sporting a huge afro haircut with a boar's tusk hanging around his neck. "You Cousteau," he says in coarse pidgin, "Max know because many boxes." Max grins happily showing a wealth of crooked teeth stained a dull red from chewing beetle nut. He looks like a head hunter. A few moments later I find out that he drives like one, too.

The truck, creating a cloud of dust and smoke, bounces and sways dangerously as it follows a winding path through the dense jungle. The chatter of the old engine, augmented by an occasional backfire, alerts the chickens and pigs on the dirt road ahead and sends them scurrying for cover. Rounding a sharp bend, I catch my first sight of *Alcyone*. The wind ship is tied alongside a small wooden pier in the quiet backwater of the little harbor. Tall, arching coconut trees lean dramatically outward toward the graceful ship. Its sleek lines and brilliant white hull are a futuristic contrast to the primitive beauty of the grass huts that line the shore. A gaggle of laughing children play in the muddy brown water at the wind ship's stern. They are diving into the still water from a small canoe made from a single hollowed out log with a bamboo outrigger.

The children happily crowd around the truck anxious to help in the porting of the gear. And that's how I arrive aboard *Alcyone*, surrounded by a mob of laughing native children clutching at my hands and pulling on my clothes.

The ship sets sail the following morning with the outgoing tide. We are headed toward an expedition of discovery across a broad chain of lush tropical islands that border the northern approaches to Papua, New Guinea. Along the way we encounter a tropical storm.

At 2 A.M., the night sky is shrouded in blackness, except for the intermittent strobe of lightning bolts that repeatedly strike the enraged ocean. The wind ship pitches and rolls in the turbulent water. A shutter runs the length of the keel as the bow slams into the oncoming waves. Thick sheets of wind-driven rain beat against the bridge windows. Inside, I am warm and dry, thanks to the twenty-first century robotics of the wind ship's futuristic design and her unique turbosails. They are automatically controlled by shipboard computers. It is a thrilling time to be standing my first helm watch on *Alcyone*.

The wind shifts ten degrees to port. I watch the turbosails react unaided by my hand and turn up the volume on the stereo. Munching a bowl of corn flakes with my feet braced against the rocking of the ship, I listen to the heavy beat of the Rolling Stones singing "I Can't Get No Satisfaction." I keep a wary eye on the sea and glance every so often at the radar screen, which is painting in bright iridescent colors the passage of successive thunderheads and squalls. At 5 A.M., the vibrant red outline of a small island appears in the screen's upper right corner. It is my clue to wake the captain. We have reached Wuuvulu island where a whale of an adventure awaits us.

The following morning there is no sign of the storm in the crystal clear sky. The diving team is in the Zodiacs en route to an underwater cave where we intend to film. Jean-Michel Cousteau is standing in the bow of the lead Zodiac, which is probably why he is the first one to see the massive black fin that cuts through the water only thirty yards away—it is at least four feet tall!

"Orcas," yells Jean-Michel just as the first spout blows.

Normally orcas are only seen in colder, less clear water. To find them in the tropics with over one hundred feet of underwater visibility is extremely rare. Here are three of the huge carnivores, two females and a young bull. The male is over twenty-two feet long.

Sitting on the side of the Zodiac, I think that it is not an easy decision to purposefully enter the water with the world's number one-ranked predator. Yet, when accompanied by other divers, it does seem a little less intimidating—though not by much. A couple of hours later there is one rather frightening moment when I find myself alone in the water. Alone that is except for the rather intimidating presence of the larger of the two female killer whales, which is idly drifting twenty feet away.

I feel totally exposed in my mask, fins, and snorkel without even the implied security of a wet suit. If she proves less than friendly, there is little I can do about it. I try to forget my worries, with little success, and concentrate on taking pictures.

It's just as I run out of film that I detect a slight change in her attitude. Her head lowers and turns toward me. My heart races as I see her tail take a couple of idle strokes. She moves slowly and deliberately in my direction. When she is only about eight feet away, she turns sideways to me. I feel somewhat reassured that I am not about to be eaten. Dwarfed by the proximity of the huge predator, I have never felt so small or so humble in my life. I wonder what that incredible mind is thinking as she stares for a moment before slowly swimming away.

When another photography team enters the water, I'm free to swim back to the Zodiac. I can't help pondering that I am only alive because that powerful animal chose not to eat me.

When the divers surface after only a few minutes, I know that something is up. Jean-Michel shouts excitedly that the orcas are catching and eating sharks! The orcas swim straight down, disappearing from sight, then return with white tip reef sharks clenched in their giant jaws. These aren't little sharks either, some are two meters (about seven feet) long, easily long enough to kill a man.

We continue to film, but it's a very scary situation. There is a long red slick of blood and shark guts floating in the dark water. At least with the orcas around we don't have to worry about other sharks. They are the main course on today's menu.

The orcas almost seem to be playing with their prey. One orca holds the shark firmly in its massive jaws while the other grabs hold. Then they rip and tear the shark in half like a couple of pit bulls fighting over a bone. Probably the most amazing aspect is that the orcas don't have to keep returning to the same spot. Yet, again and again they swim upward out of the depths directly to us. It's like they are showing off.

We stay with the orcas until the sun dips well below the horizon. Then the dark, blood-laced water becomes just too foreboding to swim in with the formidable predators actively hunting sharks. Motoring back toward *Alcyone* into a blood-red sky, I wonder what the orcas thought of us, the little awkwardly swimming creatures with heads that leaked bubbles. Suddenly realizing that their heads leaked bubbles too, I think that maybe they see us as distant relations. Then again, maybe we have been just a source of entertainment while they ate their dinner.

THE PRESENT

I am again in the water with a formidable predator, only this one isn't warm-blooded. Jean-Michel Cousteau has come up with the unique idea of seeing how a great white shark would react to an apparently cage-less diver—that being me inside a clear plastic cylinder. I soon find out how great white sharks react to an apparently cage-less diver, the sharks try to eat him—that's what happens.

Alcyone lay at anchor in the minimal shelter of Dangerous Reef in the Great South Australian Bight. I think Dangerous Reef a fitting name for the place where Jean-Michel wanted to conduct his little experiment. Dangling ten feet beneath *Alcyone*'s stern, I peer anxiously through the clear Lexan, which all but disappears underwater, at the large tuna bait that hangs two feet away. The great white shark isn't long in coming. She appears swiftly out of the gloom swimming rapidly with powerful beats of her lunate tail. Her open jaws flash white in the sunlight as the multiple rows of razor sharp teeth extend in a formidable bite that leaves half of the forty pound tuna dangling from the polypropylene line. Soon, more appear.

The sharks strike at the bait fish repeatedly, which they recognize as their natural food, all but ignoring me in the process. That is until I make the mistake of jumping into the water with a large white pointer just six feet away. We didn't see one of the sharks approaching because she swam in from underneath *Alcyone*'s stern.

It is necessary for me to leap into the open water to enter the Lexan cage because the plastic cylinder is just too tall to climb into while it's on the wind ship's deck. So, the crew lowers it down ten feet beneath the surface. I need it sunk that far in order to have room to raise the entry hatches, both of which have to be wide open, otherwise, I tend to get stuck with my legs dangling provocatively outside the cylinder, which can be very disconcerting when a hungry great white shark is in close attendance.

On this occasion I am just about to step into the water from the stern of *Alcyone* when Bruno, our French chef, sees a great white swimming out from under the wind ship's swim platform. It takes him a vital moment to translate in his mind from French to English then, a millisecond too late, he shrieks, "Look out! Shark!"

I hear his shrill warning just an instant before my head disappears beneath the water. I don't see the great white at first because of all the bubbles drifting about from my entry, but as they begin to clear away, like a silver curtain slowly opening, I have an unmistakable close-up view of a seventeen-foot great white shark swimming directly at me. I don't have time to look again as I turn my back to the huge predator and bolt for the Lexan cage. It is very disconcerting having my back exposed to the giant shark, but I know my only hope is to get into the plastic cylinder as quickly as possible. A couple of heart-fluttering seconds later, I'm reaching for the double top hatches of the cylinder and pulling myself vigorously downward. I am inside in an instant. Granted, I'm upside down in the cage with a flooded dive mask, but at least I'm inside the cage. Glancing upward while clearing my mask, I see the great white shark passing silently overhead, its black orb regarding me with the same hungry look that Cindy affects when in the proximity of chocolate. My heart is still beating frantically from the dangerous encounter.

The great white isn't long in coming back. I watch her ascending out of the gloom. The water visibility is only about thirty feet. She must have weighed well over four thousand pounds. The massive head swings side to side as she approaches closer and closer until she nudges the bottom of my plastic cylinder with her muzzle. The black (seemingly pupil-less) eye regards me coldly from inches away. I could almost sense its thoughts, which according to Cindy, who had spent the last week before my departure teasing me outrageously, might be something like this: "Hmm, crunchy on the outside, but probably soft and chewy on the inside." Confused by the invisible barrier, the shark keeps returning, though not actually attacking. That is until she is joined by a second shark and then by a third. I have apparently rung the sharks' dinner bell with my frantic entry into the cage.

The sharks grow more bold and confident in their numbers. They begin to circle my plastic cage more aggressively. I am wondering if they are able to sense my fear, when suddenly a fifteen-footer attacks. Its snout thumps the side of the Lexan cylinder solidly. I'm so intent on watching the fifteen-foot shark that I don't notice that the seventeen-footer has returned, that is until I see a large shadow passing over me. Turning abruptly, I'm shocked to see the huge shark hovering vertically alongside my cage; its pectoral fins are hugging the five foot diameter plastic cylinder as it sought to get as close to me as possible. We are separated by just the 3/16 inch wall of the clear Lexan. Her belly is rubbing against the Lexan while she seeks a way inside. Twisting her head, which is just inches from my own, I feel the shock of real fear staring into that cold, dark orb. She gnashes her teeth against the plastic then angrily peels away and swims for the bottom.

I start to breath a premature sign of relief; then suddenly the huge shark reverses her direction and begins swimming rapidly upward, like a speeding torpedo, straight toward the bottom of my cage. I am staring at her massive head moving side to side while her huge tail beats furiously. She is aiming directly for the bottom of the cylinder—its weakest point! Only a thin row of hollow Lexan tubes lying across the bottom of the cylinder stand between me and the ascending super predator. I instinctively raise my feet off the bottom of the cage just an instant before she strikes with a mighty impact. The collision drives the cage a full two feet upward. I watch wide-eyed as the Lexan tubes bend several inches apart, admitting her thick snout. Then with brute force she thrusts her massive head forward, biting furiously at the thin Lexan tubes. I am hoping that the hollow plastic tubes can hold her off. After a few moments of industrious chewing, she withdraws. My heart beats wildly against my chest.

Lexan has been known to stop a .38 bullet, but my subconscious mind isn't exactly convinced that the thin, plastic cylinder will continue to hold off this super predator, particularly if she gets me up against the side of the boat where she can throw her massive weight against it.

To distract the shark, or maybe just for his own amusement, I see the captain through the shimmering veil of the surface throw a bait fish attached to a polypropylene line into the water. The seventeen-foot great white shark goes rapidly after the bait. She swims in anxiously, her giant jaws opening incredibly wide in eager anticipation. I can see a full yard into her cavernous throat; sunlight is plainly visible, radiating through the broad gill slits. Just when she is about to seize the fish, the captain jerks it away. Her tail beats frantically as she rapidly pursues the fast retreating bait. The great white shark accelerates in spurts of speed with each rapid sweep of her massive tail as she heads directly toward the stern of *Alcyone*.

The captain rapidly hauls in on the line. Meanwhile, one of the crew members, who is standing on the swim step, is about to have the surprise of his life. The bait comes out of the water to land with a wet plop right at the bare feet of the unsuspecting crewman. The man is standing quietly, hands in his pockets, staring leisurely down into the calm water—when suddenly the great white erupts from the water, its massive jaws clashing mere inches from his bare toes.

From ten feet down, I watch the water boil directly above the cylinder with the great white thrashing at the stern of *Alcyone*. The plastic cage swings wildly in the wake of the shark-induced current. Its huge tail thrashes viciously creating a large boil of bubbles, and for a few moments, I can't see. I fear that the shark might become entangled in the cage's rope-lifting bridle, but the great white breaks for open water. Looking toward the surface, I see through the dissipating curtain of bubbles that the crewman is madly waving his arms at the captain. I have no doubt of his mood.

A few minutes later my cage is brought to the surface and helping hands haul me from the plastic cylinder. The captain is smiling at me and says something in French; everyone laughs. I look dumbly about, not sharing in the joke. My French is so bad that, according to the captain, a French poodle understands more of the language than I do.

"I said," quips the captain in his French accent, "after you saw that shark, you looked like a regular propeller butt with your fins fluttering so fast."

Later at the lunch table, Michel DeLoire, the chief of cinematography, says in accented English, "Steve, it is very exciting jumping into the open water with a white shark present, yes?" I look up from the fishhead soup I'm eating. (It's true that the French will eat almost anything. French cuisine is never wasted.)

"Yes, Michel, it's very exciting; it scared the heck out of me."

"Good," exclaims Michel; he reaches across the table to pour me a half-glass of red wine. "Because I would like to film it."

The spoon of fish head soup I am raising to my mouth pauses in mid-air. I look at Michel who is smiling. The Frenchmen on *Alcyone* are such good practical jokers. "Right, Michel," I chuckle.

"So, you will do this for me?" he asks. I realize he isn't kidding.

Two hours later I'm standing on the swim step, peering anxiously over the side. There are now four great white sharks in attendance. Sometimes they swim leisurely past the stern, at other times they rocket past in pursuit of bait or each other.

Michel is in his steel cage floating just beneath the surface. One of the divers inside the cage is holding his hand up through the bars. The hand signals one. Three is to be my signal to jump. I nervously watch a white pointer swimming in and know that Michel is filming it. The hand flashes two as the white pointer passes directly beneath me; fortunately it is at least six feet down. The hand suddenly shows three fingers. Taking a deep breath, I reluctantly jump.

The shark, hearing the splash, arrows for the bottom while I rocket for my cage. The seventeen-foot white pointer, we have named her Amy after one of the guys' ex-girlfriend, swims back up to see what is on the dinner menu. She nudges the side of my cage and then hovers against it for about ten long seconds. We are eye to orb. Her mouth opens and closes against the plastic repeatedly. Though frightful to see, this is such a wonderful opportunity to get a really good look right down inside a great white shark's mouth and cavernous throat. I notice that the great white's maul is big enough to swallow a diver in two or three bites.

After Amy departs, Michel signals happily from the steel cage. I'm glad that I won't be jumping so close to the sharks anymore.

Amy looks like she is giving my cylinder extra consideration, like she is thinking about finding a way inside.

Michel again waits until my guard is down. The Frenchmen at the table are eating steak tartar. It's a fancy name for a scoop of raw hamburger with an uncooked egg floating on top. The chef has kindly made me an omelette and quite surprisingly, he even put a bottle of catsup next to my plate. Normally, the chef is insulted by the mere sight of catsup. He's been known to pound the cutting board with a heavy meat cleaver as he snarls, "Why do you want to ruin my cuisine with catsup?"

I look around suspiciously, wondering if I'm not being had in some way, but no one seems to be paying attention. Maybe the guys are just being nice to me. Michel smiles from across the table. I smile back, not knowing that I'm being setup.

"That was very exciting this afternoon, Steve," grins Michel.

"I guess," I answer. The omelette is delicious. I add more catsup while keeping my head down; I don't want to see the revolting dish that the Frenchmen are eating.

"I only wish the shark hadn't been quite so far down," Michel says wistfully.

Pausing with a bite of omelette halfway to my mouth, I foolishly ask, "What do you mean?"

"How do you say it in English?" asks Michel, pretending like he is searching for the correct words, "Take two."

The following morning again finds me standing on the swim step peering anxiously over the side for sharks. There are seven of the nasty buggers today. The water immediately at the stern is beginning to look like the car pool express lane for sharks. The silver wetsuit-covered hand, extending from the steel cage that I wished I was in, has already struck one. Looking just beyond my flippers, I see that there is no doubt that this shark is much shallower. It is only one or two feet beneath the surface and the top of the dorsal fin is cutting through the water like a knife. Another shark is just disappearing under *Alcyone*, which means I won't know exactly where it is lurking when I hit the water. It is not exactly a comforting thought, playing hide and seek with Jaws, particularly when Jaws is present in the plural sense.

Two . . . the hand has already flashed two . . . and the shark is right beneath me. Paul, the engineer, peers over the side and says with a shrug, "It's O.K., Steve; she's only a small one."

The shark is fifteen feet long and weighs at least ten times more than I do—not exactly my idea of a "small one." The hand suddenly has three fingers in the air. *They're not paying me enough money*, I think, taking a deep breath and leaping into the cold water. I'm only a moment reaching my cage. I open the double hatches and attempt to pull myself quickly downward; but halfway in, my tank hits the side of the hatch and sticks. My whole lower torso is hanging outside the cage! For an instant I panic and swim harder, but I still don't go anywhere. I can easily imagine my frantically fluttering fins attracting the attention of the sharks. I push myself backward, freeing my tank and then am able to drop rapidly into the cage. Looking quickly about, I'm glad to see that there aren't any sharks in close attendance.

That afternoon at lunch, Michel smiles and offers to pour me a glass of wine. "No, Michel," I say quickly.

"What, you don't want any wine? But this is French wine." He is affecting a hurt look—actually he does it quite well.

"Is that all you're asking me?" I'm not in a trusting mood.

"Why, yes," grins Michel pouring my glass half full. Quietly I ignore the wine at my elbow.

Over the next six months we dive daily with the great white sharks. On one occasion we have nine of the magnificent creatures at the stern of the wind ship. When diving with that many super predators, it gets quite exciting just keeping track of them. Halfway through the dive, without any warning, the sharks go into a frenzy. At the time the door to our steel cage is standing wide open! It's necessary for the door to be open for the camera man to get the uninhibited footage he hopes for. At this particular moment, Chuck Davis, the cinematographer, is getting more exciting footage than he wants. A fifteen-foot great white is torpedoing directly at our open door!

I rapidly pull the door closed an instant before it is impacted by almost two tons of hungry shark. I desperately want to latch the door closed but can't because the shark is vigorously shaking it with his teeth. I have to keep changing my purchase on the door because the shark keeps shifting its toothy grip. A fifteen-foot great white has a bite that encompasses a diameter of two feet or more. I'm a very busy door holder as I avoid those razor sharp triangular chompers.

The cage shudders under the impact of another shark, which strikes the side of the cage nearest Chuck's head. I almost lose my grip on the door. The cage now has two sharks chewing industriously on opposing sides. I guess it's apparent that I finally latched the door closed by virtue of the fact that I still have fingers with which write about it. Yet life doesn't get much more exciting than those few shark-filled moments.

After the dive, standing on the deck of *Alcyone* and watching the great white sharks swim about the wind ship, I can't help but compare my present life with the past. I think back to my decision at Terminal Island to live an honest life based on a focus toward the good. That decision helped me to cope with prison, but now it has become a wonderful vehicle to adventure, challenge, and love. The love part is a recent development with the entrance of Cindy into my life. I have no doubt that my new wife is thoroughly enjoying her own adventure right now. While I watch for great white sharks in the Great Australian Bight, she is in the Bahamas on a Cousteau expedition of her own, swimming with a pod of friendly Atlantic spotted dolphins.

The primary focus of this book has been to warn against the hazards of drugs and how they can lead to criminal involvement or worse. There is nothing good or romantic about being a drug smuggler. Drugs can lead an otherwise good person on a downward spiraling vortex into crime that may result in a complete loss of control over one's life. Drugs disrupt the family unit and often ruin successful careers. They can destroy your mental and physical health, and sometimes they kill you outright . . . or worse yet, kill the ones you love.

Heroin is a perfect example. If an addict should die of a heroin overdose, then other addicts will beat a path to that junkie's door with the wild anticipation that if the heroin is that powerful it must be some good stuff. I cannot imagine another product that people will rush to buy just because it happened to kill the user. The term "killer dope" seems more than appropriate here.

The designer drugs are another intriguing entry in this poison market. In prison I knew some of the men who had manufactured drugs on the outside. They certainly weren't concerned about quality assurance. In fact, since most of their supplies were stolen or illicit, they just tended to mix up a batch of whatever was on hand. Some of these poisonous materials give off toxic vapors that eventually destroy the brain cells of the very people handling them. Every drug manufacturer that I ever met in the joint wasn't entirely functional upstairs. Imagine the distorted mentality of someone who sniffs paint—a lot of paint. This bozo is going to concoct a witch's brew of unknown chemical origin, and some other complete idiot is going to happily ingest or worse yet inject it for an even more toxic effect into their body? It is really quite bizarre to consider the madness that some people are willing to stoop to for an artificial high that will never bring them any real happiness, nor will the high last more than a few hours. Reality is always waiting for the serious doper, and the landing is never easy.

If there is a specific lesson to this book, it is that our only true chance for happiness in life is to be focused toward the good. It's also about never giving up hope. No matter how far one falls, through correct living and commitment, nothing is impossible. Our only limitations in life are self-imposed; some dreams can in fact become reality.

Staring into the blue, clean water, I remember the shadows of the past and compare them to my life today. The guilt which use to be my daily companion is gone. Erased by the forgiveness found through a significant relationship with a caring God.

Life should be an odyssey of adventure. To be happy is our true birthright. We should always strive to be better, to reach higher and to set goals that challenge our abilities. Each of us is a treasure to be polished until it shines, but remember, the luster comes from within.

Sometimes you don't want a story to end, and this one hasn't, at least not yet.

Standing at the stern of the wind ship, I stare at the nimbus clouds from a recent rain as they pass overhead. In the near distance I see a double rainbow painted against a vast cobalt-blue horizon. Stepping to the edge of the deck, I prepare to enter the water, then out of the corner of my eye I see a large mirror leaning against an idle shark cage. We are planning to use the mirror to see how a great white shark will react to its own reflection. I stare at my reflected image momentarily. The shiny silver of the Cousteau wetsuit is radiant in the bright sunlight. Behind me the French tricolor ripples proudly in the wind against a background of blue sky. The twin rainbows stand out clearly in the upper right corner. I'm reminded of the Lord's promise that when we see a rainbow, he has covenanted to watch over us. Taking a deep breath from my regulator, I step from the stern of the wind ship.

For an instant my splash disturbs the calm, smooth water. Then an iridescent stream of bubbles rise to the surface where they gurgle and burst before they are gone.

FINI

Indeed, if a man should live many years, let him rejoice in them all, and let him remember the days of darkness, for they shall be many. Everything that is to come will be futility.
Rejoice, young man, during your childhood, and let your heart be pleasant during the days of young manhood. And follow the impulses of your heart and the desires of your eyes. Yet know that God will bring you to judgment for all these things.

(Ecc. 11:8-9)

EPILOGUE

WHERE THEY ARE NOW

1. Susan is happily married and living in New Zealand with her husband and four young sons.

2. Sam is living in San Diego working as a waiter captain and still spends his spare time surfing his brains out.

3. Morgan Hetrick, after serving almost six years in prison, disappeared into the witness protection program.

4. Morgan's sons and the pilot I flew with have also disappeared into the witness protection program.

5. Gerald Scotti, after resigning from the DEA, is now working as a criminal defense attorney.

6. James Walsh, the prosecutor in my case, is now a personal friend.

7. Michelle has become a well-established environmental and marine artist.

8. Max Memerstein was arrested in 1986 because of incriminating evidence delivered by Morgan Hetrick and sons. Because Max cooperated, he served twenty-five months before disappearing into the witness protection program with a check from the government for $700,000 in his pocket. The Medellin Cartel has placed a three million dollar price on his head. A book has been written about Max, titled *The Man Who Made It Snow*. According to *Time* magazine, he recently testified on behalf of the government in the United State' drug trafficking case against Manuel Noriega.

9. Rafael Cardona Salazar was killed in Columbia in the drug wars.

10. John Z. DeLorean, after being acquitted on all charges, is living somewhere in California. He co-authored a book titled *DeLorean*.

11. Ralph was released after spending over six years in prison. When he was arrested at the age of 18 and sentenced to twenty years, he thought he would see cars flying before he would be free again.

12. The author lives in Rancho Palos Verdes in southern California with his wife Cindy, daughter Stetcin Lee, and their two cats Scooter Bug and Grumbles. He continues to go on expedition with the Cousteau Society and is presently working on a second book.